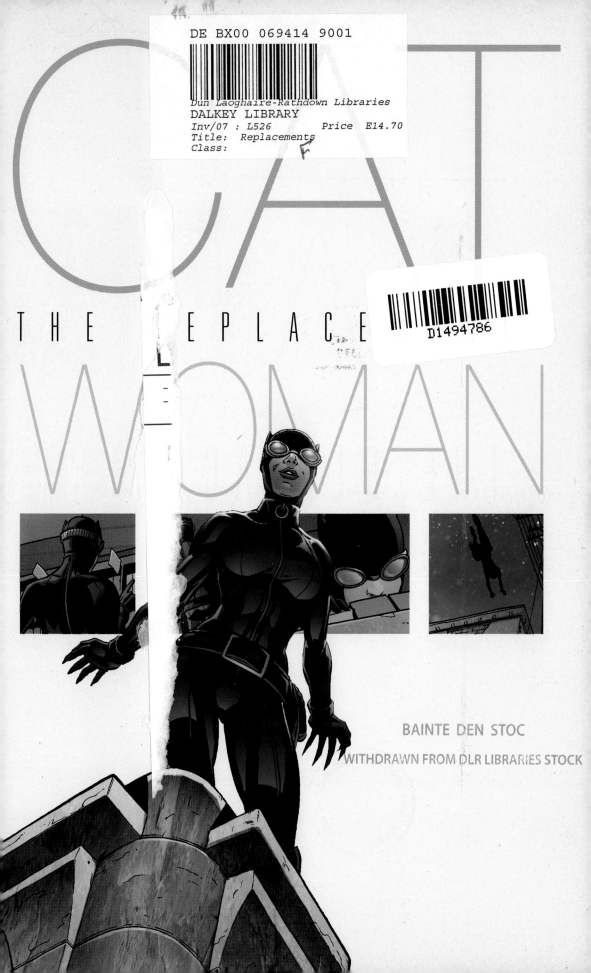

CAT WOMAN

THE REPLACEMENTS

CATW

THE REPLACEMENTS

OMAN

WILL **PFEIFER** WRITER   DAVID **LOPEZ** PENCILLER   ALVARO **LOPEZ** INKER

JEROMY **COX** BRAD **ANDERSON** COLORISTS   JARED K. **FLETCHER** LETTERER

ADAM **HUGHES** ORIGINAL COVERS

DC Comics, 1700 Broadway, New York, NY 10019
A Warner Bros. Entertainment Company
Printed in Canada. First Printing.
ISBN: 1-4012-1213-1
ISBN 13: 978-1-4012-1213-1

Following the world-shattering event known as the Infinite Crisis,
the stories of the DC Universe catapulted ahead one year where the
World's Greatest Super-Heroes continue their adventures in new
settings and situations!

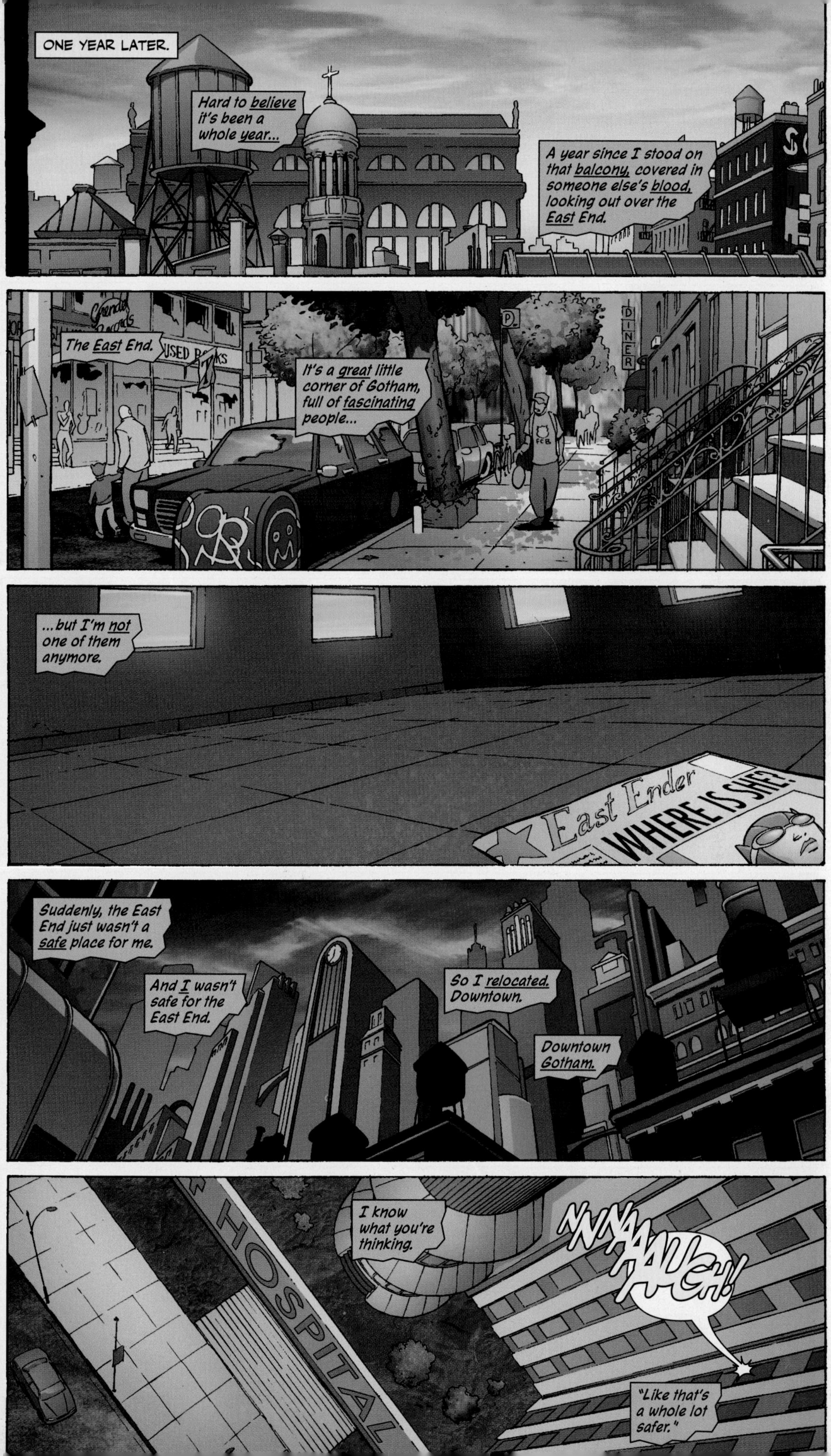
ONE YEAR LATER.
Hard to believe it's been a whole year...
A year since I stood on that balcony, covered in someone else's blood, looking out over the East End.
The East End.
DINER
It's a great little corner of Gotham, full of fascinating people...
...but I'm not one of them anymore.
East Ender
WHERE IS SHE?!
Suddenly, the East End just wasn't a safe place for me.
And I wasn't safe for the East End.
So I relocated. Downtown.
Downtown Gotham.
HOSPITAL
I know what you're thinking.
NNNAAAUGH!!
"Like that's a whole lot safer."

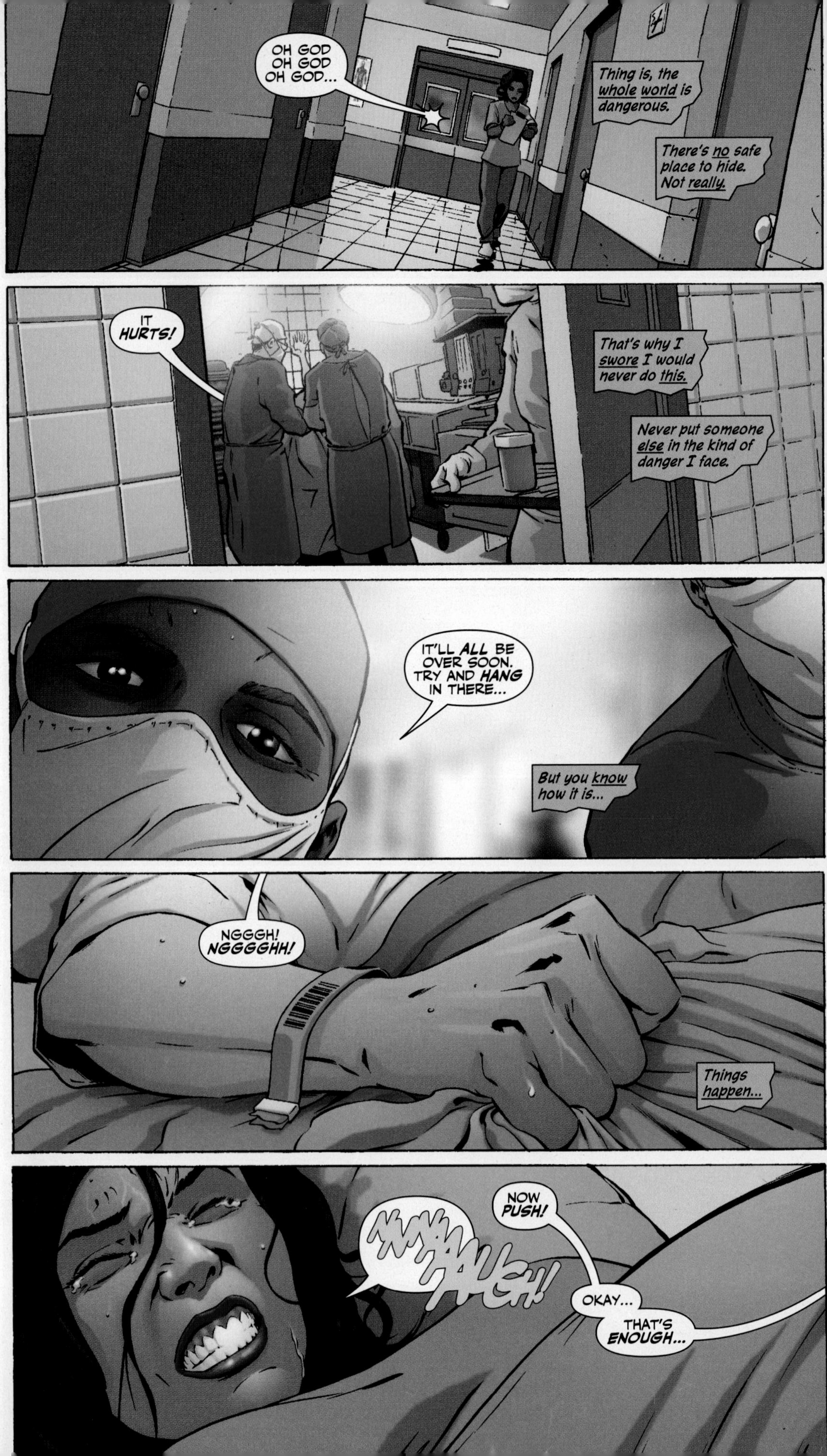
OH GOD
OH GOD
OH GOD...
Thing is, the whole world is dangerous.
There's no safe place to hide. Not really.
IT HURTS!
That's why I swore I would never do this.
Never put someone else in the kind of danger I face.
IT'LL ALL BE OVER SOON. TRY AND HANG IN THERE...
But you know how it is...
NGGGH! NGGGGHH!
Things happen...
NOW PUSH!
NNNAAAUGH!
OKAY...
THAT'S ENOUGH...

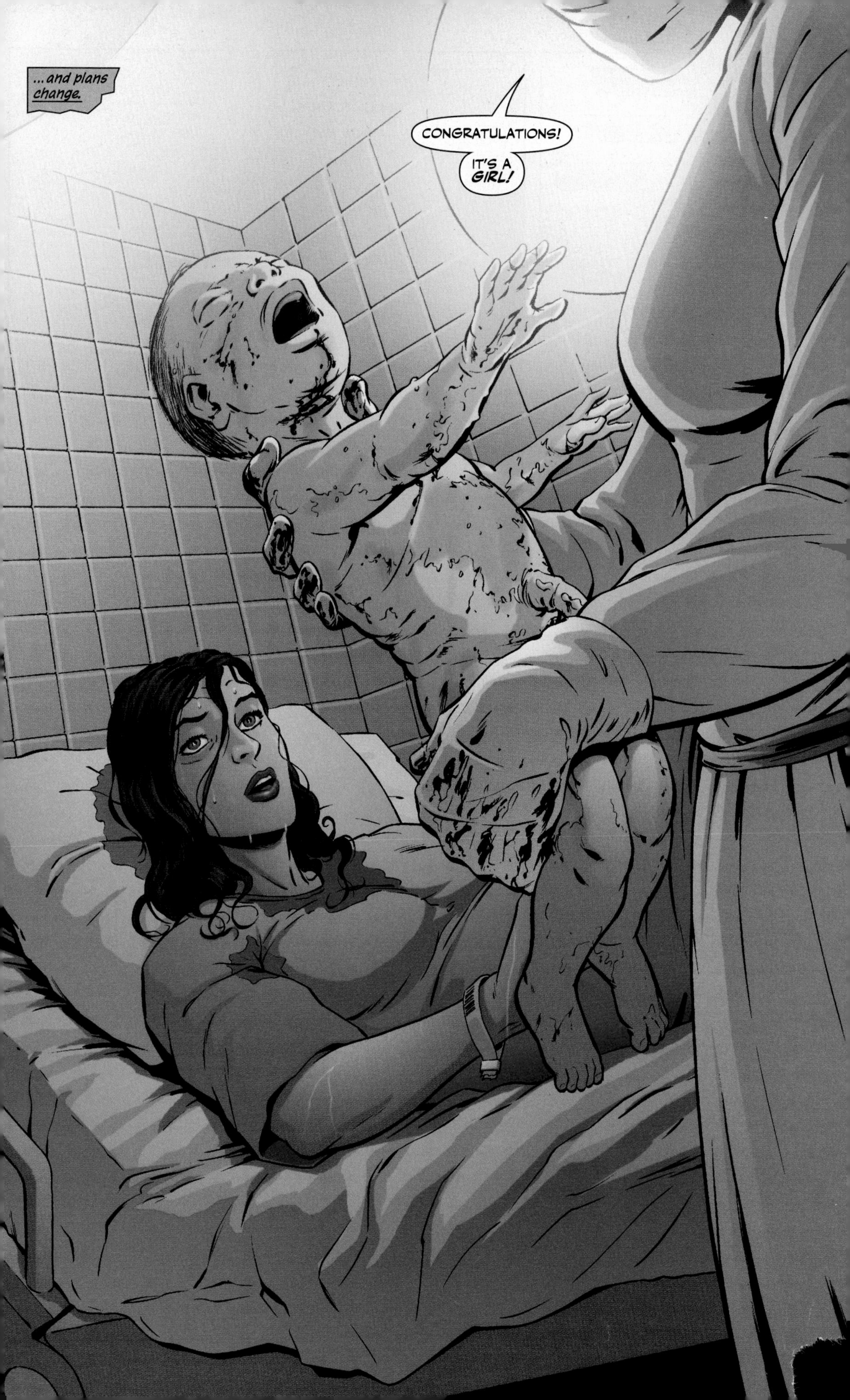
...and plans change.
CONGRATULATIONS!
IT'S A GIRL!

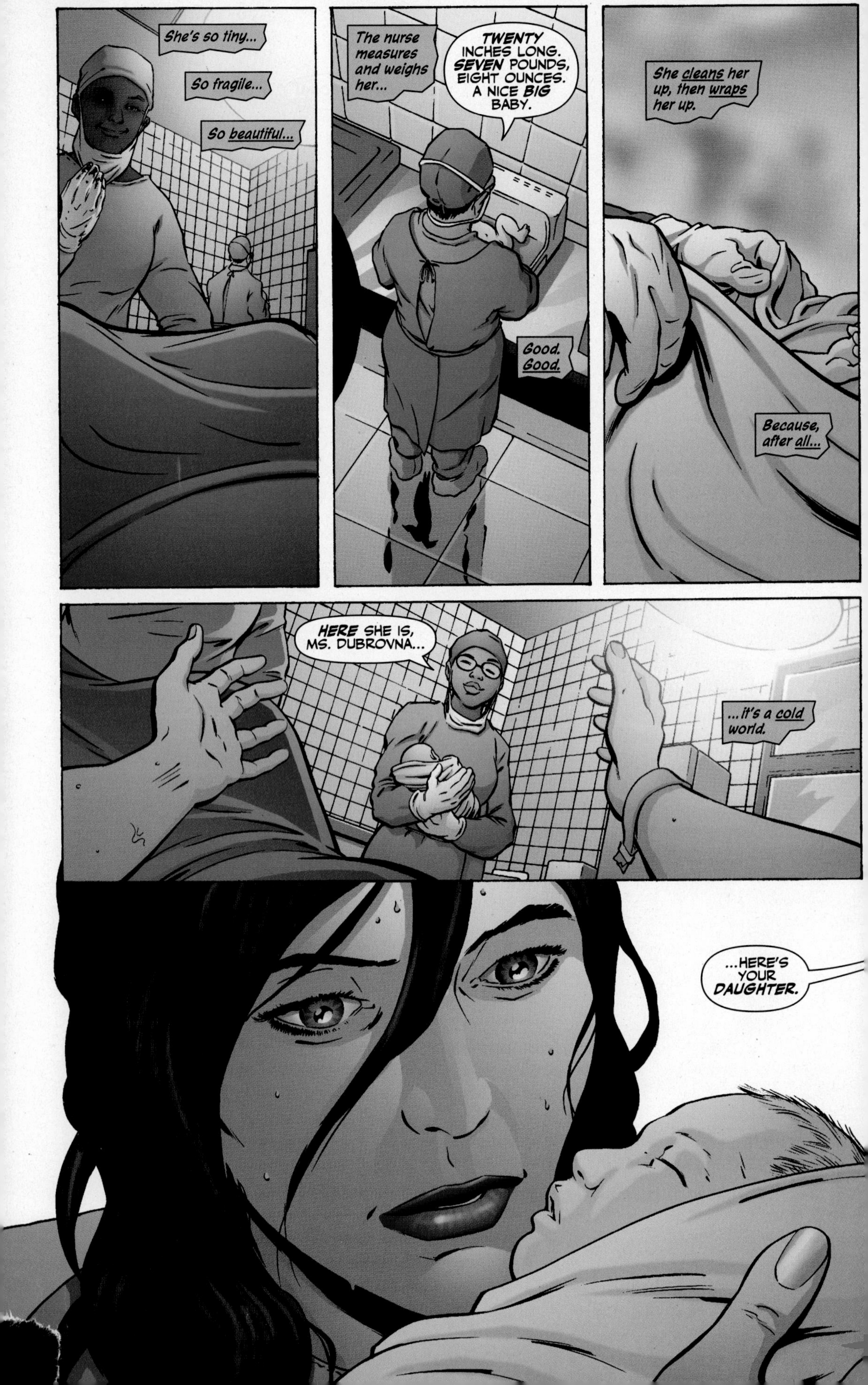
She's so tiny...
So fragile...
So beautiful...
The nurse measures and weighs her...
TWENTY INCHES LONG. SEVEN POUNDS, EIGHT OUNCES. A NICE BIG BABY.
Good. Good.
She cleans her up, then wraps her up.
Because, after all...
HERE SHE IS, MS. DUBROVNA...
...it's a cold world.
...HERE'S YOUR DAUGHTER.

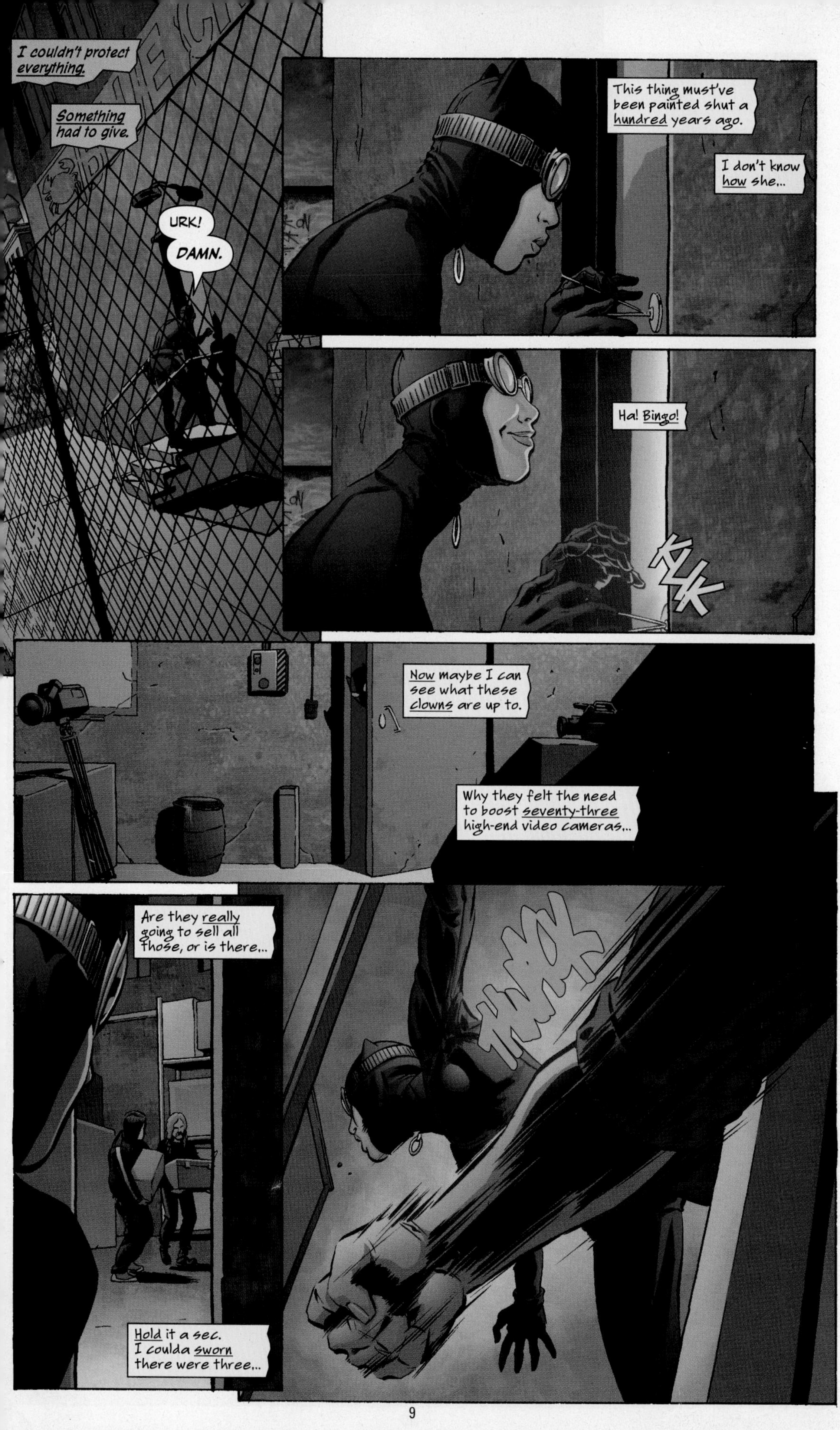
I couldn't protect everything.
Something had to give.
URK!
DAMN.
This thing must've been painted shut a hundred years ago.
I don't know how she...
Ha! Bingo!
KLIK
Now maybe I can see what these clowns are up to.
Why they felt the need to boost seventy-three high-end video cameras...
Are they really going to sell all those, or is there...
Hold it a sec. I coulda sworn there were three...

NICE SHOT, DON. *VERY* NICE.

THANKS, OTTO. SO, YOU THINK IT'S *REALLY* HER?

HELL, SHE'S WEARING THE *COSTUME*...

...WHO *ELSE* IS IT GONNA BE?

Uh-oh.

This is not— I repeat— not good.

THERE'S *ALWAYS* A *HIDDEN ADVANTAGE.* SOMETHING JUST *WAITING* TO BE USED IN YOUR FAVOR.

YOU JUST HAVE TO *FIND* IT.

C'mon, think! Think!

THIS HAS GOTTA BE WORTH *SOMETHING,* RIGHT? I MEAN, SOMETHING *BIG!*

YOU KNOW WHAT *EDISON* WOULD SAY. WE NEED TO GET IT ON *CAMERA.*

I MEAN, THE CINEMATIC *POSSIBILITIES* OF THIS MOMENT? *C'MON!*

Bingo.

WELL, HELL. WE'VE GOT A WHOLE *WAREHOUSE* FULL OF—

THUNK

GAHHH!

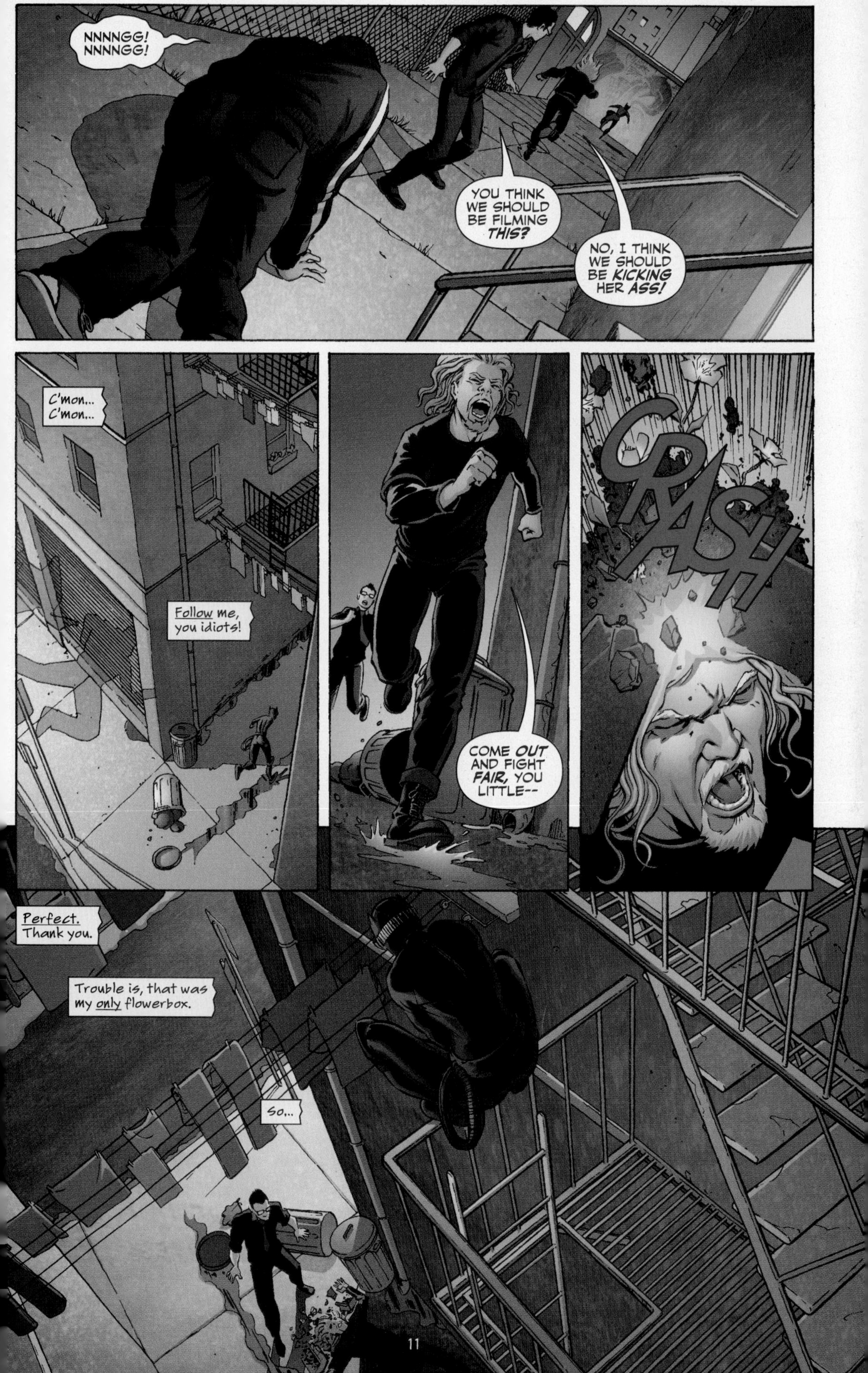
NNNNGG! NNNNGG!
YOU THINK WE SHOULD BE FILMING THIS?
NO, I THINK WE SHOULD BE KICKING HER ASS!
C'mon... C'mon...
Follow me, you idiots!
COME OUT AND FIGHT FAIR, YOU LITTLE--
CRASH
Perfect. Thank you.
Trouble is, that was my only flowerbox.
So...

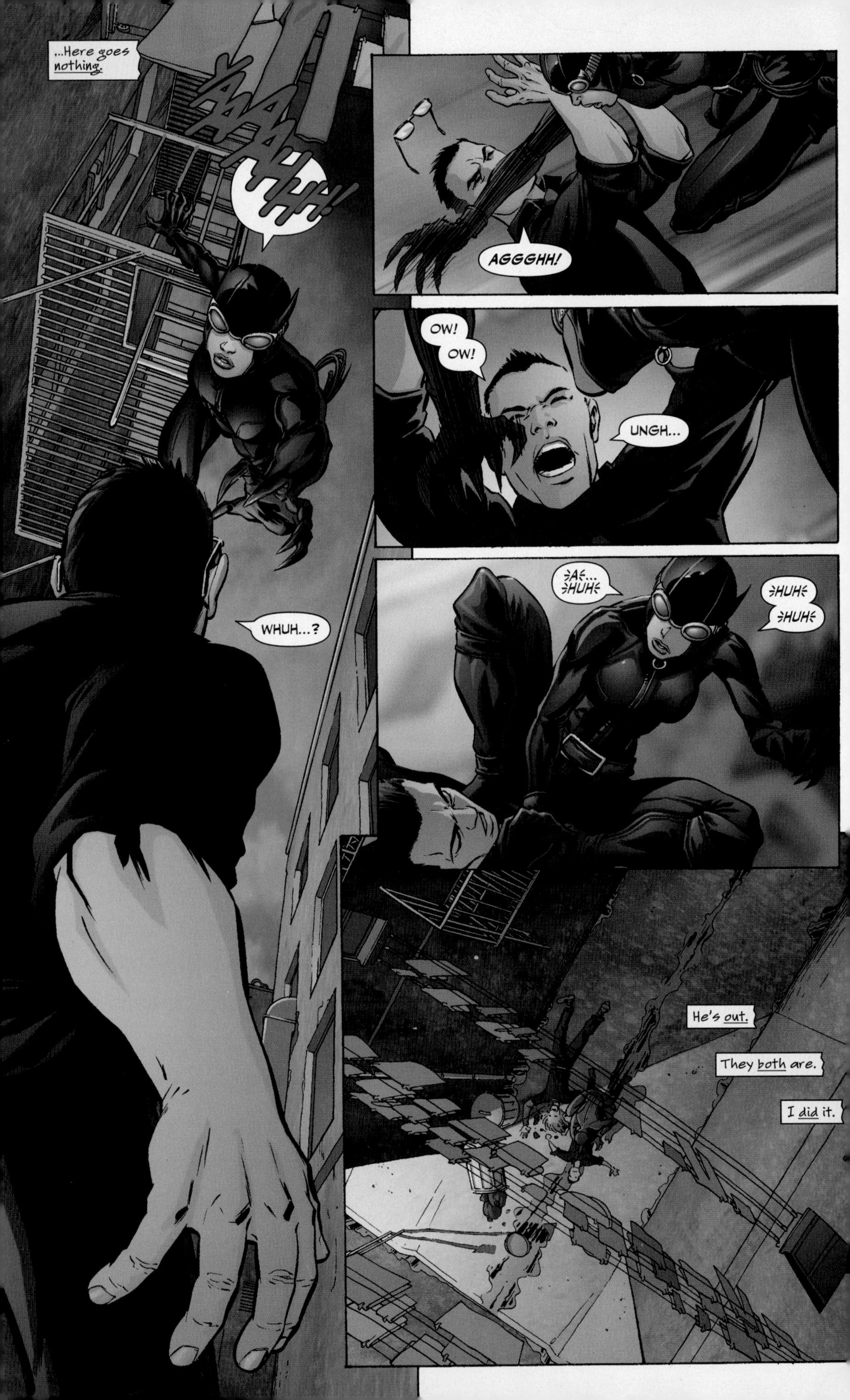
...Here goes nothing.
YAAAHHH!
WHUH...?
AGGGHH!
OW!
OW!
UNGH...
A... HUH
HUH
HUH
He's out.
They both are.
I did it.

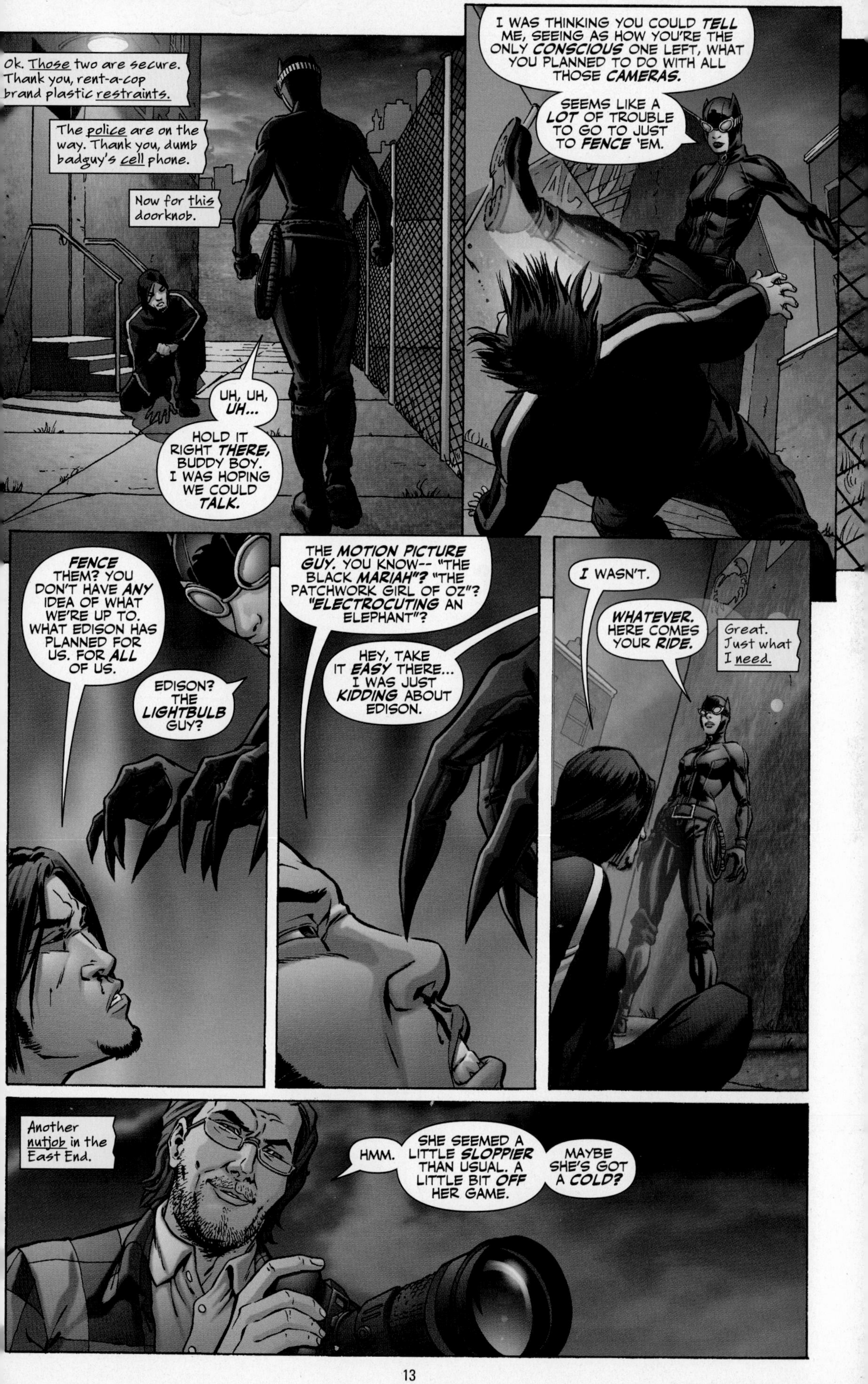

Ok. Those two are secure. Thank you, rent-a-cop brand plastic restraints.
The police are on the way. Thank you, dumb badguy's cell phone.
Now for this doorknob.
UH, UH, UH...
HOLD IT RIGHT THERE, BUDDY BOY. I WAS HOPING WE COULD TALK.
I WAS THINKING YOU COULD TELL ME, SEEING AS HOW YOU'RE THE ONLY CONSCIOUS ONE LEFT, WHAT YOU PLANNED TO DO WITH ALL THOSE CAMERAS.
SEEMS LIKE A LOT OF TROUBLE TO GO TO JUST TO FENCE 'EM.
FENCE THEM? YOU DON'T HAVE ANY IDEA OF WHAT WE'RE UP TO. WHAT EDISON HAS PLANNED FOR US. FOR ALL OF US.
EDISON? THE LIGHTBULB GUY?
THE MOTION PICTURE GUY. YOU KNOW-- "THE BLACK MARIAH"? "THE PATCHWORK GIRL OF OZ"? "ELECTROCUTING AN ELEPHANT"?
HEY, TAKE IT EASY THERE... I WAS JUST KIDDING ABOUT EDISON.
I WASN'T.
WHATEVER. HERE COMES YOUR RIDE.
Great. Just what I need.
Another nutjob in the East End.
HMM.
SHE SEEMED A LITTLE SLOPPIER THAN USUAL. A LITTLE BIT OFF HER GAME.
MAYBE SHE'S GOT A COLD?

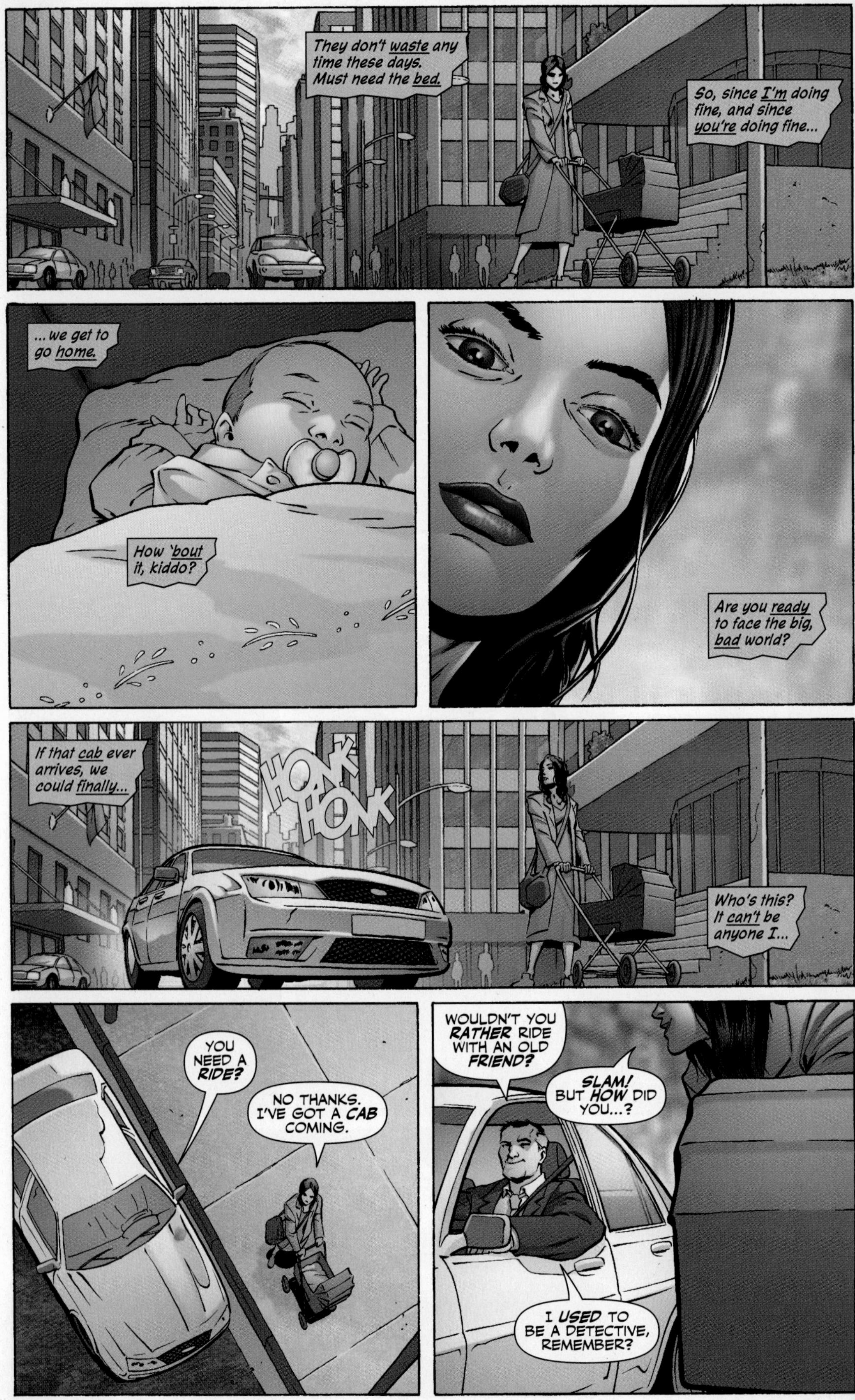
They don't waste any time these days. Must need the bed.
So, since I'm doing fine, and since you're doing fine...
...we get to go home.
How 'bout it, kiddo?
Are you ready to face the big, bad world?
If that cab ever arrives, we could finally...
HONK HONK
Who's this? It can't be anyone I...
YOU NEED A RIDE?
NO THANKS. I'VE GOT A CAB COMING.
WOULDN'T YOU RATHER RIDE WITH AN OLD FRIEND?
SLAM! BUT HOW DID YOU...?
I USED TO BE A DETECTIVE, REMEMBER?

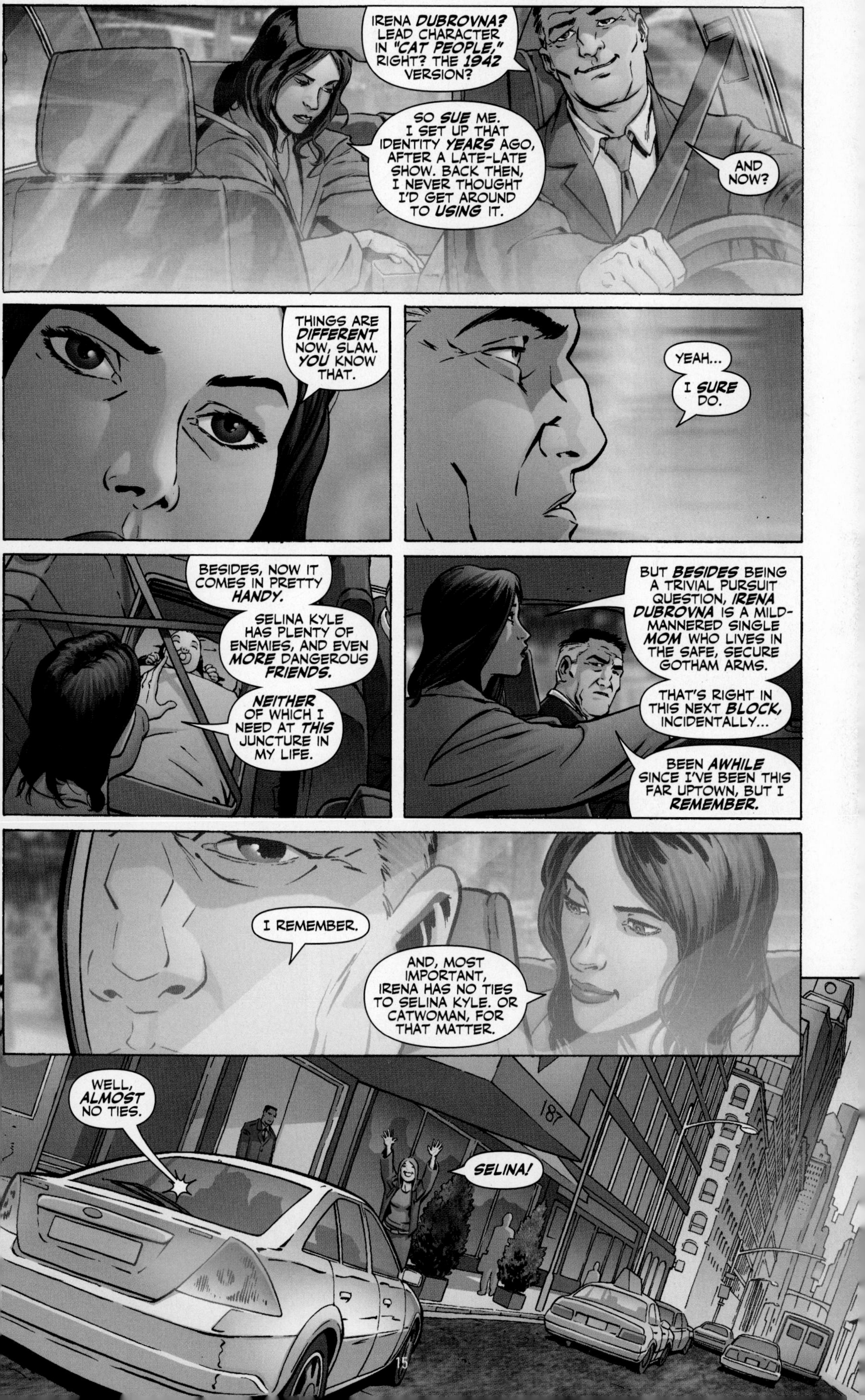

IRENA DUBROVNA? LEAD CHARACTER IN "CAT PEOPLE," RIGHT? THE 1942 VERSION?
SO SUE ME. I SET UP THAT IDENTITY YEARS AGO, AFTER A LATE-LATE SHOW. BACK THEN, I NEVER THOUGHT I'D GET AROUND TO USING IT.
AND NOW?
THINGS ARE DIFFERENT NOW, SLAM. YOU KNOW THAT.
YEAH...
I SURE DO.
BESIDES, NOW IT COMES IN PRETTY HANDY.
SELINA KYLE HAS PLENTY OF ENEMIES, AND EVEN MORE DANGEROUS FRIENDS.
NEITHER OF WHICH I NEED AT THIS JUNCTURE IN MY LIFE.
BUT BESIDES BEING A TRIVIAL PURSUIT QUESTION, IRENA DUBROVNA IS A MILD-MANNERED SINGLE MOM WHO LIVES IN THE SAFE, SECURE GOTHAM ARMS.
THAT'S RIGHT IN THIS NEXT BLOCK, INCIDENTALLY...
BEEN AWHILE SINCE I'VE BEEN THIS FAR UPTOWN, BUT I REMEMBER.
I REMEMBER.
AND, MOST IMPORTANT, IRENA HAS NO TIES TO SELINA KYLE. OR CATWOMAN, FOR THAT MATTER.
WELL, ALMOST NO TIES.
SELINA!
187

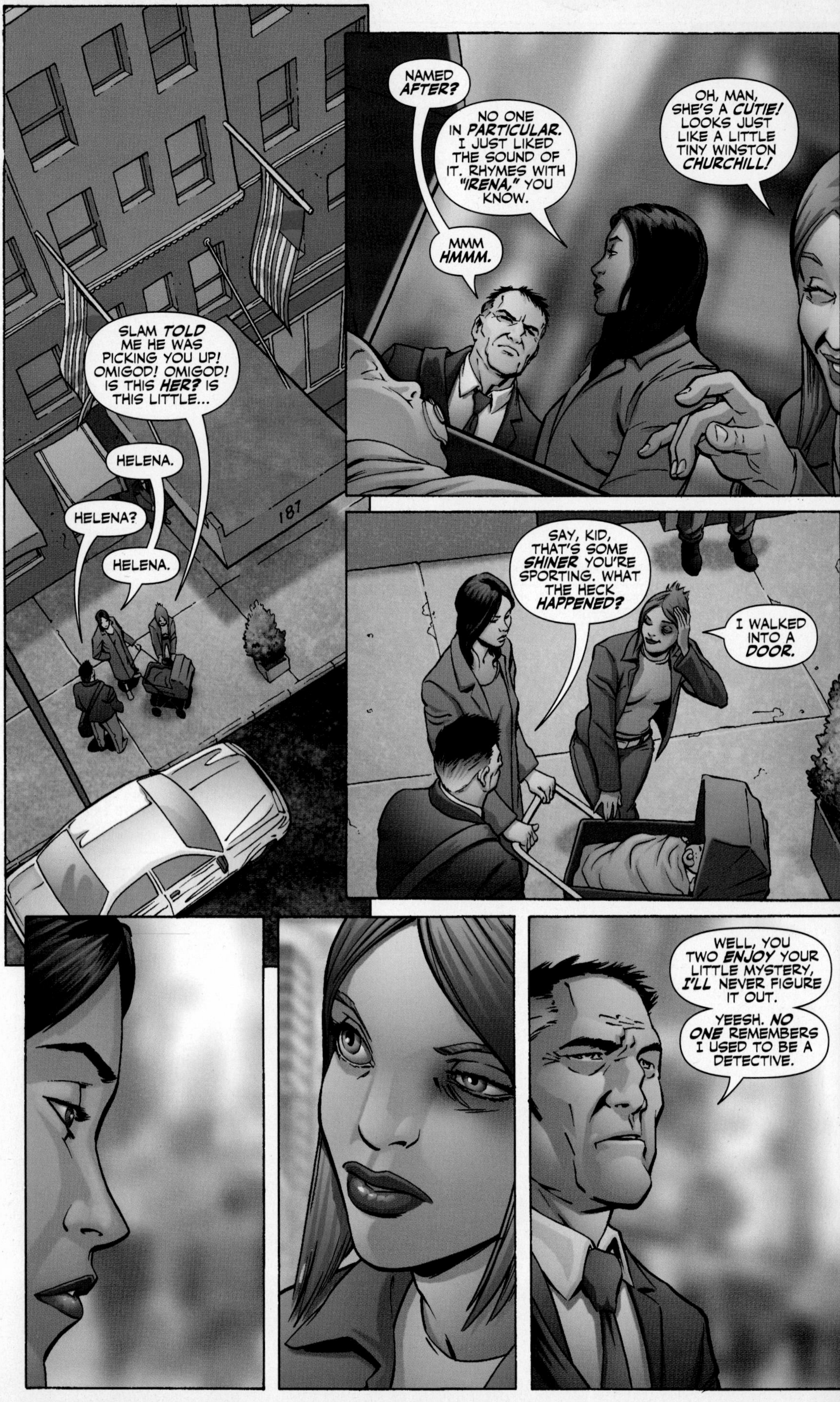
SLAM TOLD ME HE WAS PICKING YOU UP! OMIGOD! OMIGOD! IS THIS HER? IS THIS LITTLE...
HELENA.
HELENA?
HELENA.
NAMED AFTER?
NO ONE IN PARTICULAR. I JUST LIKED THE SOUND OF IT. RHYMES WITH "IRENA," YOU KNOW.
MMM HMMM.
OH, MAN, SHE'S A CUTIE! LOOKS JUST LIKE A LITTLE TINY WINSTON CHURCHILL!
SAY, KID, THAT'S SOME SHINER YOU'RE SPORTING. WHAT THE HECK HAPPENED?
I WALKED INTO A DOOR.
WELL, YOU TWO ENJOY YOUR LITTLE MYSTERY, I'LL NEVER FIGURE IT OUT.
YEESH. NO ONE REMEMBERS I USED TO BE A DETECTIVE.

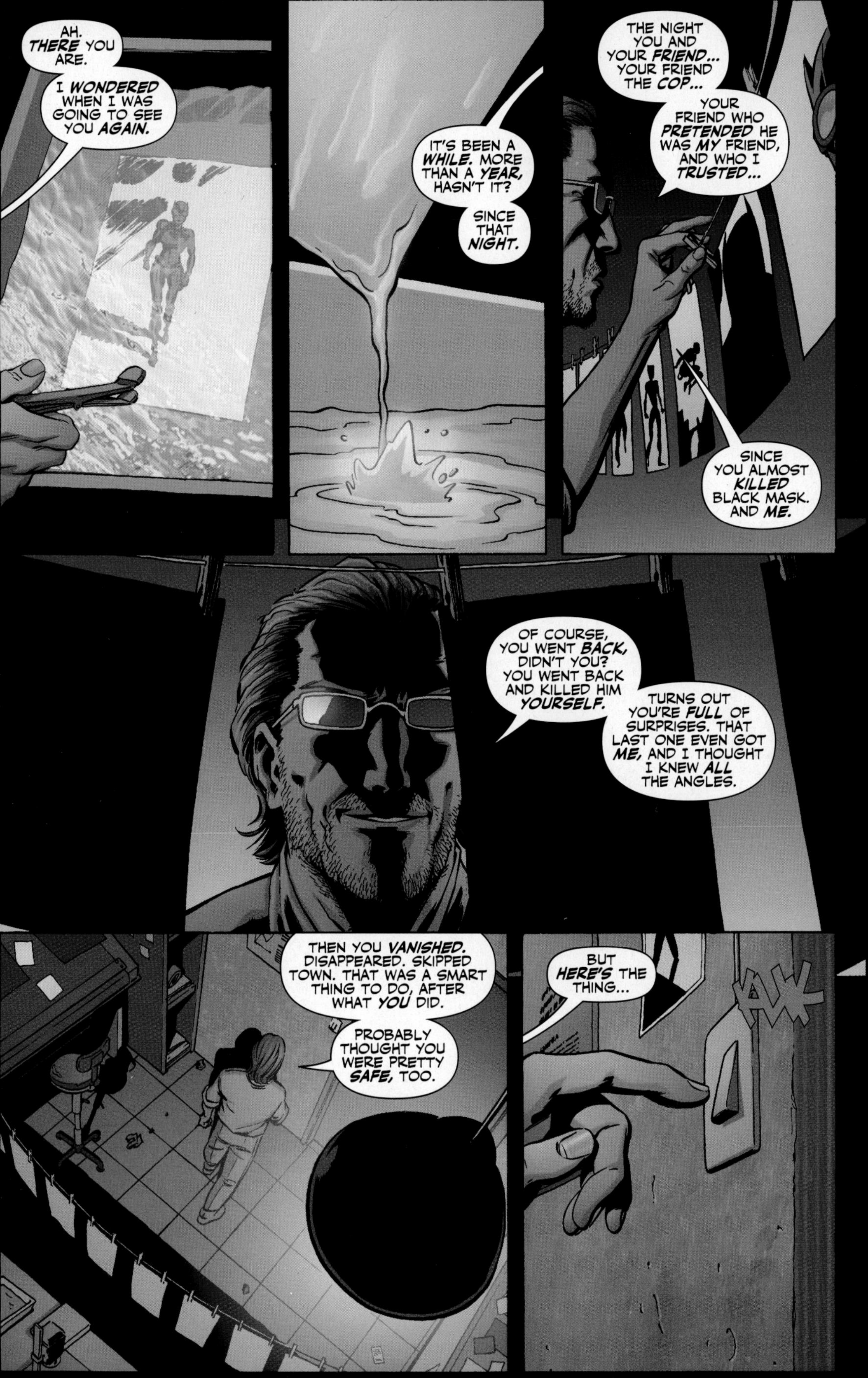
AH. THERE YOU ARE.
I WONDERED WHEN I WAS GOING TO SEE YOU AGAIN.
IT'S BEEN A WHILE. MORE THAN A YEAR, HASN'T IT?
SINCE THAT NIGHT.
THE NIGHT YOU AND YOUR FRIEND... YOUR FRIEND THE COP...
YOUR FRIEND WHO PRETENDED HE WAS MY FRIEND, AND WHO I TRUSTED...
SINCE YOU ALMOST KILLED BLACK MASK. AND ME.
OF COURSE, YOU WENT BACK, DIDN'T YOU? YOU WENT BACK AND KILLED HIM YOURSELF.
TURNS OUT YOU'RE FULL OF SURPRISES. THAT LAST ONE EVEN GOT ME, AND I THOUGHT I KNEW ALL THE ANGLES.
THEN YOU VANISHED. DISAPPEARED. SKIPPED TOWN. THAT WAS A SMART THING TO DO, AFTER WHAT YOU DID.
PROBABLY THOUGHT YOU WERE PRETTY SAFE, TOO.
BUT HERE'S THE THING...
KLIK

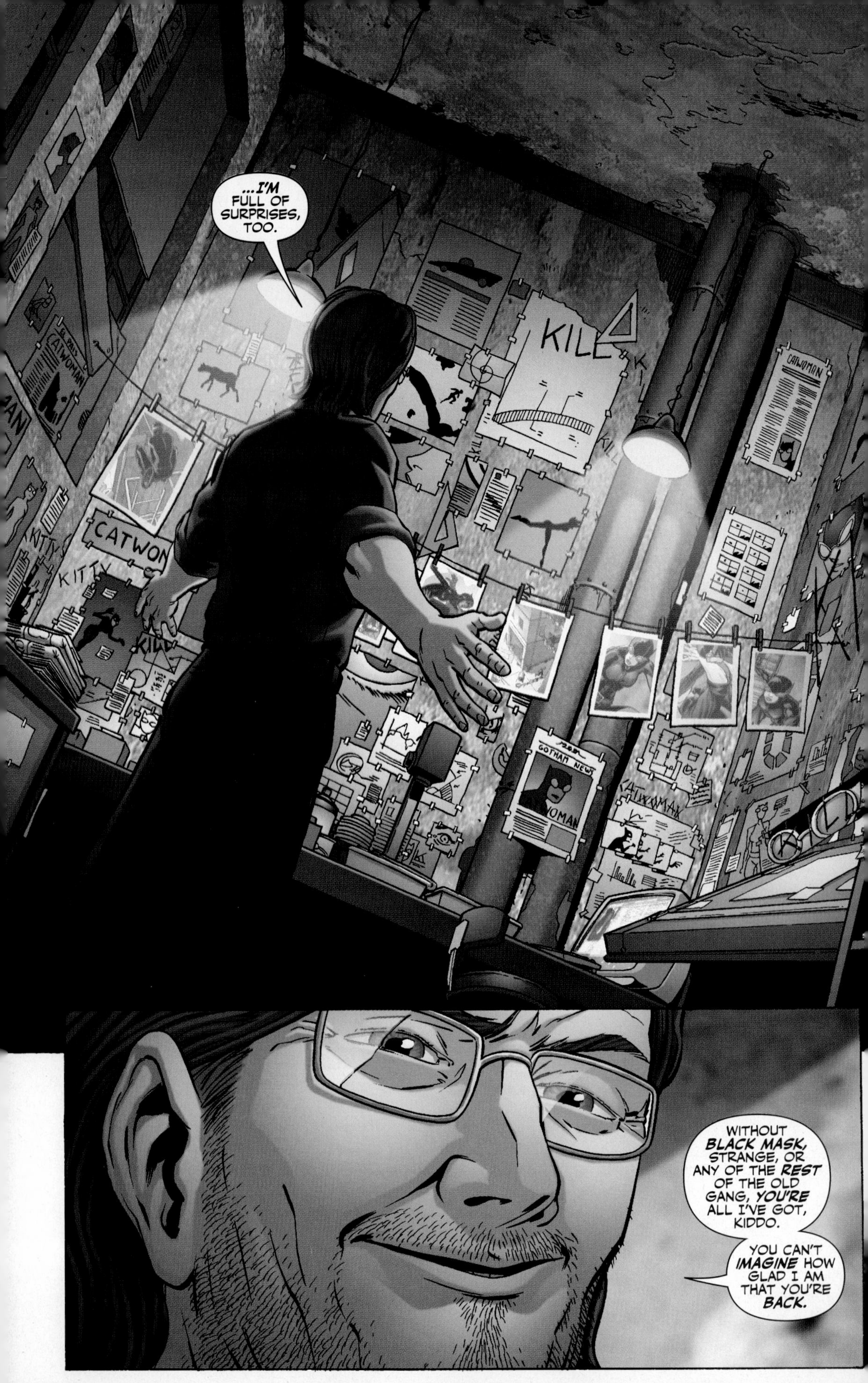
...I'M FULL OF SURPRISES, TOO.
WITHOUT BLACK MASK, STRANGE, OR ANY OF THE REST OF THE OLD GANG, YOU'RE ALL I'VE GOT, KIDDO.
YOU CAN'T IMAGINE HOW GLAD I AM THAT YOU'RE BACK.

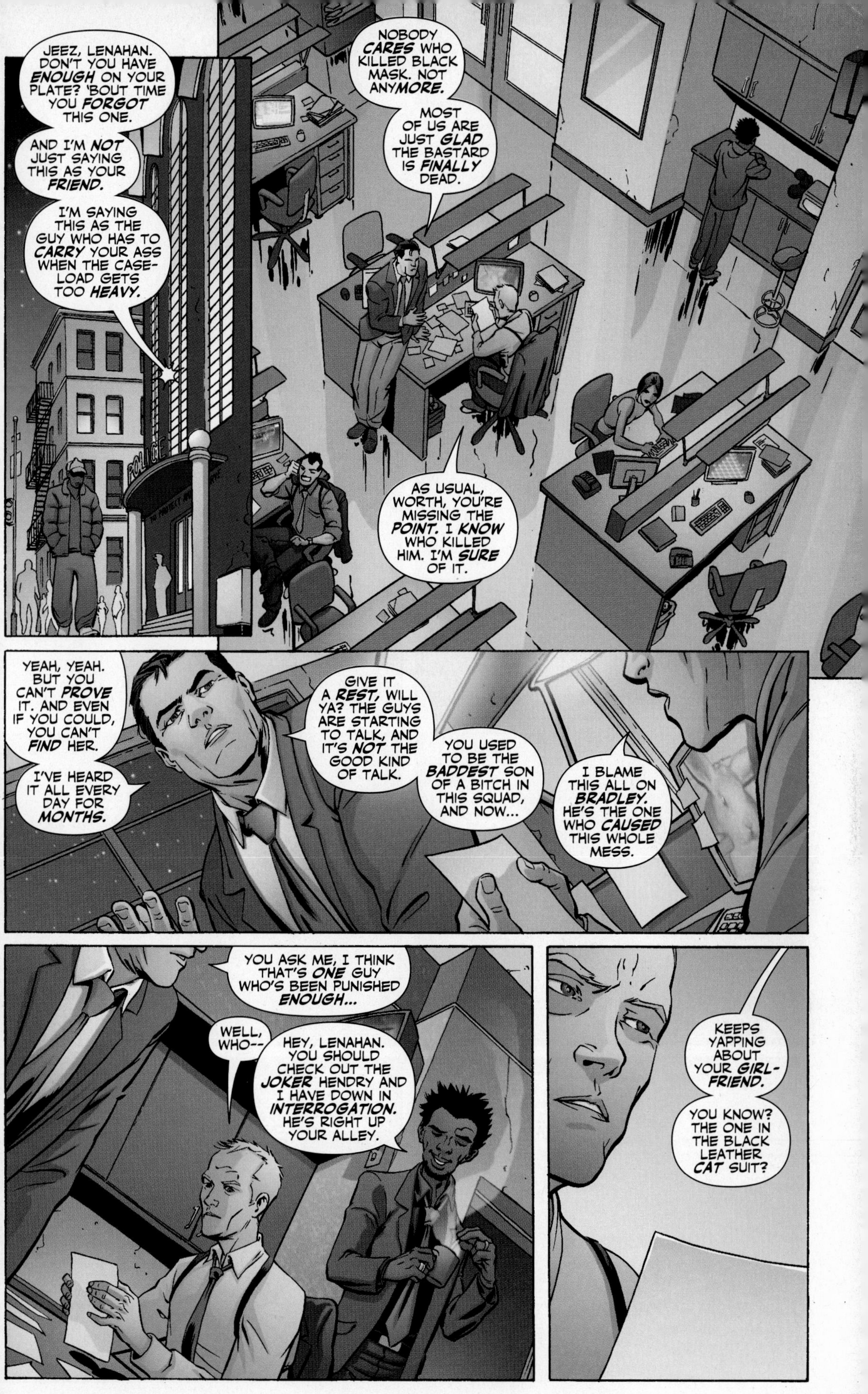

JEEZ, LENAHAN. DON'T YOU HAVE ENOUGH ON YOUR PLATE? 'BOUT TIME YOU FORGOT THIS ONE.
AND I'M NOT JUST SAYING THIS AS YOUR FRIEND.
I'M SAYING THIS AS THE GUY WHO HAS TO CARRY YOUR ASS WHEN THE CASE-LOAD GETS TOO HEAVY.
NOBODY CARES WHO KILLED BLACK MASK. NOT ANYMORE.
MOST OF US ARE JUST GLAD THE BASTARD IS FINALLY DEAD.
AS USUAL, WORTH, YOU'RE MISSING THE POINT. I KNOW WHO KILLED HIM. I'M SURE OF IT.
YEAH, YEAH. BUT YOU CAN'T PROVE IT. AND EVEN IF YOU COULD, YOU CAN'T FIND HER.
I'VE HEARD IT ALL EVERY DAY FOR MONTHS.
GIVE IT A REST, WILL YA? THE GUYS ARE STARTING TO TALK, AND IT'S NOT THE GOOD KIND OF TALK.
YOU USED TO BE THE BADDEST SON OF A BITCH IN THIS SQUAD, AND NOW...
I BLAME THIS ALL ON BRADLEY. HE'S THE ONE WHO CAUSED THIS WHOLE MESS.
YOU ASK ME, I THINK THAT'S ONE GUY WHO'S BEEN PUNISHED ENOUGH...
WELL, WHO--
HEY, LENAHAN. YOU SHOULD CHECK OUT THE JOKER HENDRY AND I HAVE DOWN IN INTERROGATION. HE'S RIGHT UP YOUR ALLEY.
KEEPS YAPPING ABOUT YOUR GIRL-FRIEND.
YOU KNOW? THE ONE IN THE BLACK LEATHER CAT SUIT?

YOU TOLD IT TO *ME*, KID. NOW TELL IT TO *HIM*.

TELL HIM *WHO* BROKE UP YOUR LITTLE *CAMERA* CLUB.

I DON'T *THINK* SO. IF IT'S *IMPORTANT* ENOUGH TO BRING ANOTHER COP IN ON, IT MUST BE IMPORTANT ENOUGH TO GET ME SOME SORT OF *DEAL*.

SO *THAT'S* WHAT I WANT-- A *DEAL*.

FINE. NO PROBLEM.

YAAA!

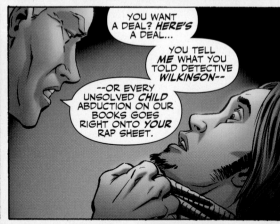

YOU WANT A DEAL? *HERE'S* A DEAL...

YOU TELL *ME* WHAT YOU TOLD DETECTIVE *WILKINSON*--

--OR EVERY UNSOLVED *CHILD* ABDUCTION ON OUR BOOKS GOES RIGHT ONTO *YOUR* RAP SHEET.

AND YOU *KNOW* HOW THAT'LL PLAY UPSTATE...

OKAY! *OKAY!* IT WAS *HER!* IT WAS *CATWOMAN!*

WELCOME *BACK,* LENAHAN.

NICE TO SEE YOU HAVEN'T LOST YOUR *DELICATE* TOUCH.

≥WHIMPER≤

20

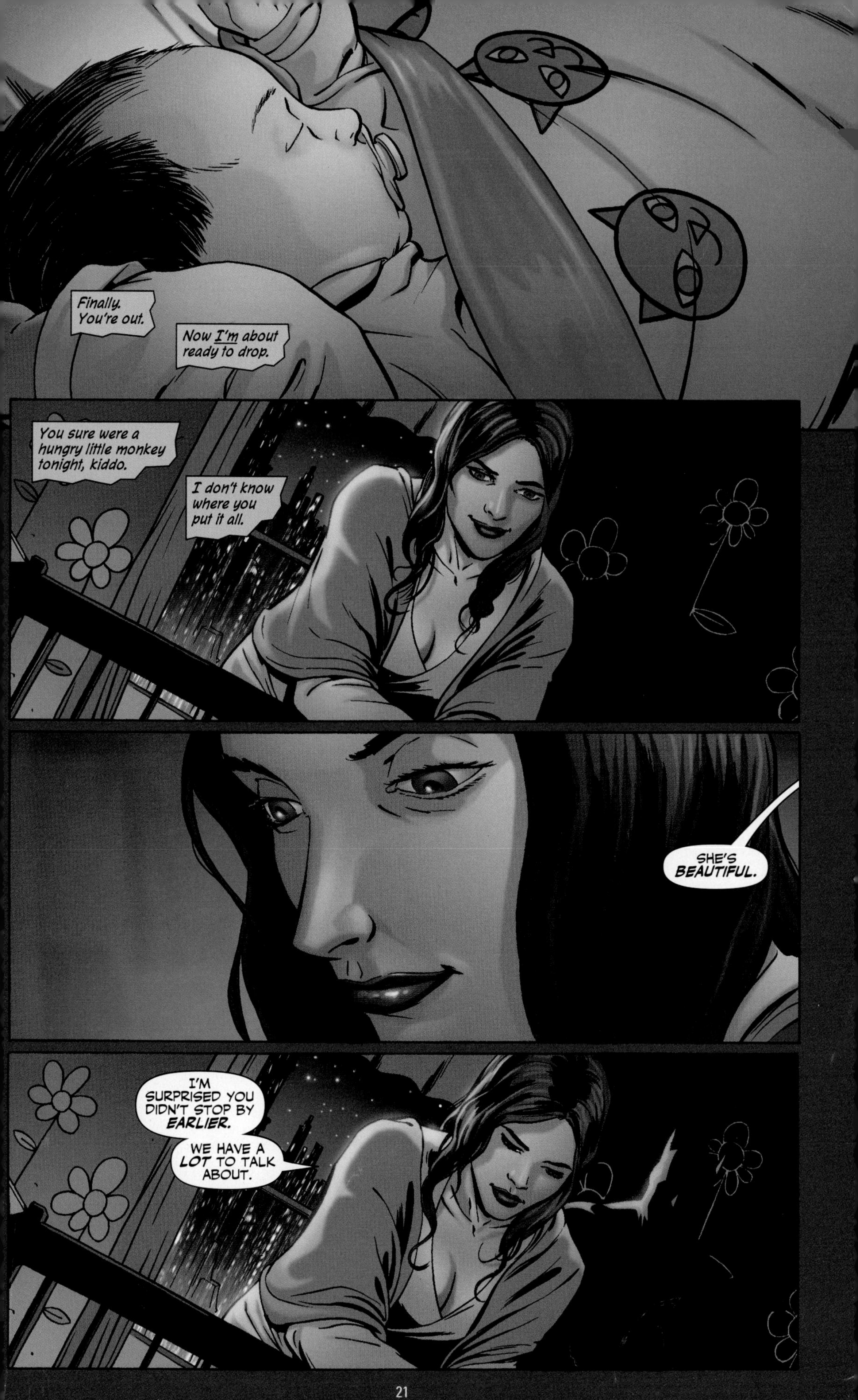
Finally. You're out.
Now I'm about ready to drop.
You sure were a hungry little monkey tonight, kiddo.
I don't know where you put it all.
SHE'S BEAUTIFUL.
I'M SURPRISED YOU DIDN'T STOP BY EARLIER.
WE HAVE A LOT TO TALK ABOUT.

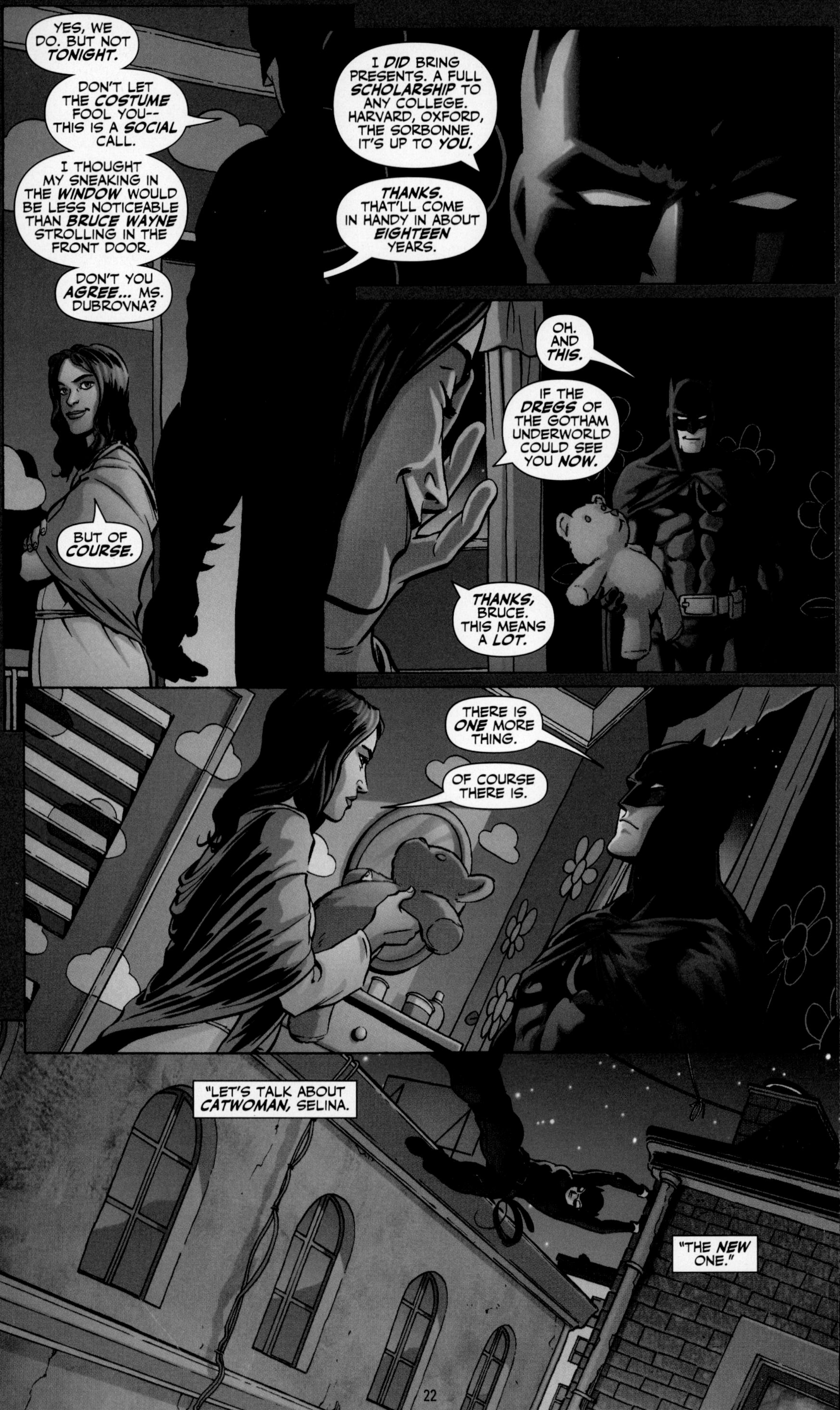
YES, WE DO. BUT NOT TONIGHT.
DON'T LET THE COSTUME FOOL YOU-- THIS IS A SOCIAL CALL.
I THOUGHT MY SNEAKING IN THE WINDOW WOULD BE LESS NOTICEABLE THAN BRUCE WAYNE STROLLING IN THE FRONT DOOR.
DON'T YOU AGREE... MS. DUBROVNA?
BUT OF COURSE.
I DID BRING PRESENTS. A FULL SCHOLARSHIP TO ANY COLLEGE. HARVARD, OXFORD, THE SORBONNE. IT'S UP TO YOU.
THANKS. THAT'LL COME IN HANDY IN ABOUT EIGHTEEN YEARS.
OH. AND THIS.
IF THE DREGS OF THE GOTHAM UNDERWORLD COULD SEE YOU NOW.
THANKS, BRUCE. THIS MEANS A LOT.
THERE IS ONE MORE THING.
OF COURSE THERE IS.
"LET'S TALK ABOUT CATWOMAN, SELINA.
"THE NEW ONE."

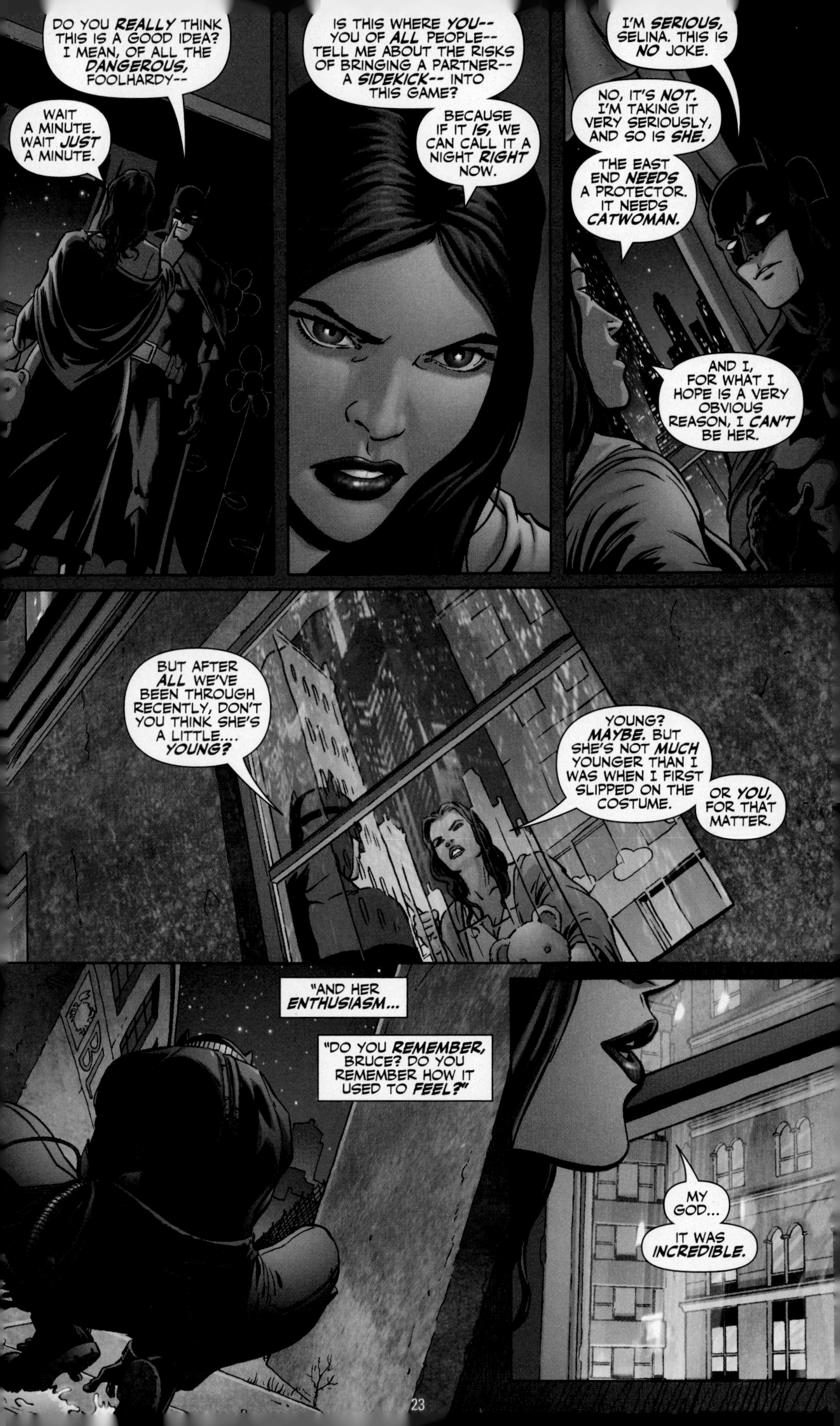

DO YOU REALLY THINK THIS IS A GOOD IDEA? I MEAN, OF ALL THE DANGEROUS, FOOLHARDY--
WAIT A MINUTE. WAIT JUST A MINUTE.
IS THIS WHERE YOU-- YOU OF ALL PEOPLE-- TELL ME ABOUT THE RISKS OF BRINGING A PARTNER-- A SIDEKICK-- INTO THIS GAME?
BECAUSE IF IT IS, WE CAN CALL IT A NIGHT RIGHT NOW.
I'M SERIOUS, SELINA. THIS IS NO JOKE.
NO, IT'S NOT. I'M TAKING IT VERY SERIOUSLY, AND SO IS SHE.
THE EAST END NEEDS A PROTECTOR. IT NEEDS CATWOMAN.
AND I, FOR WHAT I HOPE IS A VERY OBVIOUS REASON, I CAN'T BE HER.
BUT AFTER ALL WE'VE BEEN THROUGH RECENTLY, DON'T YOU THINK SHE'S A LITTLE.... YOUNG?
YOUNG? MAYBE. BUT SHE'S NOT MUCH YOUNGER THAN I WAS WHEN I FIRST SLIPPED ON THE COSTUME.
OR YOU, FOR THAT MATTER.
"AND HER ENTHUSIASM...
"DO YOU REMEMBER, BRUCE? DO YOU REMEMBER HOW IT USED TO FEEL?"
MY GOD... IT WAS INCREDIBLE.

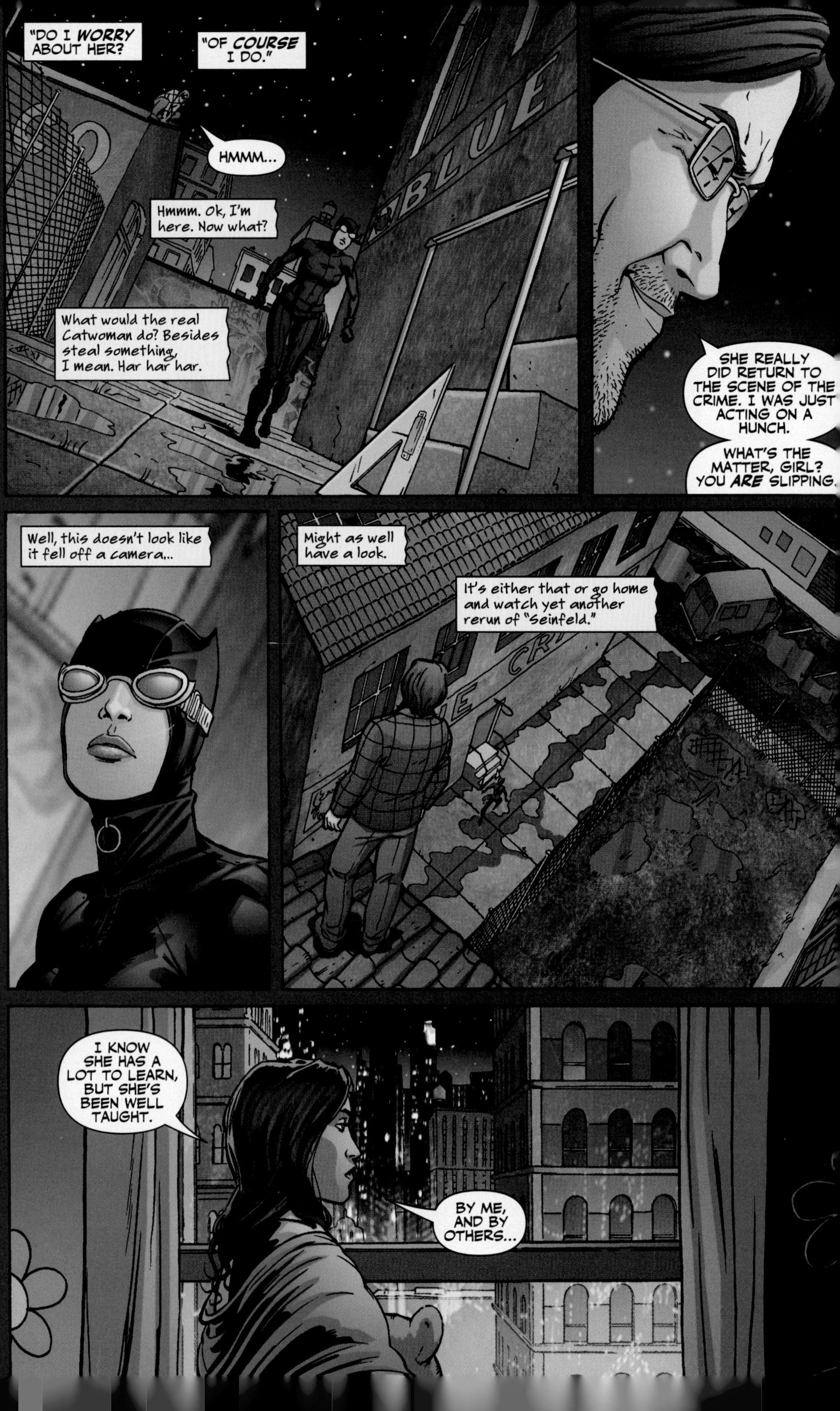

"DO I WORRY ABOUT HER?
"OF COURSE I DO."
HMMM...
Hmmm. Ok, I'm here. Now what?
What would the real Catwoman do? Besides steal something, I mean. Har har har.
SHE REALLY DID RETURN TO THE SCENE OF THE CRIME. I WAS JUST ACTING ON A HUNCH.
WHAT'S THE MATTER, GIRL? YOU ARE SLIPPING.
Well, this doesn't look like it fell off a camera...
Might as well have a look.
It's either that or go home and watch yet another rerun of "Seinfeld."
I KNOW SHE HAS A LOT TO LEARN, BUT SHE'S BEEN WELL TAUGHT.
BY ME, AND BY OTHERS...

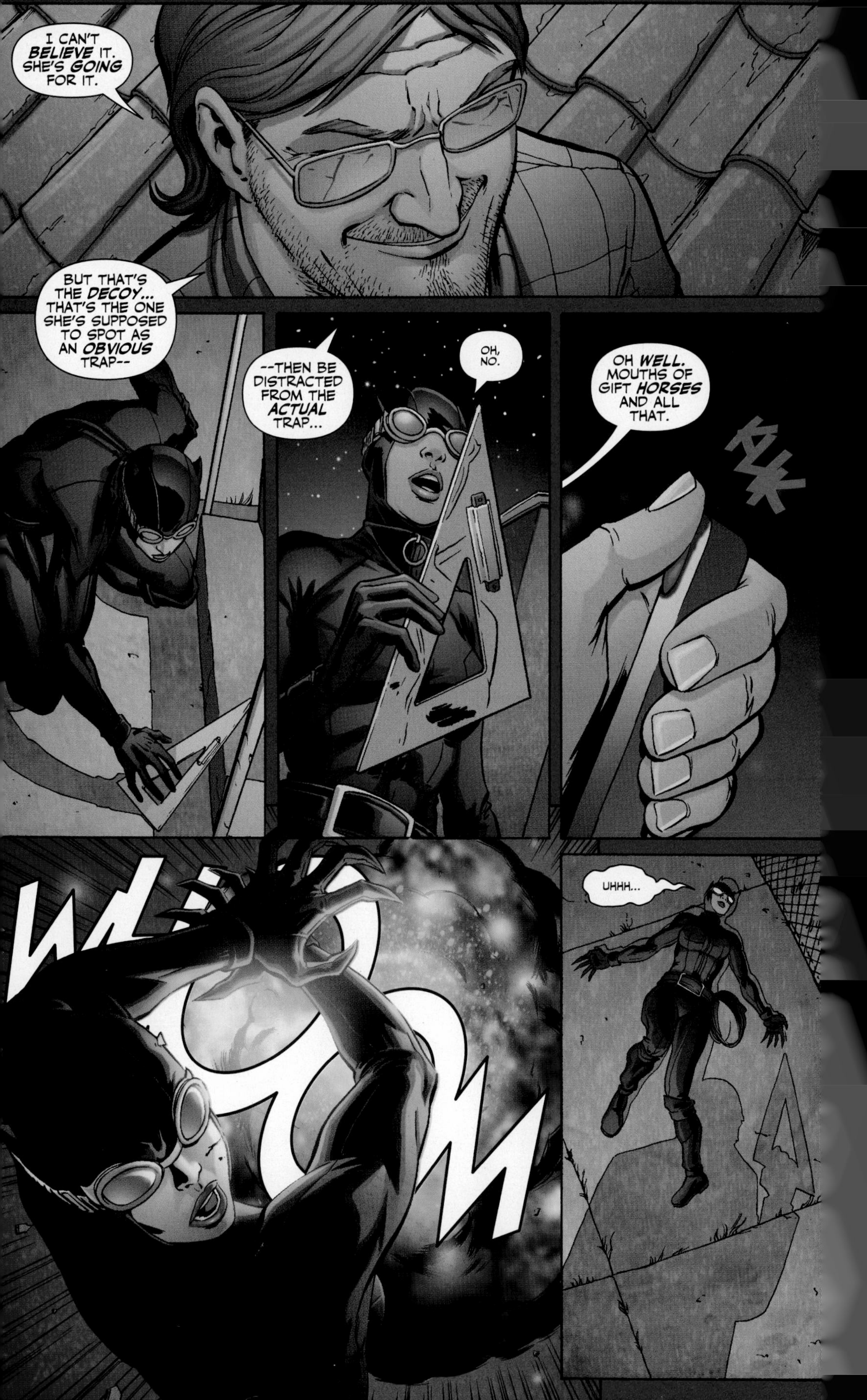

I CAN'T BELIEVE IT. SHE'S GOING FOR IT.
BUT THAT'S THE DECOY... THAT'S THE ONE SHE'S SUPPOSED TO SPOT AS AN OBVIOUS TRAP--
--THEN BE DISTRACTED FROM THE ACTUAL TRAP...
OH, NO.
OH WELL. MOUTHS OF GIFT HORSES AND ALL THAT.
KLIK
UHHH...

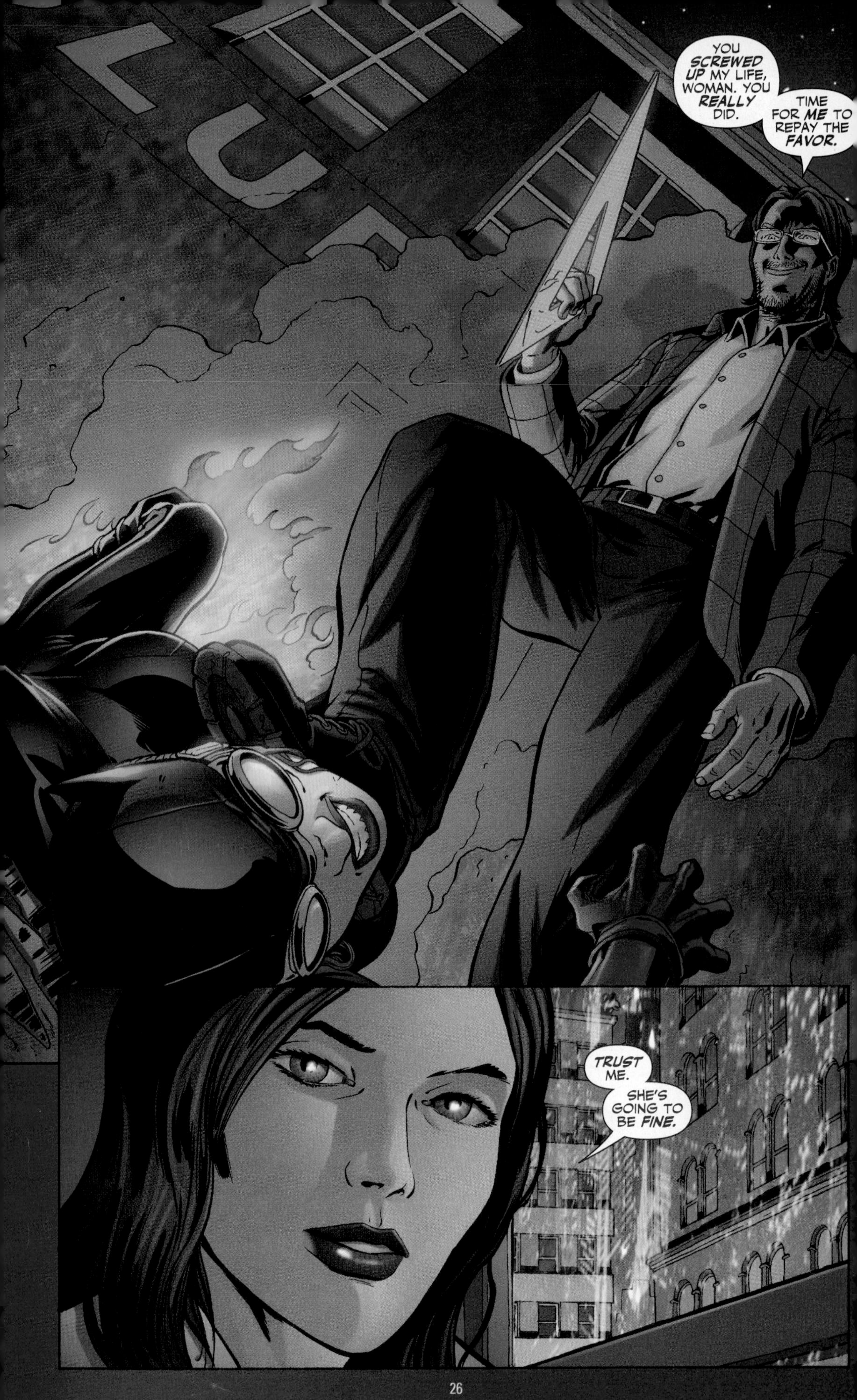
YOU SCREWED UP MY LIFE, WOMAN. YOU REALLY DID.
TIME FOR ME TO REPAY THE FAVOR.
TRUST ME.
SHE'S GOING TO BE FINE.

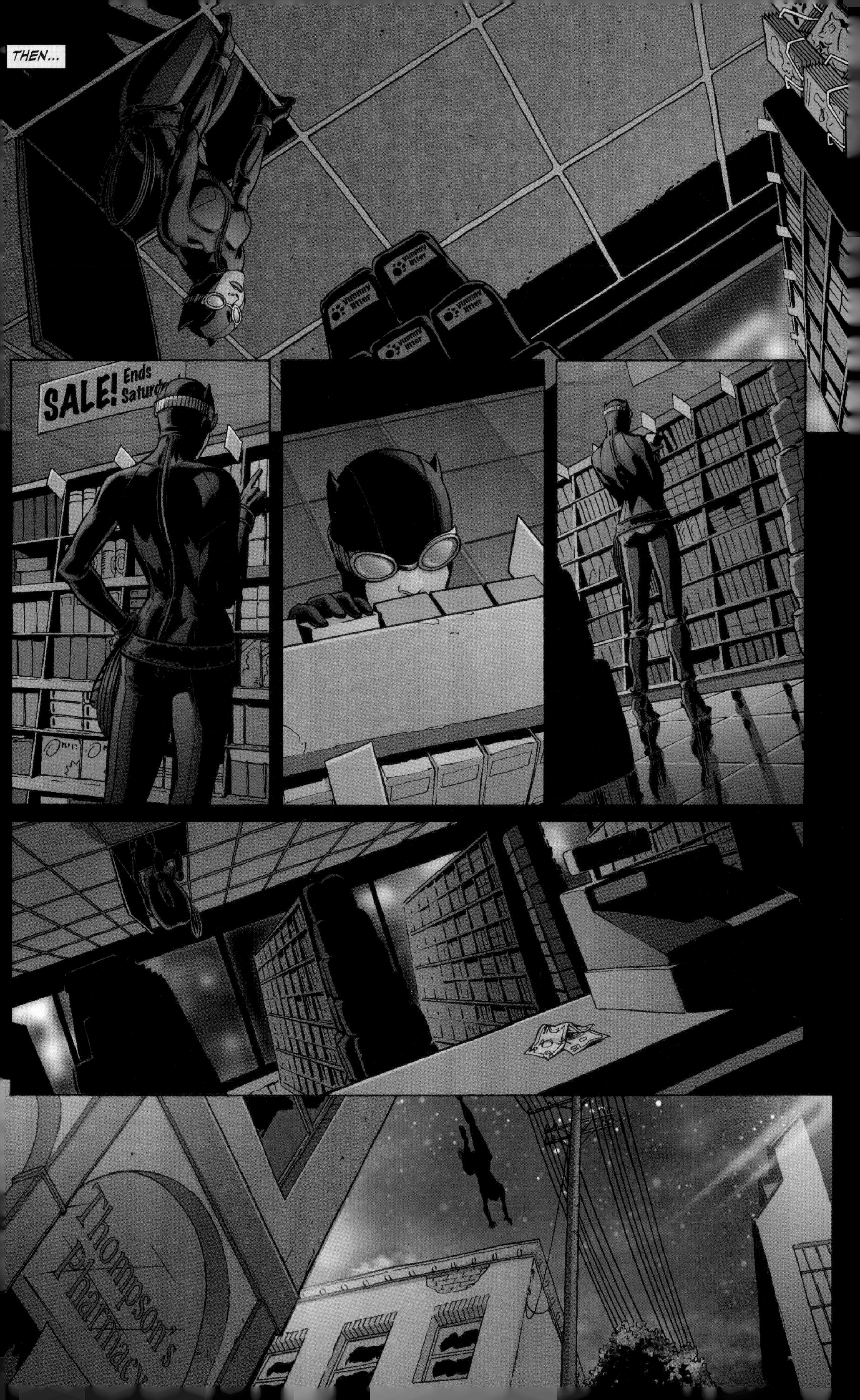
THEN...
yummy litter
SALE! Ends Saturd
Thompson's Pharmacy

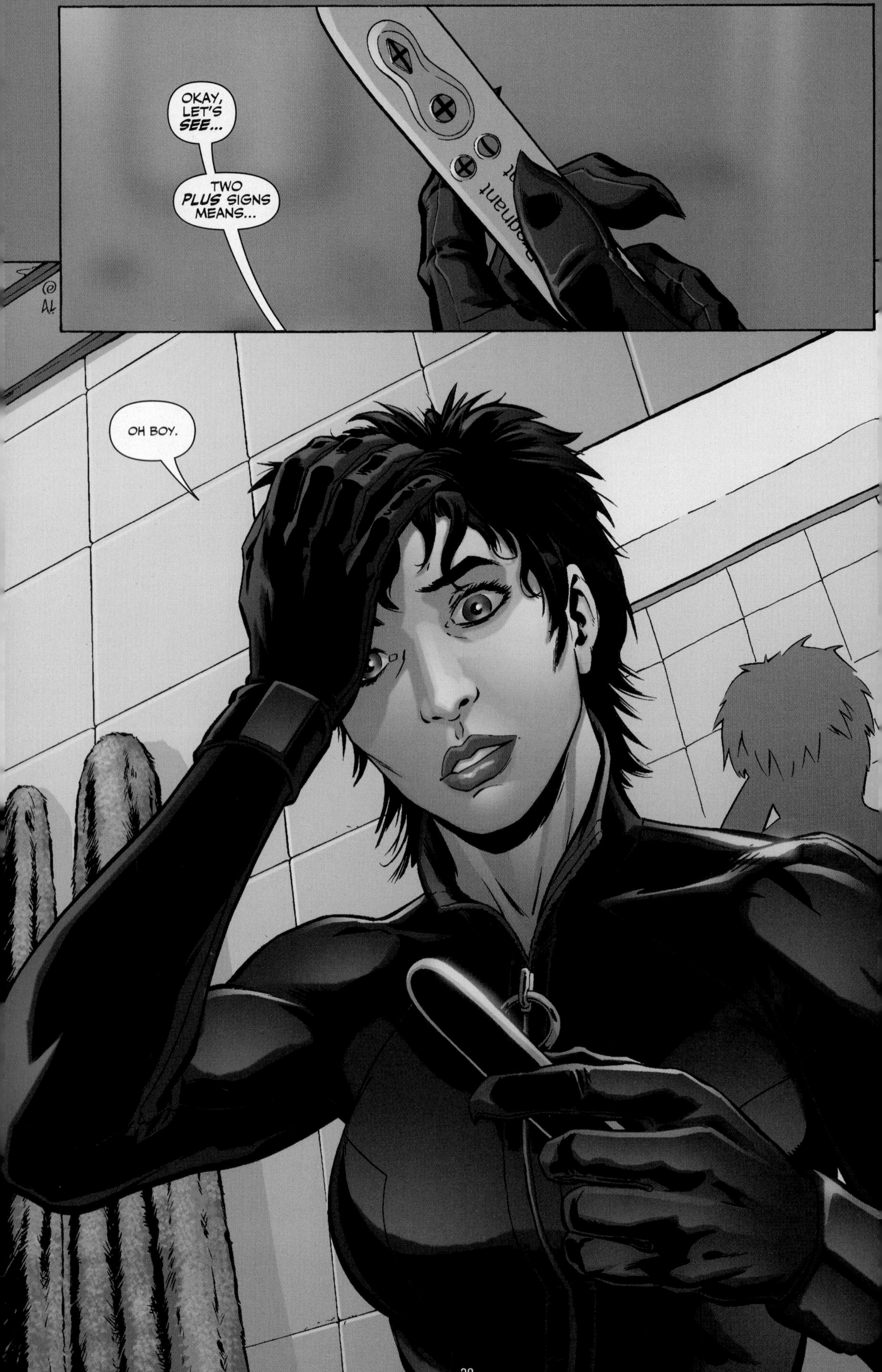
OKAY, LET'S SEE...
TWO PLUS SIGNS MEANS...
OH BOY.

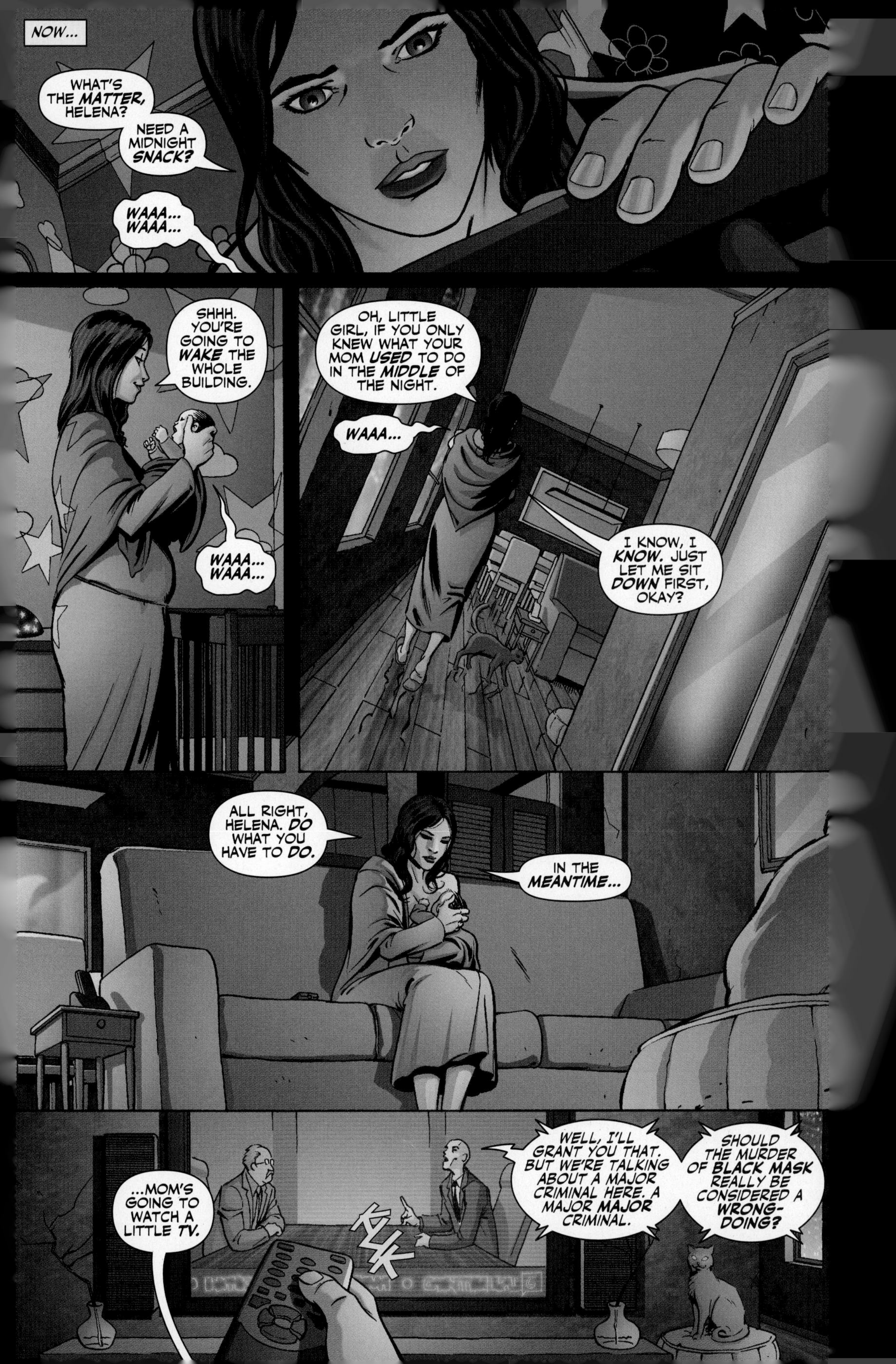
NOW...
WHAT'S THE MATTER, HELENA?
NEED A MIDNIGHT SNACK?
WAAA... WAAA...
SHHH. YOU'RE GOING TO WAKE THE WHOLE BUILDING.
WAAA... WAAA...
OH, LITTLE GIRL, IF YOU ONLY KNEW WHAT YOUR MOM USED TO DO IN THE MIDDLE OF THE NIGHT.
WAAA...
I KNOW, I KNOW. JUST LET ME SIT DOWN FIRST, OKAY?
ALL RIGHT, HELENA. DO WHAT YOU HAVE TO DO.
IN THE MEANTIME...
...MOM'S GOING TO WATCH A LITTLE TV.
KLIK
WELL, I'LL GRANT YOU THAT. BUT WE'RE TALKING ABOUT A MAJOR CRIMINAL HERE. A MAJOR MAJOR CRIMINAL.
SHOULD THE MURDER OF BLACK MASK REALLY BE CONSIDERED A WRONG-DOING?

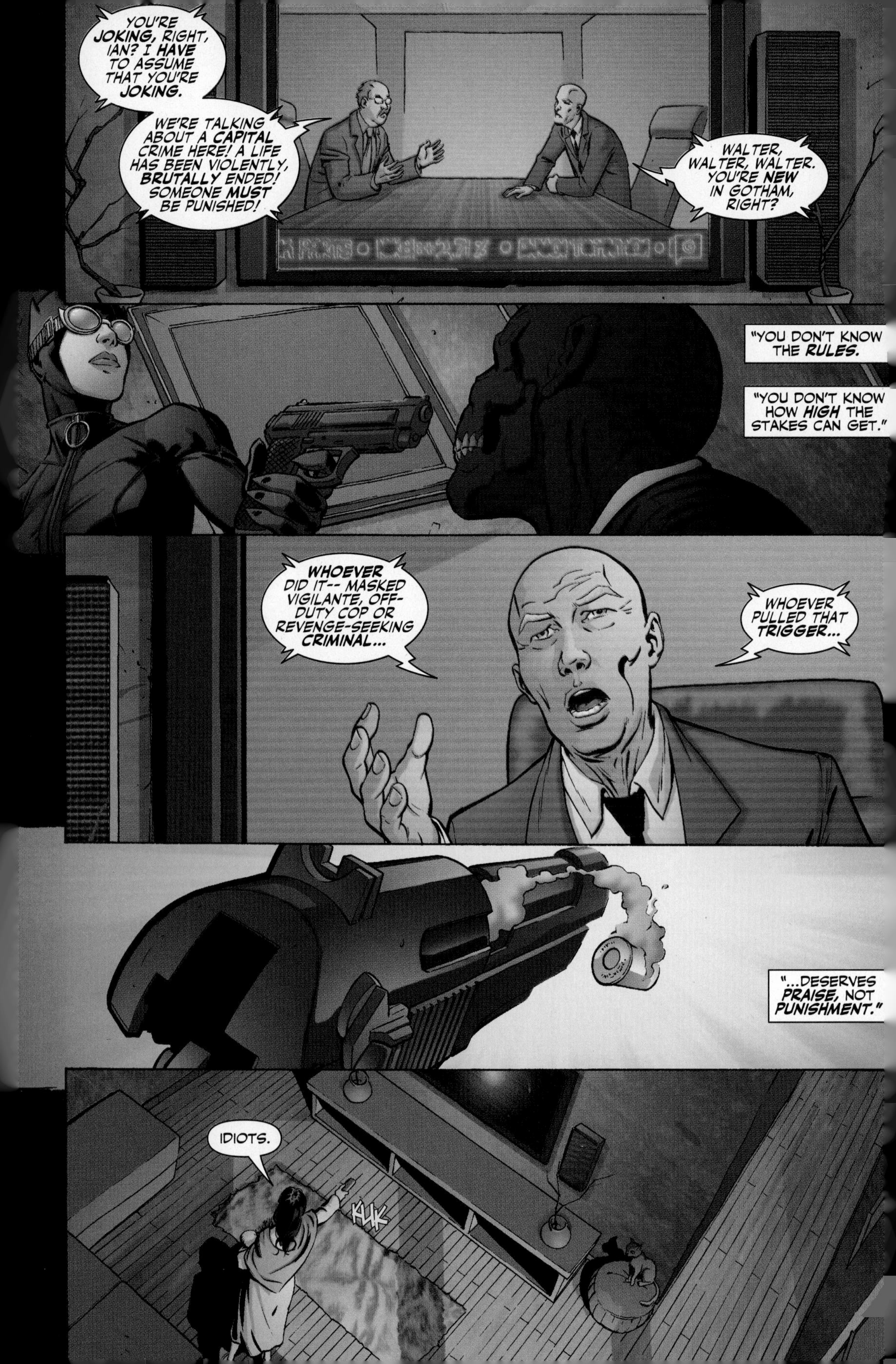

YOU'RE JOKING, RIGHT, IAN? I HAVE TO ASSUME THAT YOU'RE JOKING.
WE'RE TALKING ABOUT A CAPITAL CRIME HERE! A LIFE HAS BEEN VIOLENTLY, BRUTALLY ENDED! SOMEONE MUST BE PUNISHED!
WALTER, WALTER, WALTER. YOU'RE NEW IN GOTHAM, RIGHT?
"YOU DON'T KNOW THE RULES.
"YOU DON'T KNOW HOW HIGH THE STAKES CAN GET."
WHOEVER DID IT-- MASKED VIGILANTE, OFF-DUTY COP OR REVENGE-SEEKING CRIMINAL...
WHOEVER PULLED THAT TRIGGER...
"...DESERVES PRAISE, NOT PUNISHMENT."
IDIOTS.
KLIK

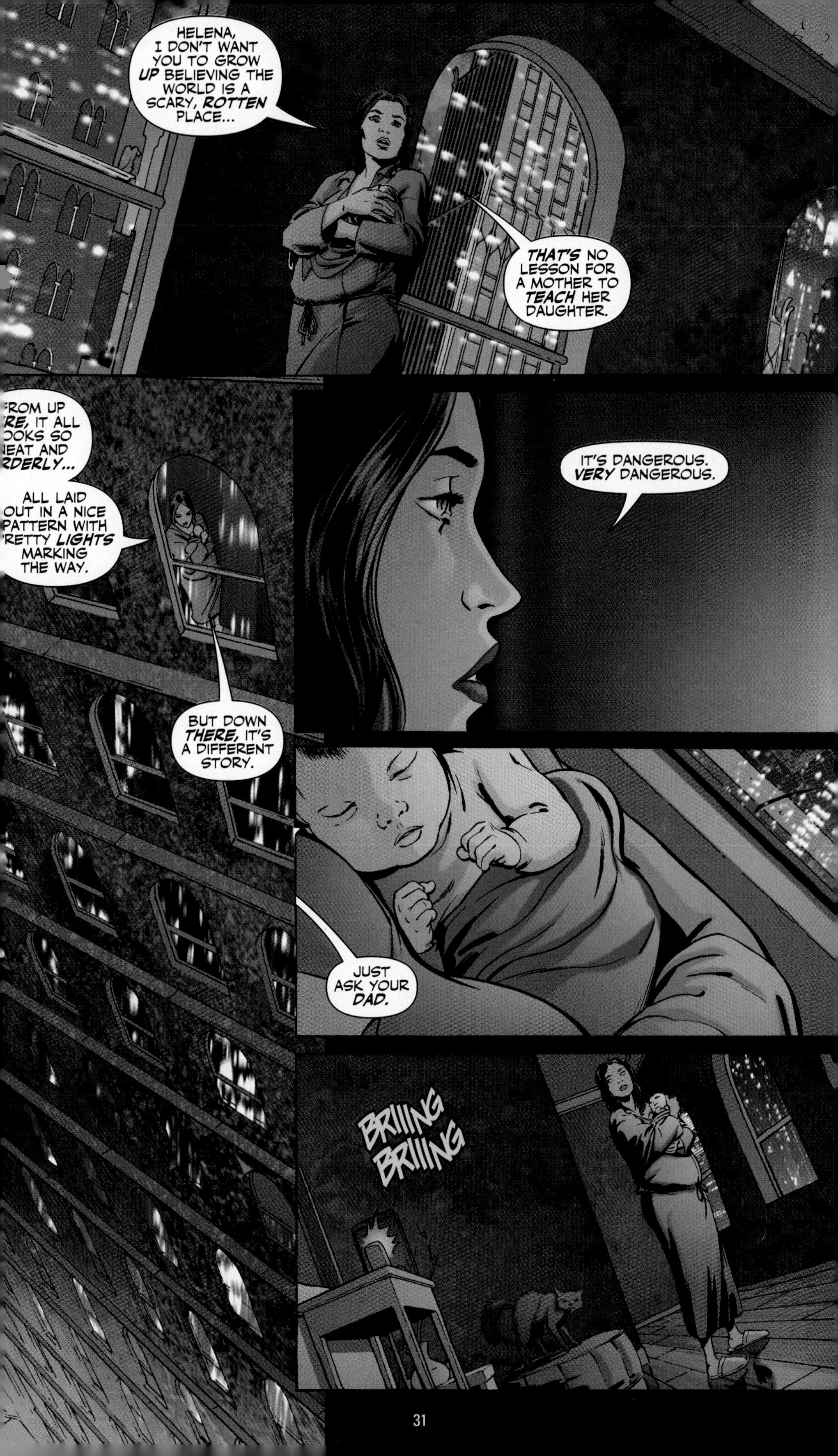
HELENA, I DON'T WANT YOU TO GROW *UP* BELIEVING THE WORLD IS A SCARY, *ROTTEN* PLACE...
THAT'S NO LESSON FOR A MOTHER TO *TEACH* HER DAUGHTER.
FROM UP *RE,* IT ALL OOKS SO EAT AND *RDERLY...*
ALL LAID OUT IN A NICE PATTERN WITH RETTY *LIGHTS* MARKING THE WAY.
BUT DOWN *THERE,* IT'S A DIFFERENT STORY.
IT'S DANGEROUS. *VERY* DANGEROUS.
JUST ASK YOUR *DAD.*
BRIIING BRIIING

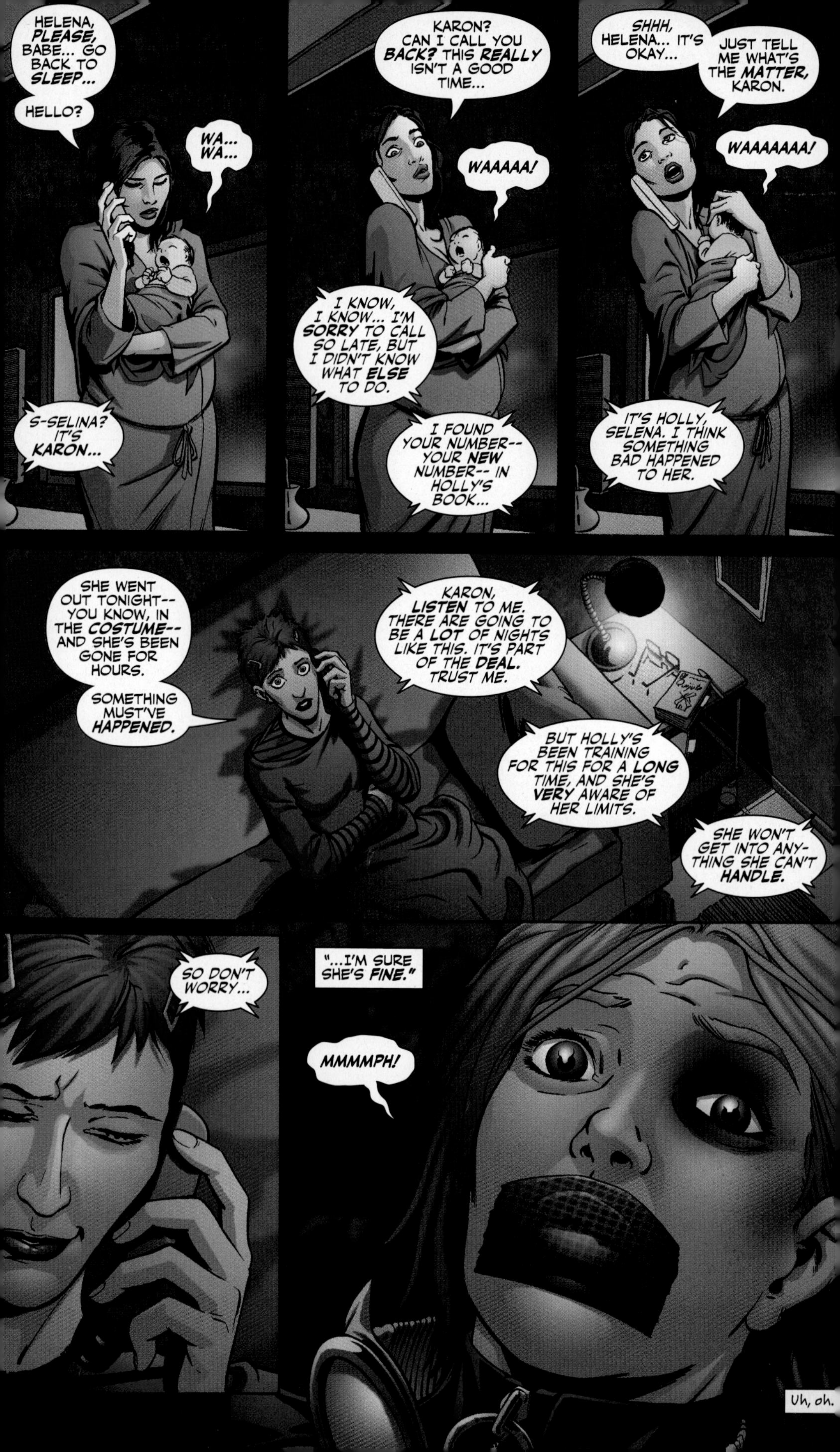
HELENA, PLEASE, BABE... GO BACK TO SLEEP...
HELLO?
WA... WA...
S-SELINA? IT'S KARON...
KARON? CAN I CALL YOU BACK? THIS REALLY ISN'T A GOOD TIME...
WAAAAA!
I KNOW, I KNOW... I'M SORRY TO CALL SO LATE, BUT I DIDN'T KNOW WHAT ELSE TO DO.
I FOUND YOUR NUMBER-- YOUR NEW NUMBER-- IN HOLLY'S BOOK...
SHHH, HELENA... IT'S OKAY...
JUST TELL ME WHAT'S THE MATTER, KARON.
WAAAAAAA!
IT'S HOLLY, SELENA. I THINK SOMETHING BAD HAPPENED TO HER.
SHE WENT OUT TONIGHT-- YOU KNOW, IN THE COSTUME-- AND SHE'S BEEN GONE FOR HOURS.
SOMETHING MUST'VE HAPPENED.
KARON, LISTEN TO ME. THERE ARE GOING TO BE A LOT OF NIGHTS LIKE THIS. IT'S PART OF THE DEAL. TRUST ME.
BUT HOLLY'S BEEN TRAINING FOR THIS FOR A LONG TIME, AND SHE'S VERY AWARE OF HER LIMITS.
SHE WON'T GET INTO ANYTHING SHE CAN'T HANDLE.
SO DON'T WORRY...
"...I'M SURE SHE'S FINE."
MMMMPH!
Uh, oh.

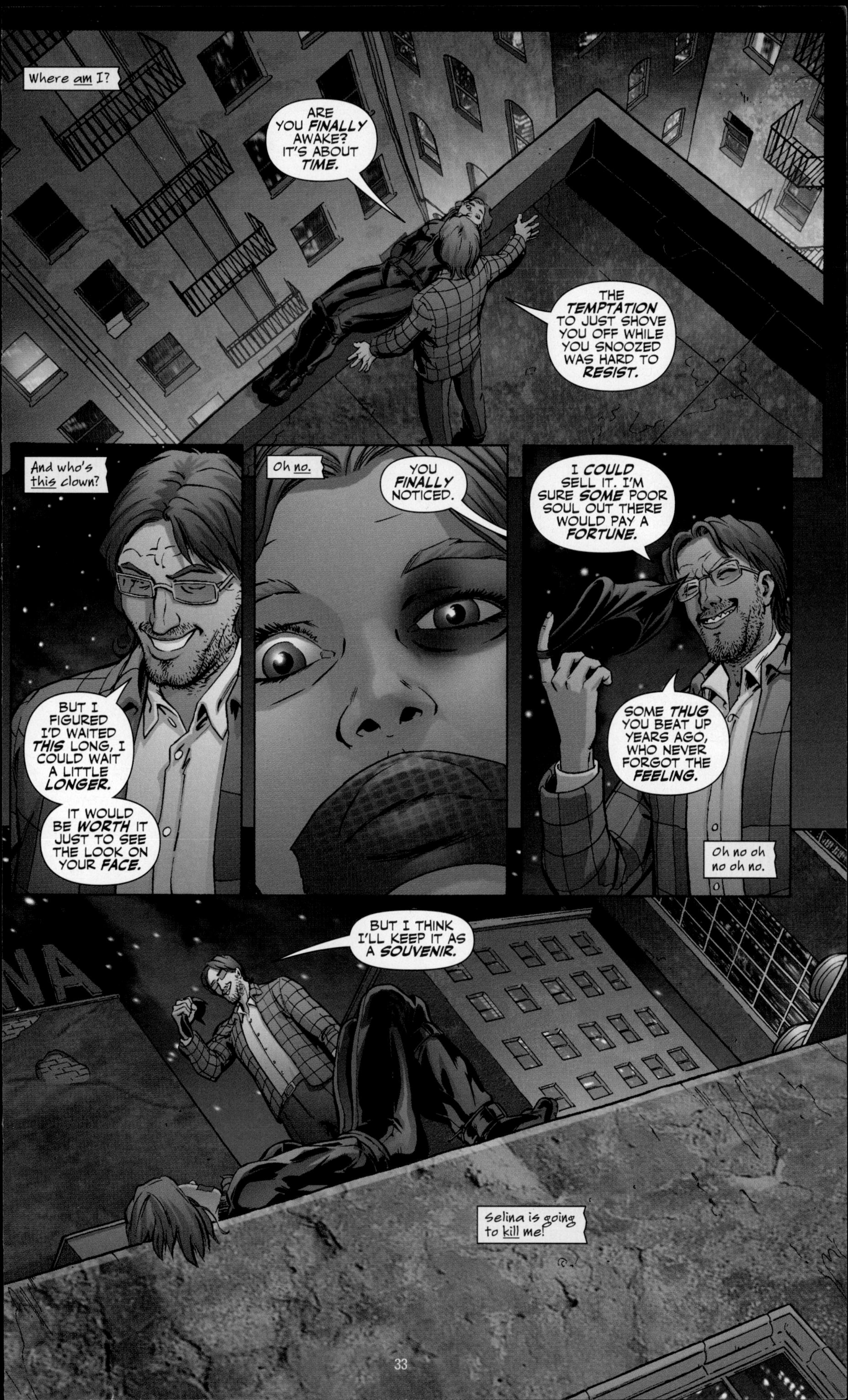
Where am I?
ARE YOU FINALLY AWAKE? IT'S ABOUT TIME.
THE TEMPTATION TO JUST SHOVE YOU OFF WHILE YOU SNOOZED WAS HARD TO RESIST.
And who's this clown?
BUT I FIGURED I'D WAITED THIS LONG, I COULD WAIT A LITTLE LONGER.
IT WOULD BE WORTH IT JUST TO SEE THE LOOK ON YOUR FACE.
Oh no.
YOU FINALLY NOTICED.
I COULD SELL IT. I'M SURE SOME POOR SOUL OUT THERE WOULD PAY A FORTUNE.
SOME THUG YOU BEAT UP YEARS AGO, WHO NEVER FORGOT THE FEELING.
Oh no oh no oh no.
BUT I THINK I'LL KEEP IT AS A SOUVENIR.
Selina is going to kill me!

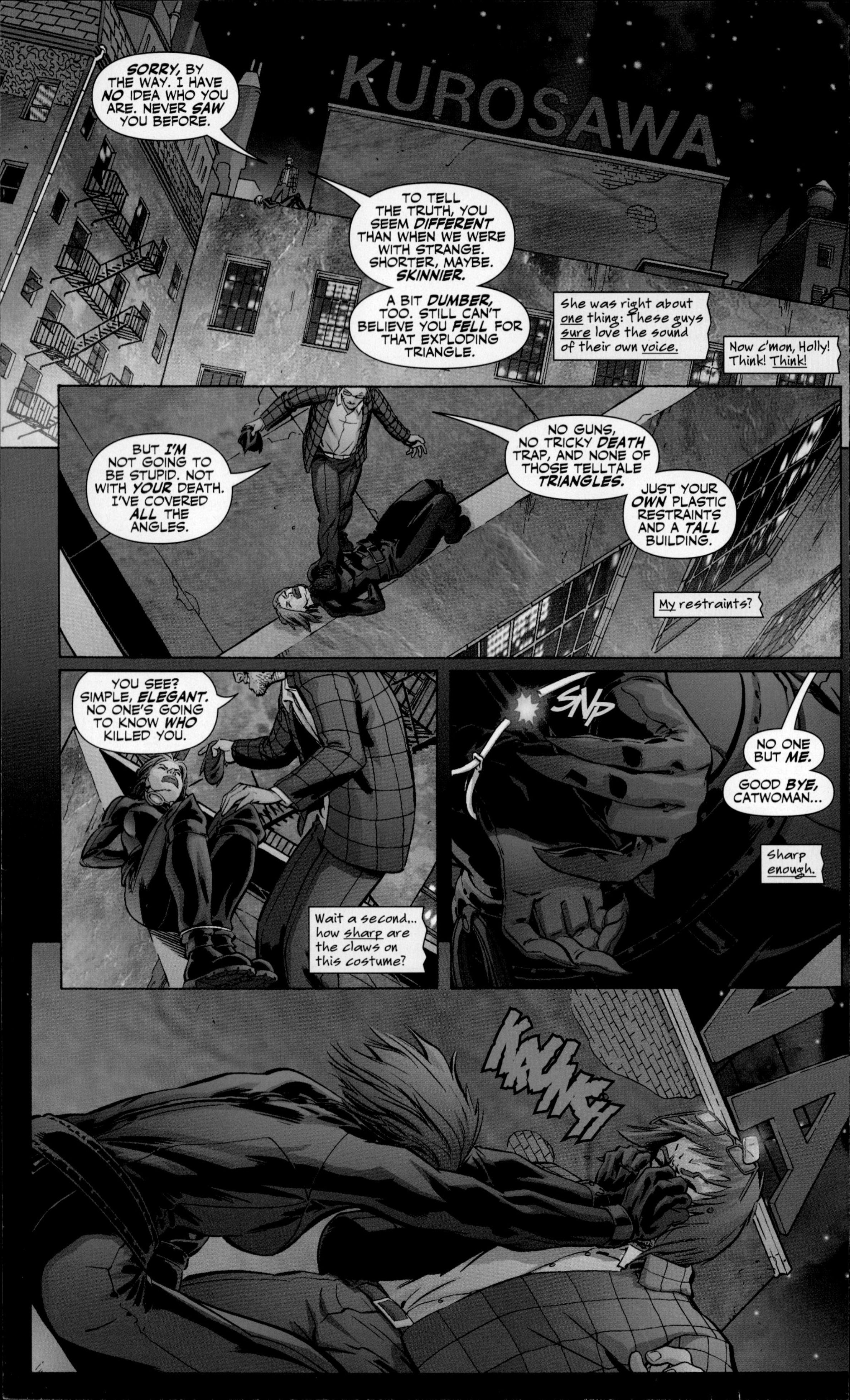
KUROSAWA
SORRY, BY THE WAY. I HAVE NO IDEA WHO YOU ARE. NEVER SAW YOU BEFORE.
TO TELL THE TRUTH, YOU SEEM DIFFERENT THAN WHEN WE WERE WITH STRANGE. SHORTER, MAYBE. SKINNIER.
A BIT DUMBER, TOO. STILL CAN'T BELIEVE YOU FELL FOR THAT EXPLODING TRIANGLE.
She was right about one thing: These guys sure love the sound of their own voice.
Now c'mon, Holly! Think! Think!
BUT I'M NOT GOING TO BE STUPID. NOT WITH YOUR DEATH. I'VE COVERED ALL THE ANGLES.
NO GUNS, NO TRICKY DEATH TRAP, AND NONE OF THOSE TELLTALE TRIANGLES.
JUST YOUR OWN PLASTIC RESTRAINTS AND A TALL BUILDING.
My restraints?
YOU SEE? SIMPLE, ELEGANT. NO ONE'S GOING TO KNOW WHO KILLED YOU.
Wait a second... how sharp are the claws on this costume?
SNP
NO ONE BUT ME.
GOOD BYE, CATWOMAN...
Sharp enough.
KRUNCH

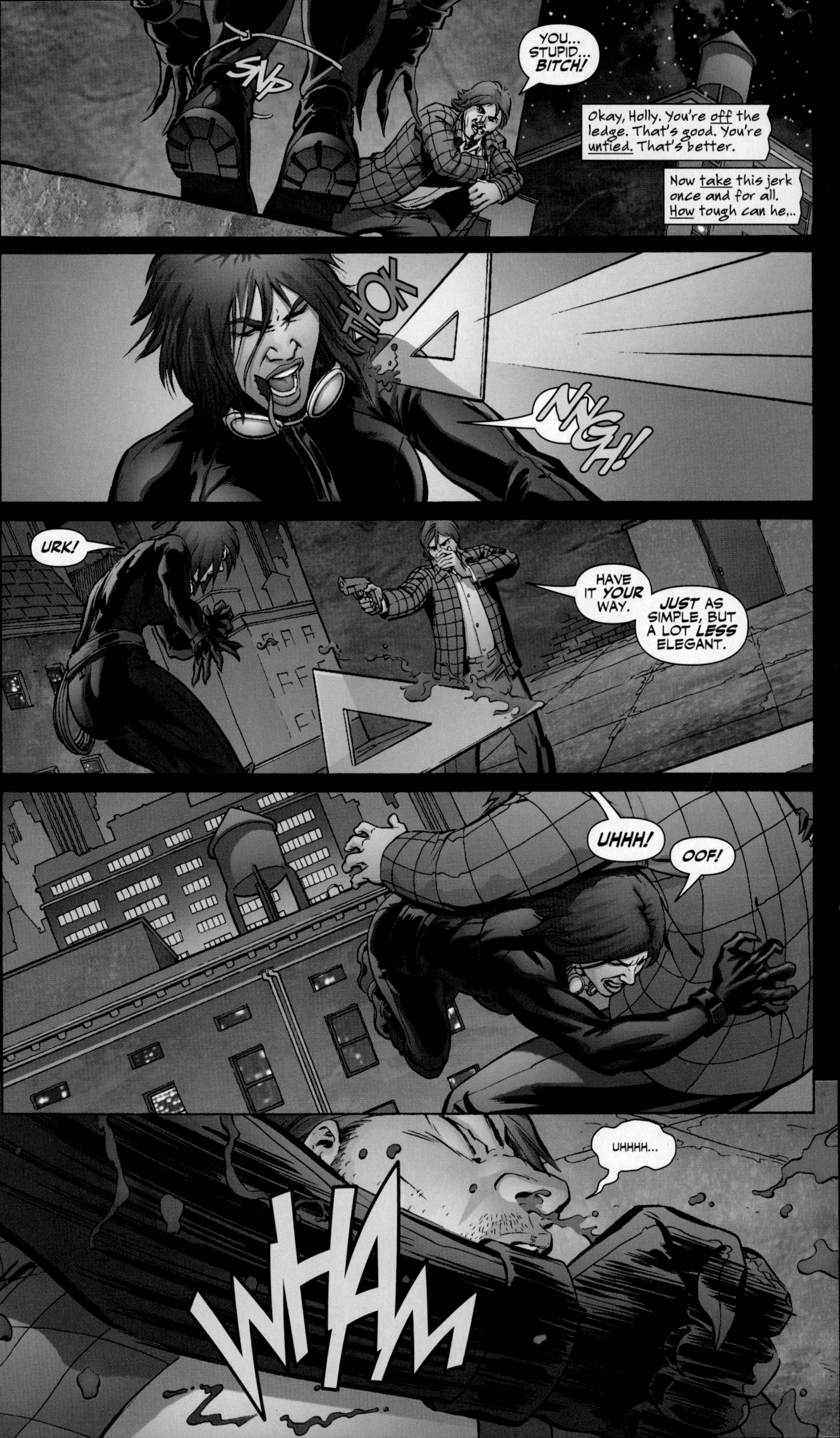
SNP
YOU... STUPID... BITCH!
Okay, Holly. You're off the ledge. That's good. You're untied. That's better.
Now take this jerk once and for all. How tough can he...
THOK
NNGH!
URK!
HAVE IT YOUR WAY.
JUST AS SIMPLE, BUT A LOT LESS ELEGANT.
UHHH!
OOF!
UHHHH...
WHAM

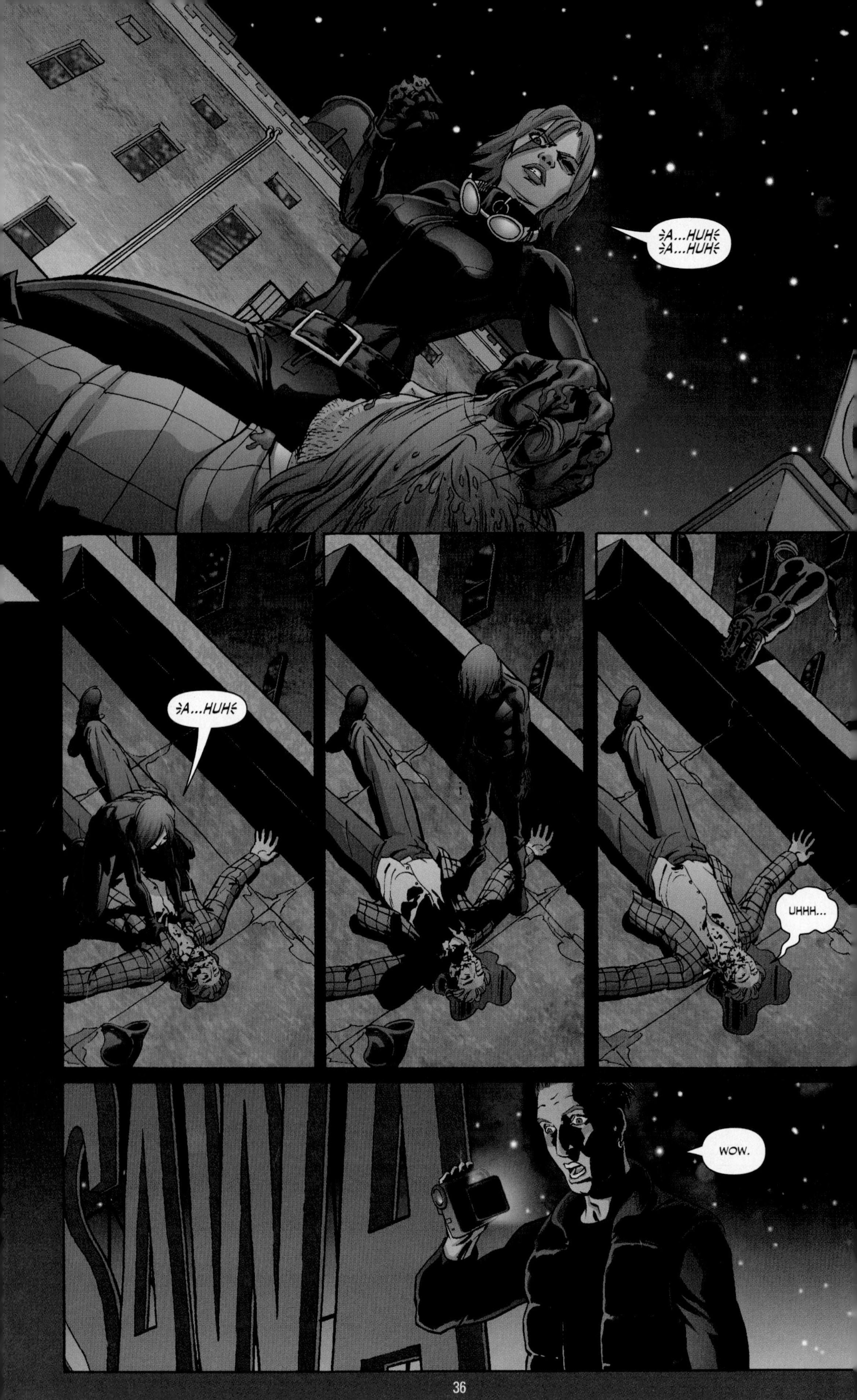
A...HUH A...HUH
A...HUH
UHHH...
WOW.

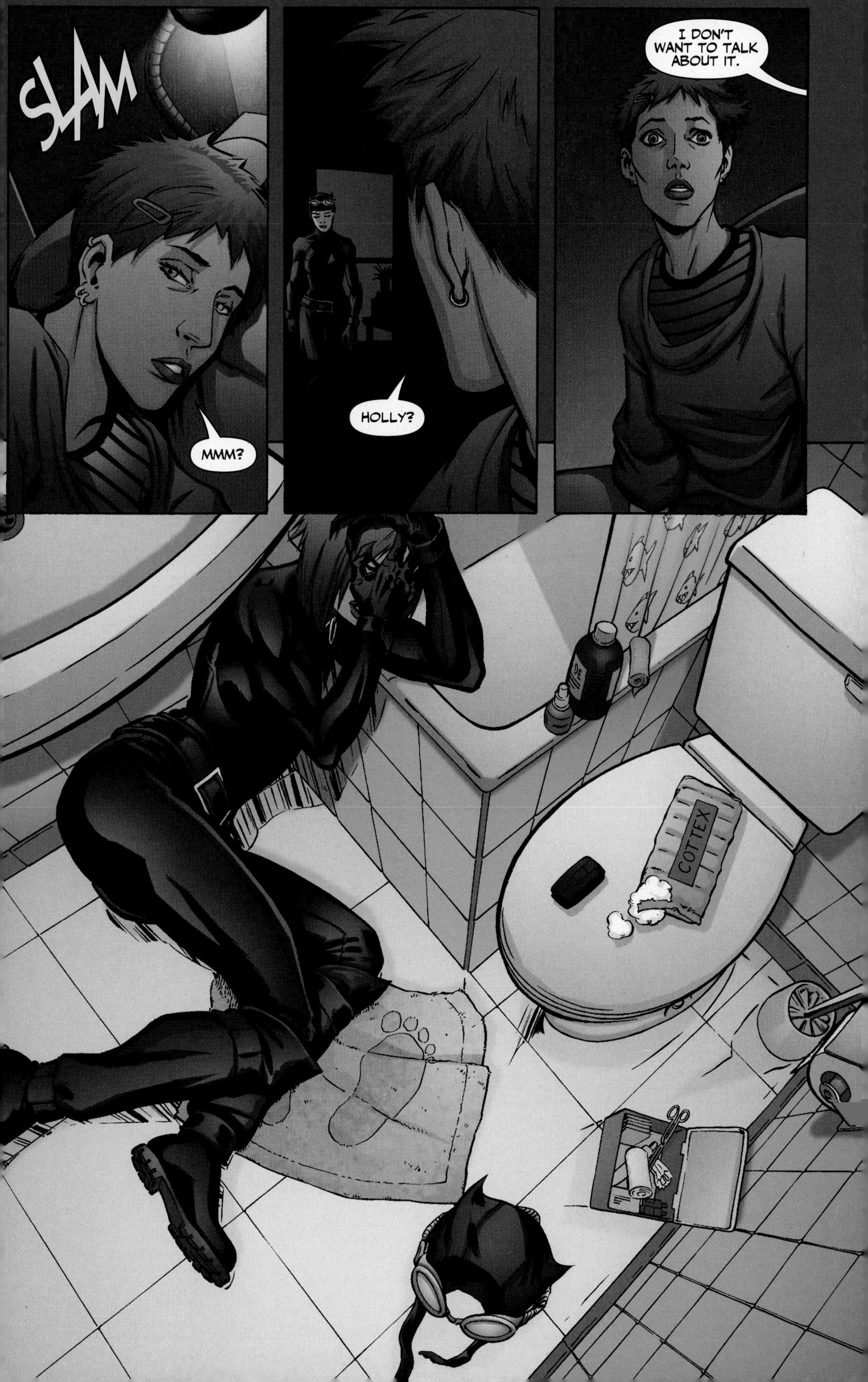
SLAM
MMM?
HOLLY?
I DON'T WANT TO TALK ABOUT IT.
COTTEX

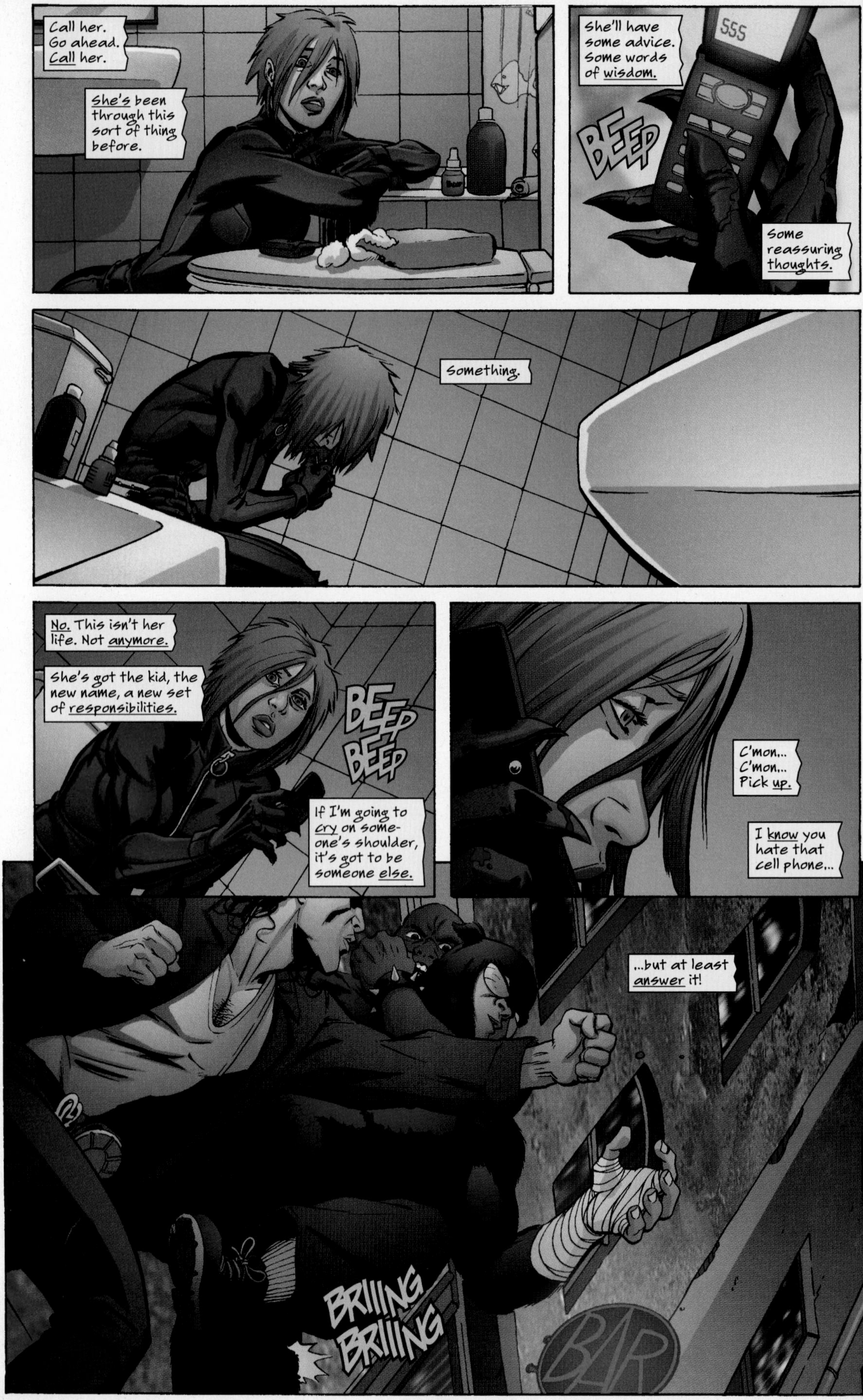
Call her.
Go ahead.
Call her.
She's been through this sort of thing before.
She'll have some advice. Some words of wisdom.
555
BEEP
Some reassuring thoughts.
Something.
No. This isn't her life. Not anymore.
She's got the kid, the new name, a new set of responsibilities.
BEEP BEEP
If I'm going to cry on some-one's shoulder, it's got to be someone else.
C'mon... C'mon... Pick up.
I know you hate that cell phone...
...but at least answer it!
BRIIING BRIIING
BAR

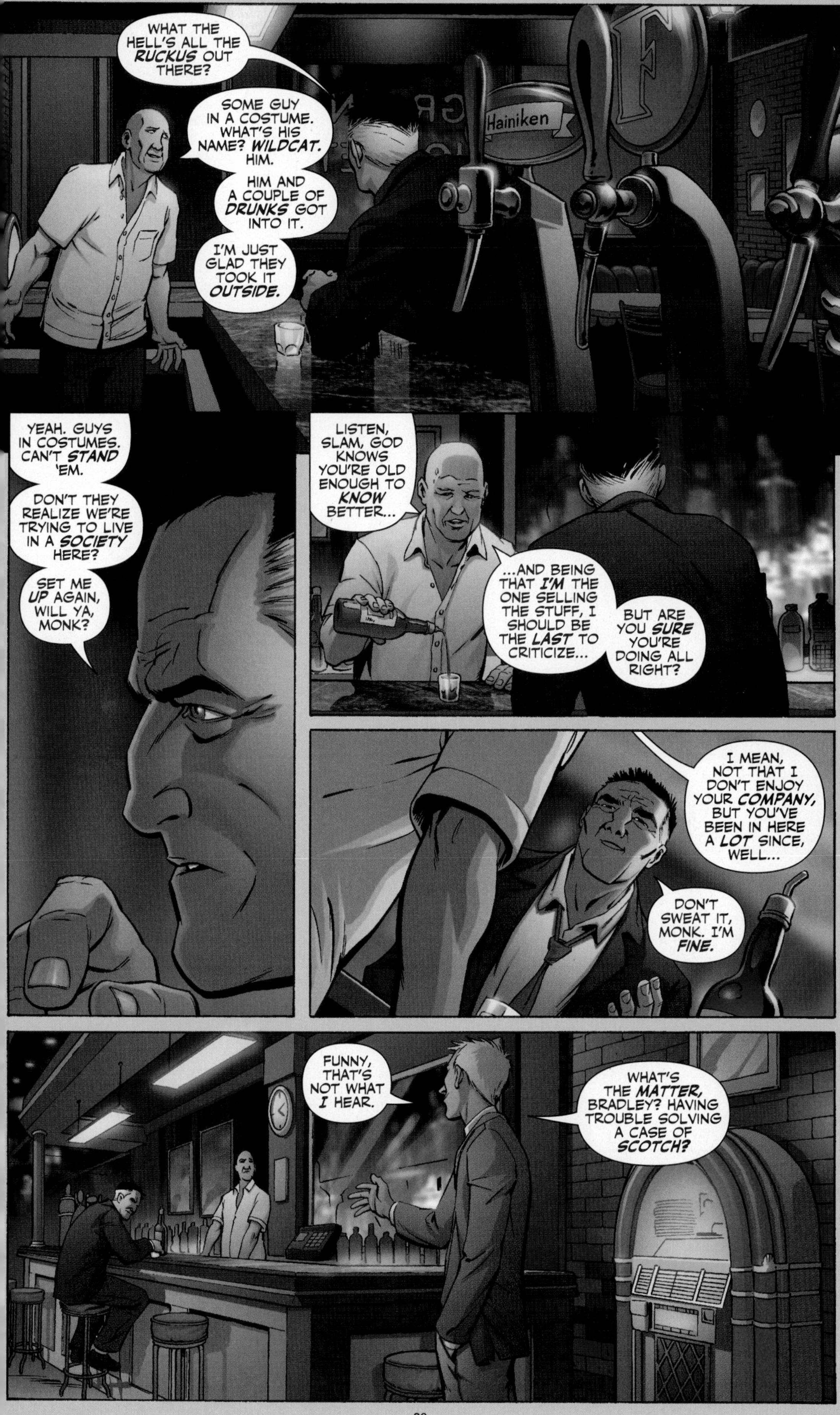
WHAT THE HELL'S ALL THE RUCKUS OUT THERE?
SOME GUY IN A COSTUME. WHAT'S HIS NAME? WILDCAT. HIM.
HIM AND A COUPLE OF DRUNKS GOT INTO IT.
I'M JUST GLAD THEY TOOK IT OUTSIDE.
Hainiken
YEAH. GUYS IN COSTUMES. CAN'T STAND 'EM.
DON'T THEY REALIZE WE'RE TRYING TO LIVE IN A SOCIETY HERE?
SET ME UP AGAIN, WILL YA, MONK?
LISTEN, SLAM, GOD KNOWS YOU'RE OLD ENOUGH TO KNOW BETTER...
...AND BEING THAT I'M THE ONE SELLING THE STUFF, I SHOULD BE THE LAST TO CRITICIZE...
BUT ARE YOU SURE YOU'RE DOING ALL RIGHT?
I MEAN, NOT THAT I DON'T ENJOY YOUR COMPANY, BUT YOU'VE BEEN IN HERE A LOT SINCE, WELL...
DON'T SWEAT IT, MONK. I'M FINE.
FUNNY, THAT'S NOT WHAT I HEAR.
WHAT'S THE MATTER, BRADLEY? HAVING TROUBLE SOLVING A CASE OF SCOTCH?

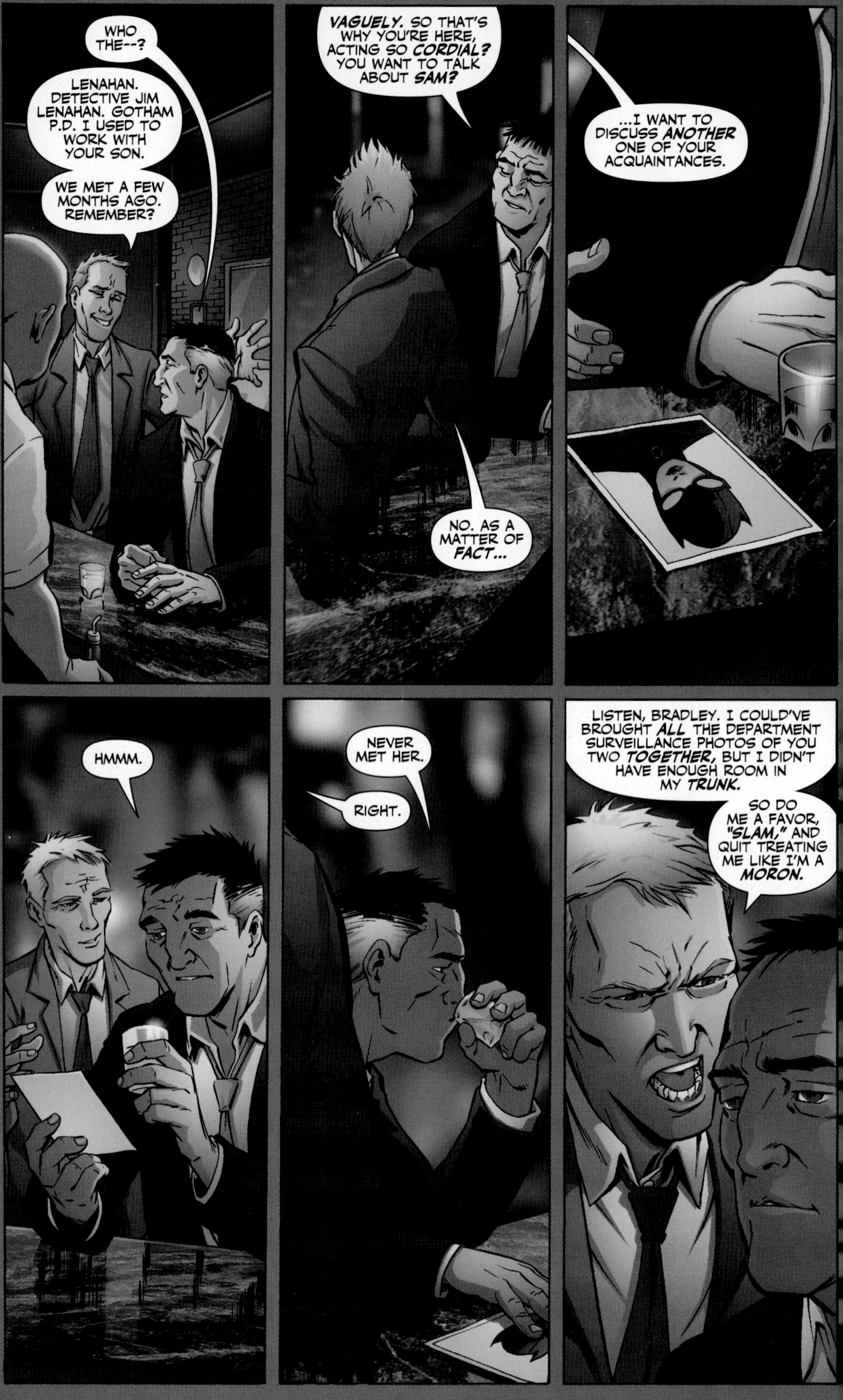
WHO THE--?
LENAHAN. DETECTIVE JIM LENAHAN. GOTHAM P.D. I USED TO WORK WITH YOUR SON.
WE MET A FEW MONTHS AGO. REMEMBER?
VAGUELY. SO THAT'S WHY YOU'RE HERE, ACTING SO CORDIAL? YOU WANT TO TALK ABOUT SAM?
NO. AS A MATTER OF FACT...
...I WANT TO DISCUSS ANOTHER ONE OF YOUR ACQUAINTANCES.
HMMM.
NEVER MET HER.
RIGHT.
LISTEN, BRADLEY. I COULD'VE BROUGHT ALL THE DEPARTMENT SURVEILLANCE PHOTOS OF YOU TWO TOGETHER, BUT I DIDN'T HAVE ENOUGH ROOM IN MY TRUNK.
SO DO ME A FAVOR, "SLAM," AND QUIT TREATING ME LIKE I'M A MORON.

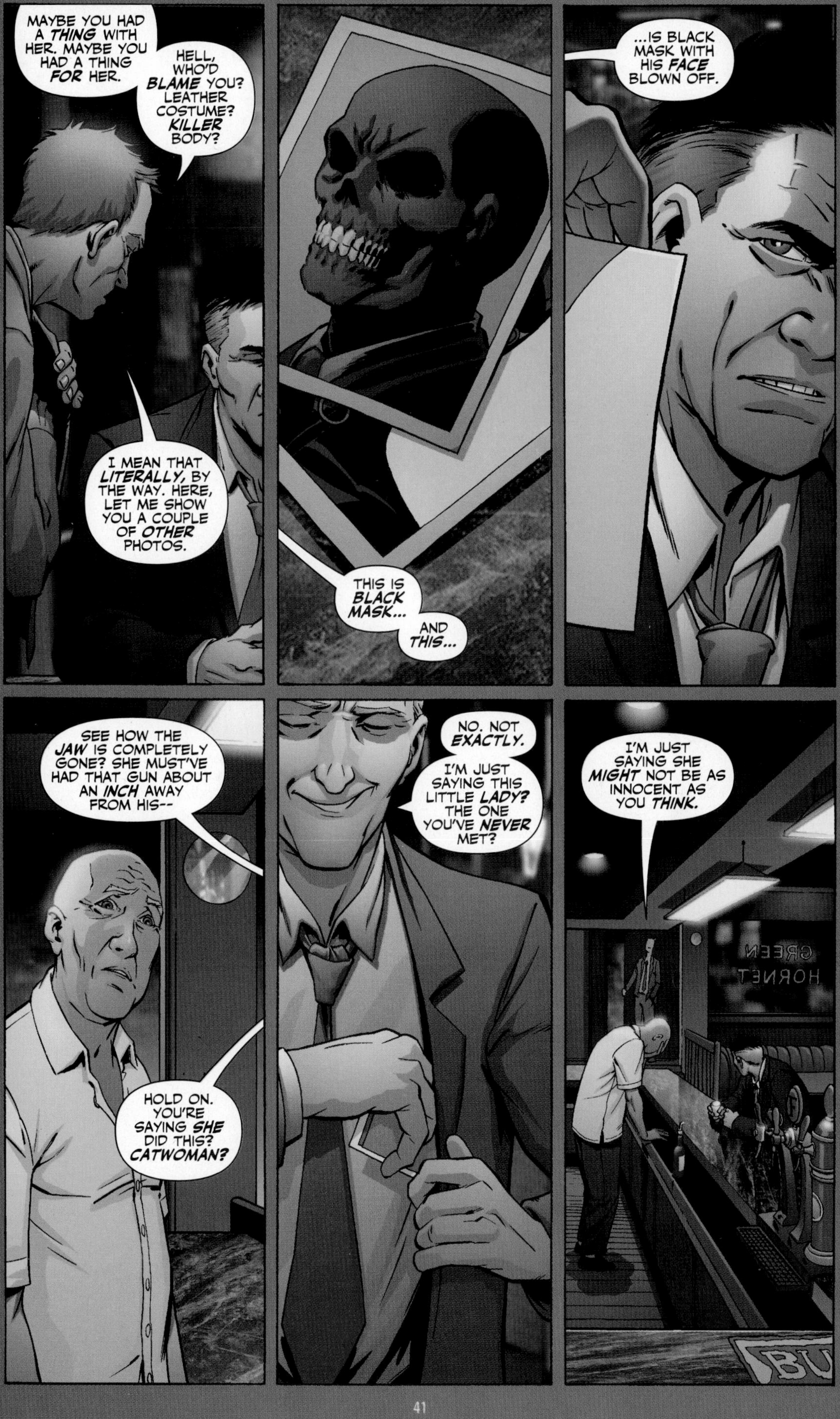
MAYBE YOU HAD A THING WITH HER. MAYBE YOU HAD A THING FOR HER.
HELL, WHO'D BLAME YOU? LEATHER COSTUME? KILLER BODY?
I MEAN THAT LITERALLY, BY THE WAY. HERE, LET ME SHOW YOU A COUPLE OF OTHER PHOTOS.
THIS IS BLACK MASK...
AND THIS...
...IS BLACK MASK WITH HIS FACE BLOWN OFF.
SEE HOW THE JAW IS COMPLETELY GONE? SHE MUST'VE HAD THAT GUN ABOUT AN INCH AWAY FROM HIS--
HOLD ON. YOU'RE SAYING SHE DID THIS? CATWOMAN?
NO. NOT EXACTLY.
I'M JUST SAYING THIS LITTLE LADY? THE ONE YOU'VE NEVER MET?
I'M JUST SAYING SHE MIGHT NOT BE AS INNOCENT AS YOU THINK.
GREEN HORNET

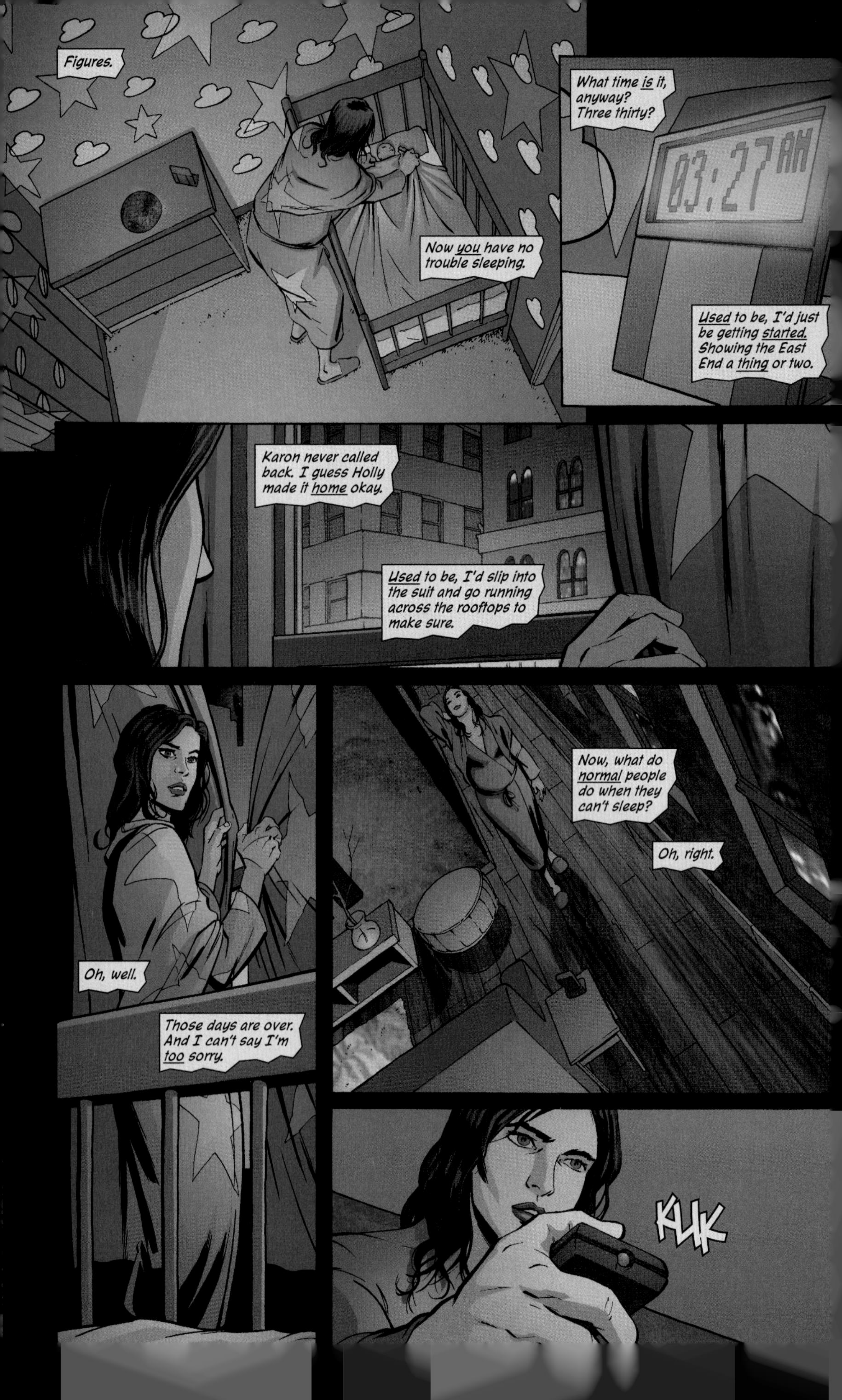
Figures.
Now you have no trouble sleeping.
What time is it, anyway? Three thirty?
03:27 AM
Used to be, I'd just be getting started. Showing the East End a thing or two.
Karon never called back. I guess Holly made it home okay.
Used to be, I'd slip into the suit and go running across the rooftops to make sure.
Oh, well.
Those days are over. And I can't say I'm too sorry.
Now, what do normal people do when they can't sleep?
Oh, right.
KLIK

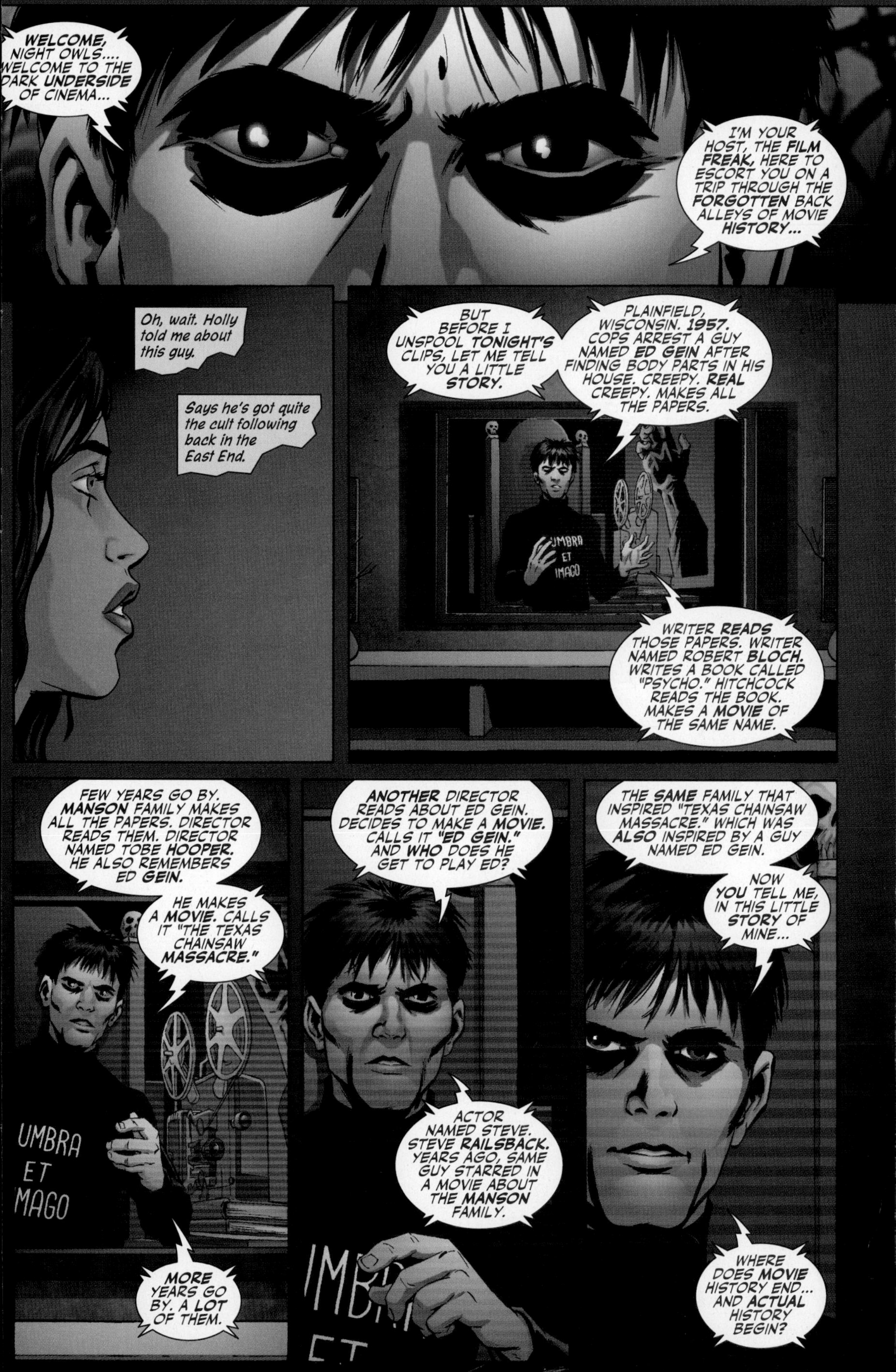
WELCOME, NIGHT OWLS.... WELCOME TO THE DARK UNDERSIDE OF CINEMA...
I'M YOUR HOST, THE FILM FREAK, HERE TO ESCORT YOU ON A TRIP THROUGH THE FORGOTTEN BACK ALLEYS OF MOVIE HISTORY...
Oh, wait. Holly told me about this guy.
Says he's got quite the cult following back in the East End.
BUT BEFORE I UNSPOOL TONIGHT'S CLIPS, LET ME TELL YOU A LITTLE STORY.
PLAINFIELD, WISCONSIN. 1957. COPS ARREST A GUY NAMED ED GEIN AFTER FINDING BODY PARTS IN HIS HOUSE. CREEPY. REAL CREEPY. MAKES ALL THE PAPERS.
UMBRA ET IMAGO
WRITER READS THOSE PAPERS. WRITER NAMED ROBERT BLOCH. WRITES A BOOK CALLED "PSYCHO." HITCHCOCK READS THE BOOK. MAKES A MOVIE OF THE SAME NAME.
FEW YEARS GO BY. MANSON FAMILY MAKES ALL THE PAPERS. DIRECTOR READS THEM. DIRECTOR NAMED TOBE HOOPER. HE ALSO REMEMBERS ED GEIN.
HE MAKES A MOVIE. CALLS IT "THE TEXAS CHAINSAW MASSACRE."
UMBRA ET IMAGO
MORE YEARS GO BY. A LOT OF THEM.
ANOTHER DIRECTOR READS ABOUT ED GEIN. DECIDES TO MAKE A MOVIE. CALLS IT "ED GEIN." AND WHO DOES HE GET TO PLAY ED?
ACTOR NAMED STEVE. STEVE RAILSBACK. YEARS AGO, SAME GUY STARRED IN A MOVIE ABOUT THE MANSON FAMILY.
THE SAME FAMILY THAT INSPIRED "TEXAS CHAINSAW MASSACRE." WHICH WAS ALSO INSPIRED BY A GUY NAMED ED GEIN.
NOW YOU TELL ME, IN THIS LITTLE STORY OF MINE...
WHERE DOES MOVIE HISTORY END... AND ACTUAL HISTORY BEGIN?

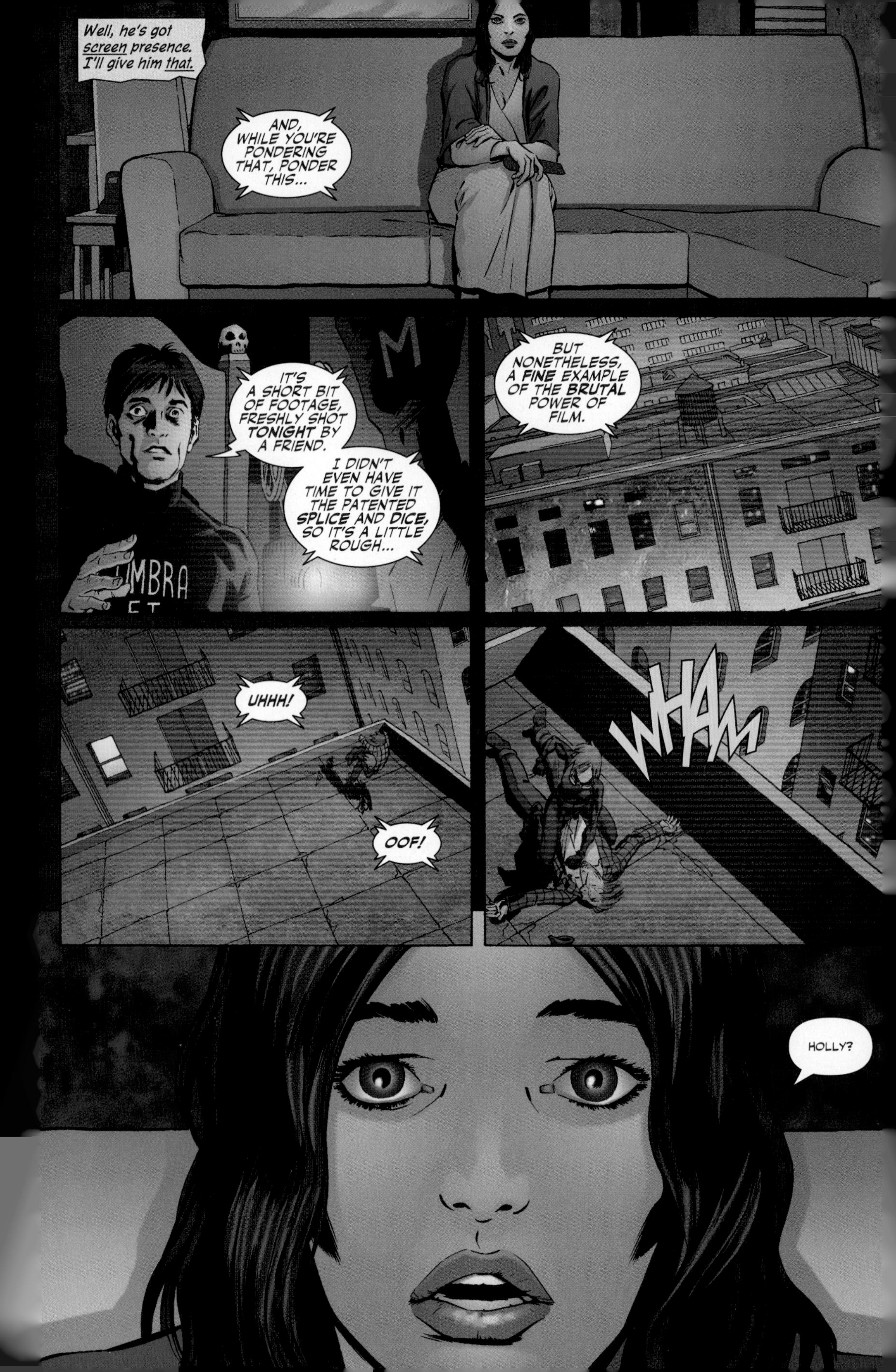
Well, he's got screen presence. I'll give him that.
AND, WHILE YOU'RE PONDERING THAT, PONDER THIS...
IT'S A SHORT BIT OF FOOTAGE, FRESHLY SHOT TONIGHT BY A FRIEND.
I DIDN'T EVEN HAVE TIME TO GIVE IT THE PATENTED SPLICE AND DICE, SO IT'S A LITTLE ROUGH...
MBRA
BUT NONETHELESS, A FINE EXAMPLE OF THE BRUTAL POWER OF FILM.
UHHH!
OOF!
WHAM
HOLLY?

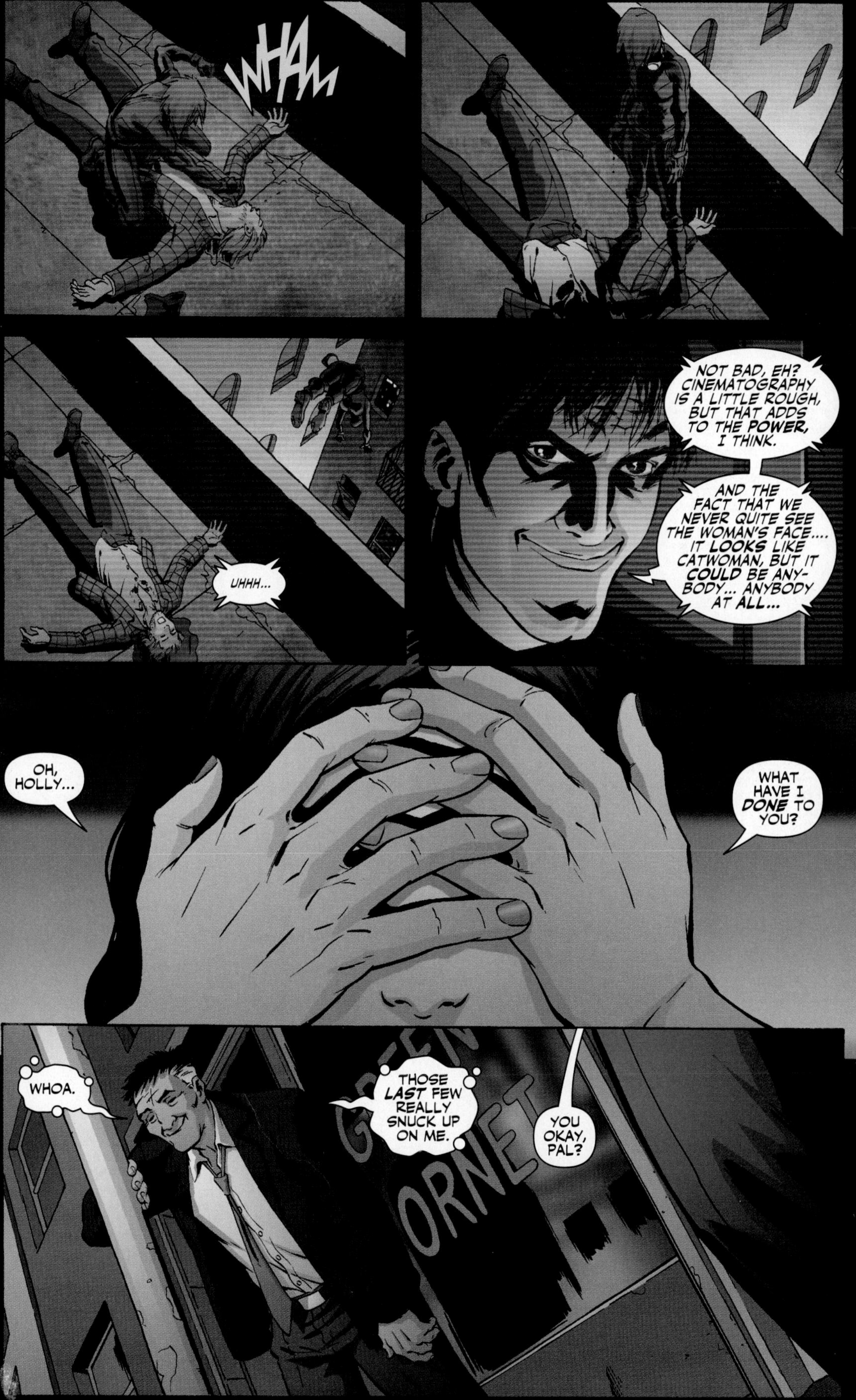
WHAM
UHHH...
NOT BAD, EH? CINEMATOGRAPHY IS A LITTLE ROUGH, BUT THAT ADDS TO THE POWER, I THINK.
AND THE FACT THAT WE NEVER QUITE SEE THE WOMAN'S FACE.... IT LOOKS LIKE CATWOMAN, BUT IT COULD BE ANYBODY... ANYBODY AT ALL...
OH, HOLLY...
WHAT HAVE I DONE TO YOU?
WHOA.
THOSE LAST FEW REALLY SNUCK UP ON ME.
YOU OKAY, PAL?
GREEN HORNET

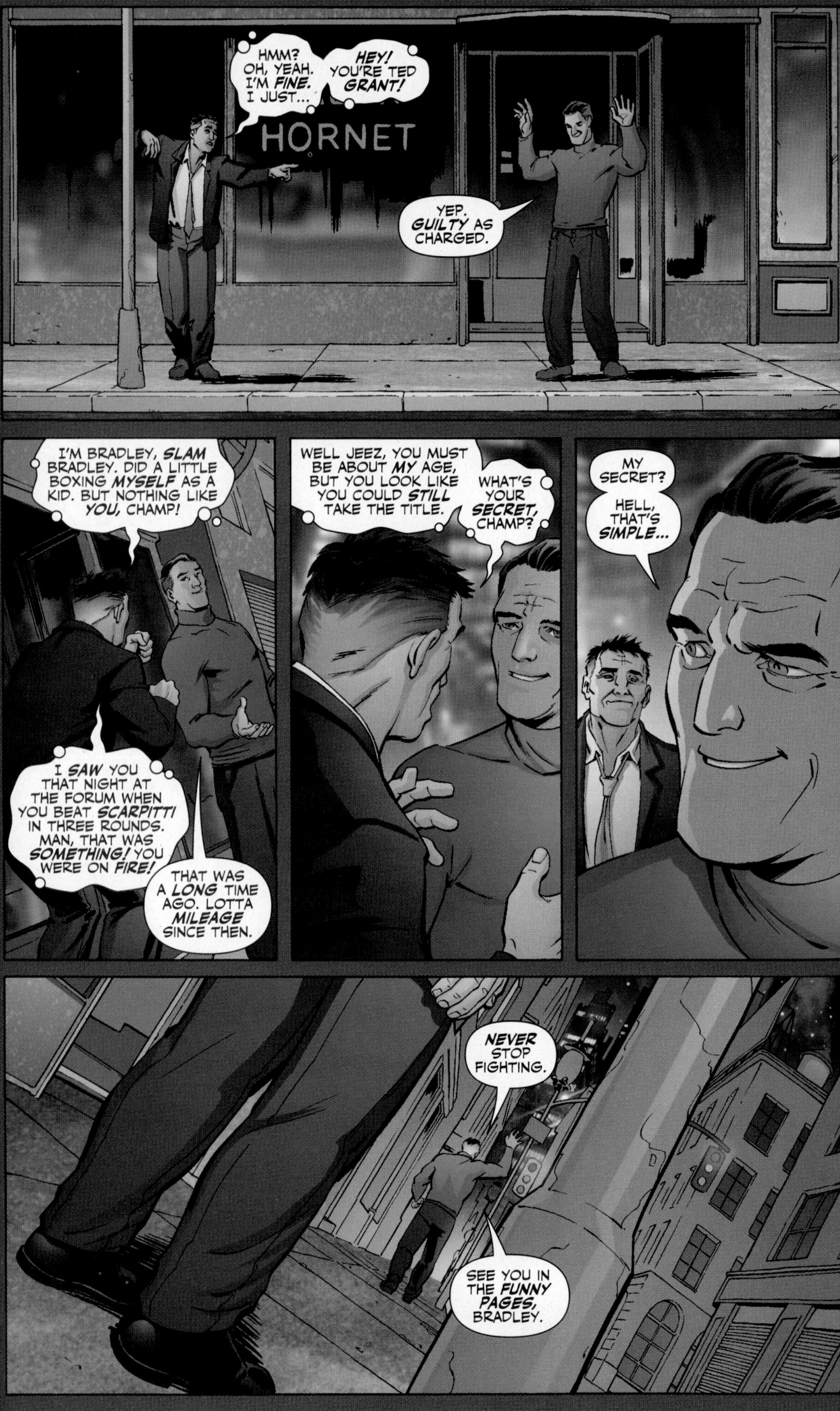

HMM? OH, YEAH. I'M FINE. I JUST...
HEY! YOU'RE TED GRANT!
HORNET
YEP. GUILTY AS CHARGED.
I'M BRADLEY, SLAM BRADLEY. DID A LITTLE BOXING MYSELF AS A KID. BUT NOTHING LIKE YOU, CHAMP!
I SAW YOU THAT NIGHT AT THE FORUM WHEN YOU BEAT SCARPITTI IN THREE ROUNDS. MAN, THAT WAS SOMETHING! YOU WERE ON FIRE!
THAT WAS A LONG TIME AGO. LOTTA MILEAGE SINCE THEN.
WELL JEEZ, YOU MUST BE ABOUT MY AGE, BUT YOU LOOK LIKE YOU COULD STILL TAKE THE TITLE.
WHAT'S YOUR SECRET, CHAMP?
MY SECRET?
HELL, THAT'S SIMPLE...
NEVER STOP FIGHTING.
SEE YOU IN THE FUNNY PAGES, BRADLEY.

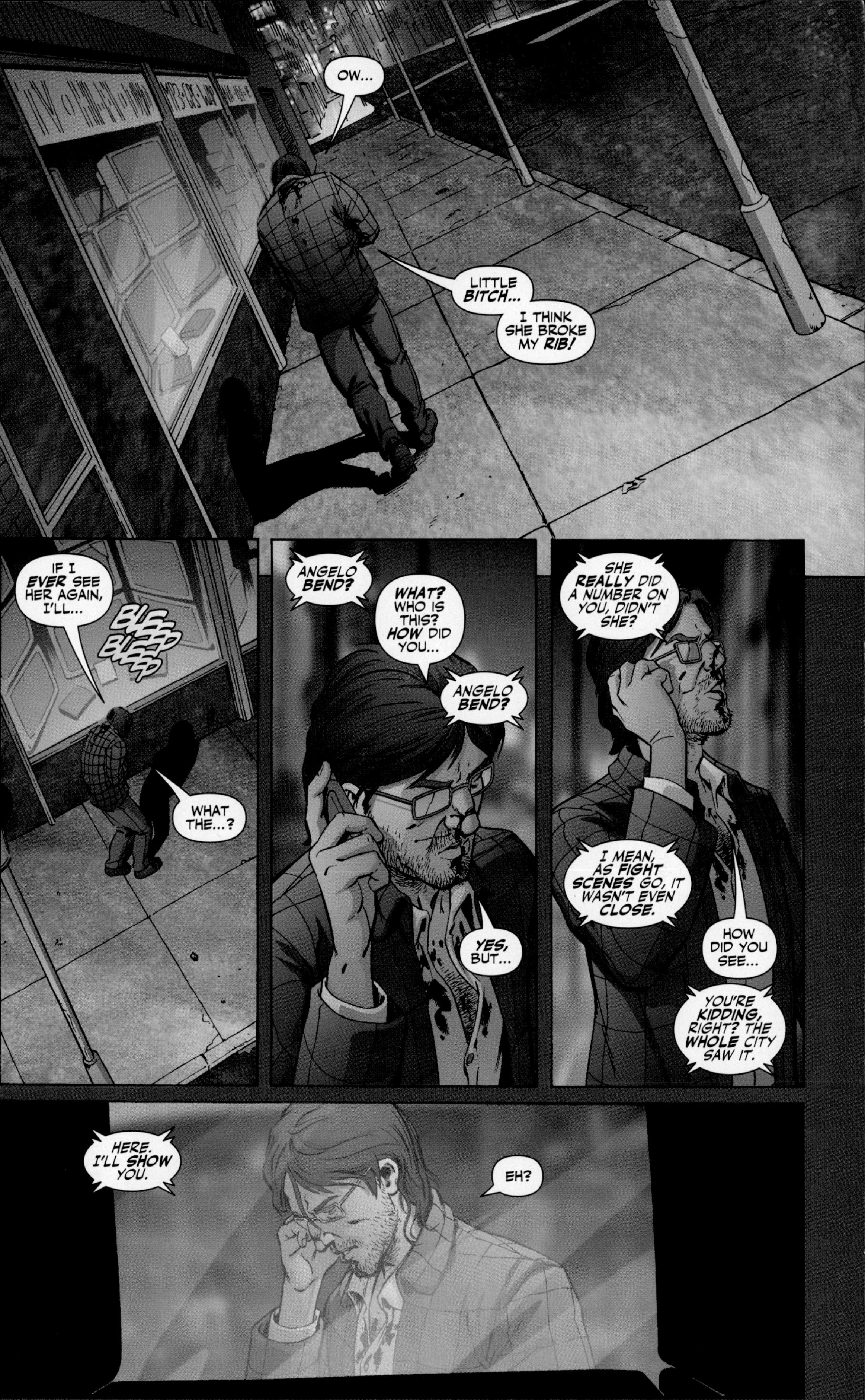
OW...
LITTLE BITCH...
I THINK SHE BROKE MY RIB!
IF I EVER SEE HER AGAIN, I'LL...
BLEEP BLEEP
WHAT THE...?
ANGELO BEND?
WHAT? WHO IS THIS? HOW DID YOU...
ANGELO BEND?
YES, BUT...
SHE REALLY DID A NUMBER ON YOU, DIDN'T SHE?
I MEAN, AS FIGHT SCENES GO, IT WASN'T EVEN CLOSE.
HOW DID YOU SEE...
YOU'RE KIDDING, RIGHT? THE WHOLE CITY SAW IT.
HERE. I'LL SHOW YOU.
EH?

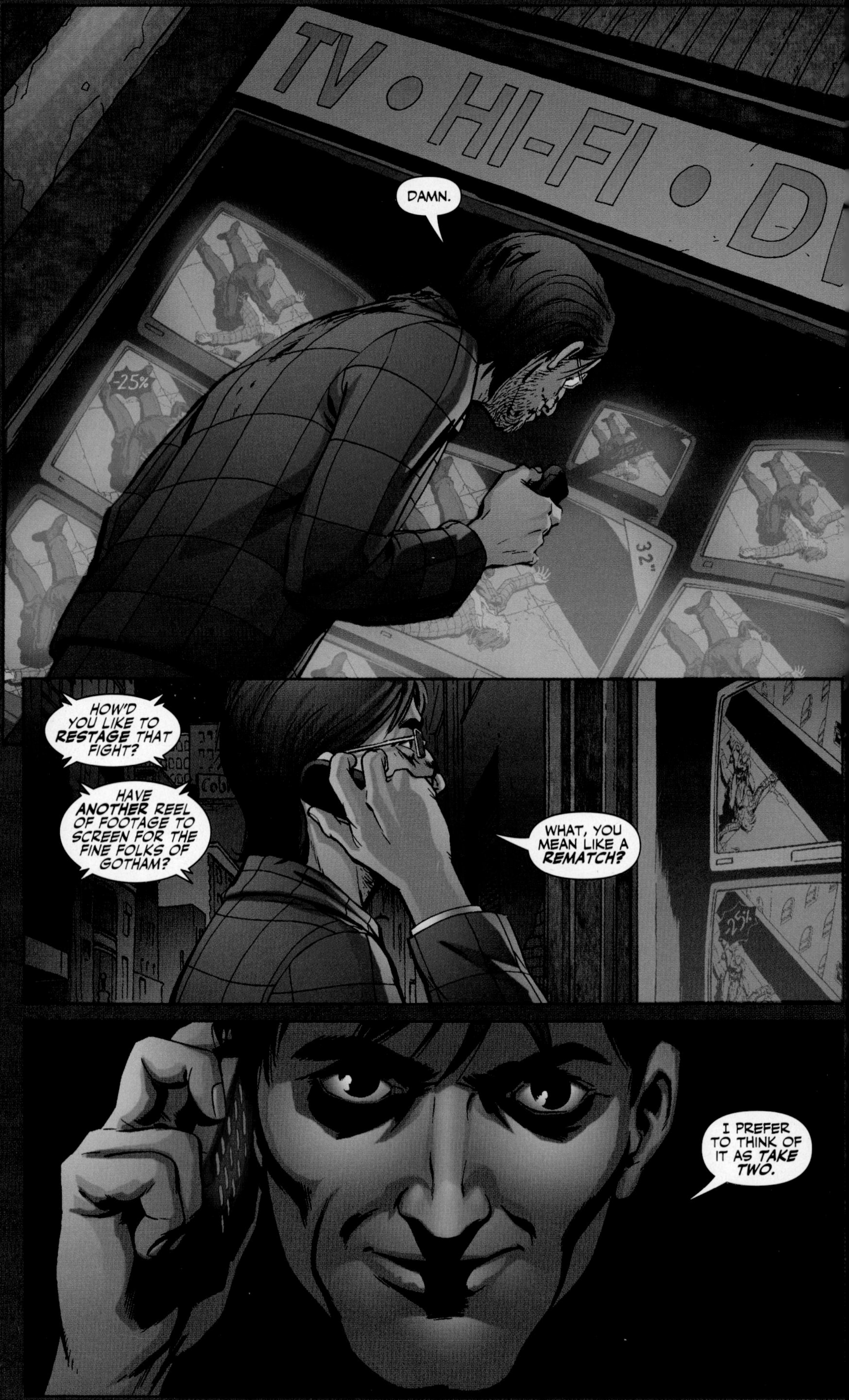
TV • HI-FI • D
DAMN.
-25%
32"
HOW'D YOU LIKE TO RESTAGE THAT FIGHT?
HAVE ANOTHER REEL OF FOOTAGE TO SCREEN FOR THE FINE FOLKS OF GOTHAM?
WHAT, YOU MEAN LIKE A REMATCH?
I PREFER TO THINK OF IT AS TAKE TWO.

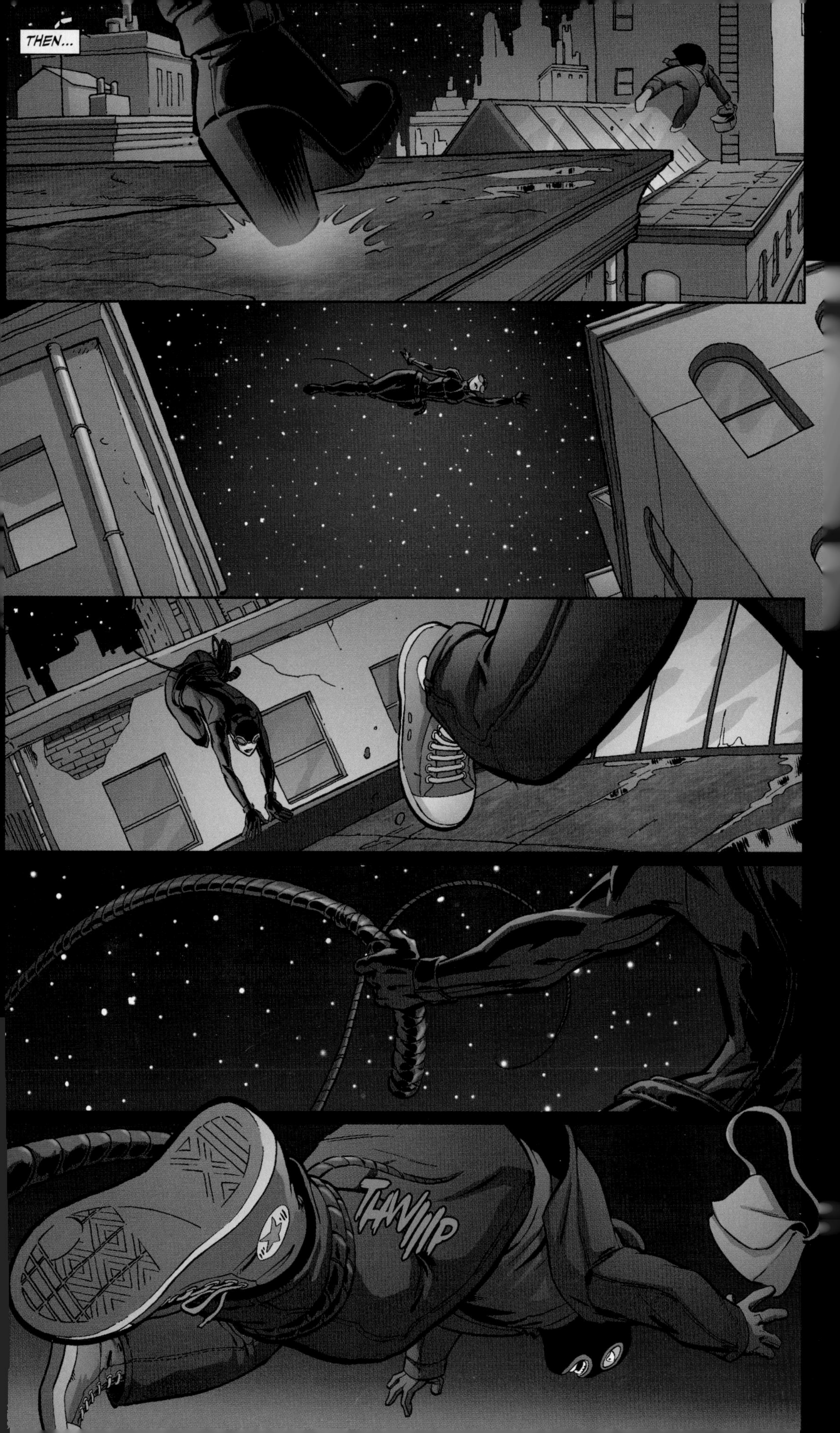
THEN...
THWIIIP

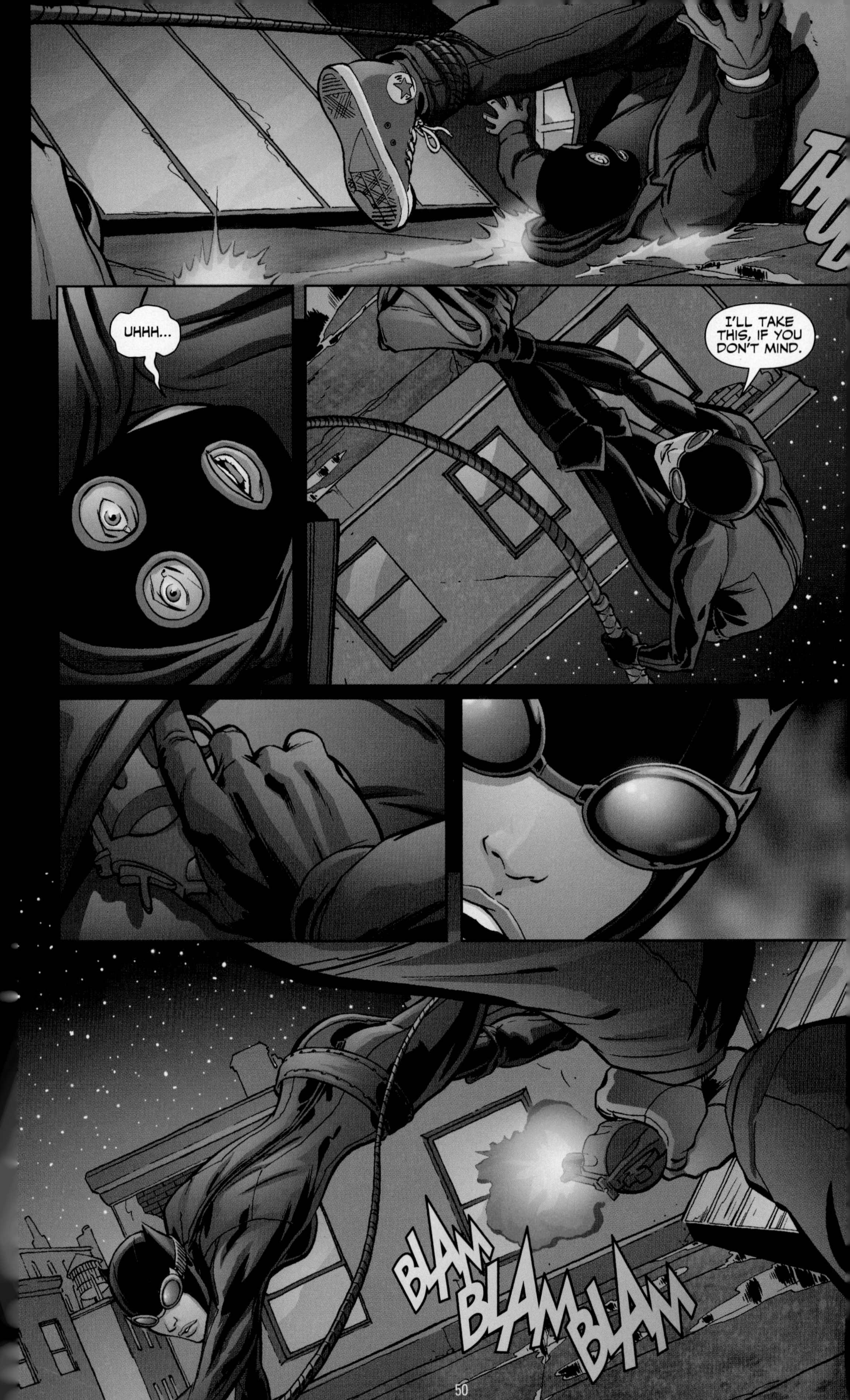
THUD
UHHH...
I'LL TAKE THIS, IF YOU DON'T MIND.
BLAM BLAM BLAM

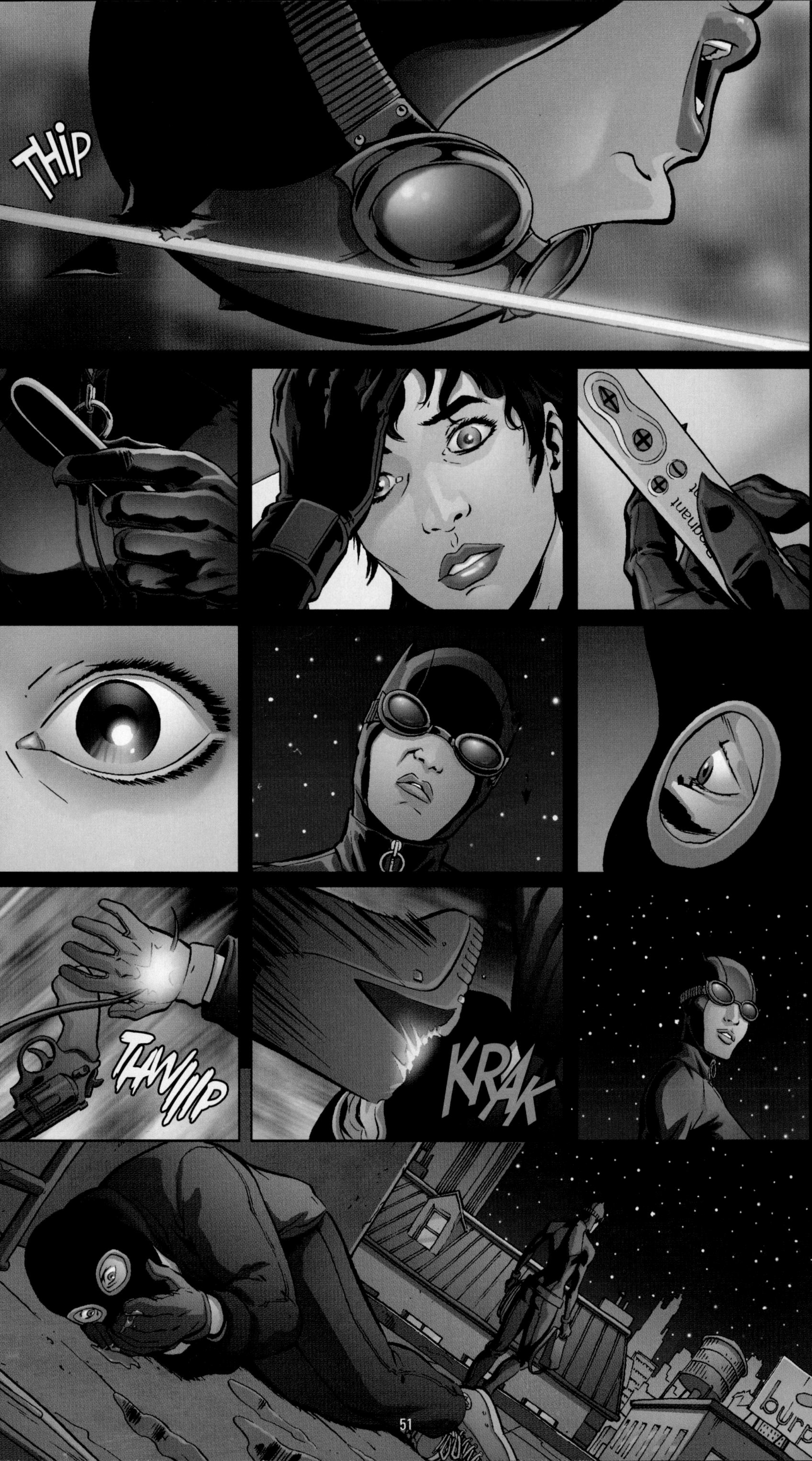
THIP
THWIIIP
KRAK
burps

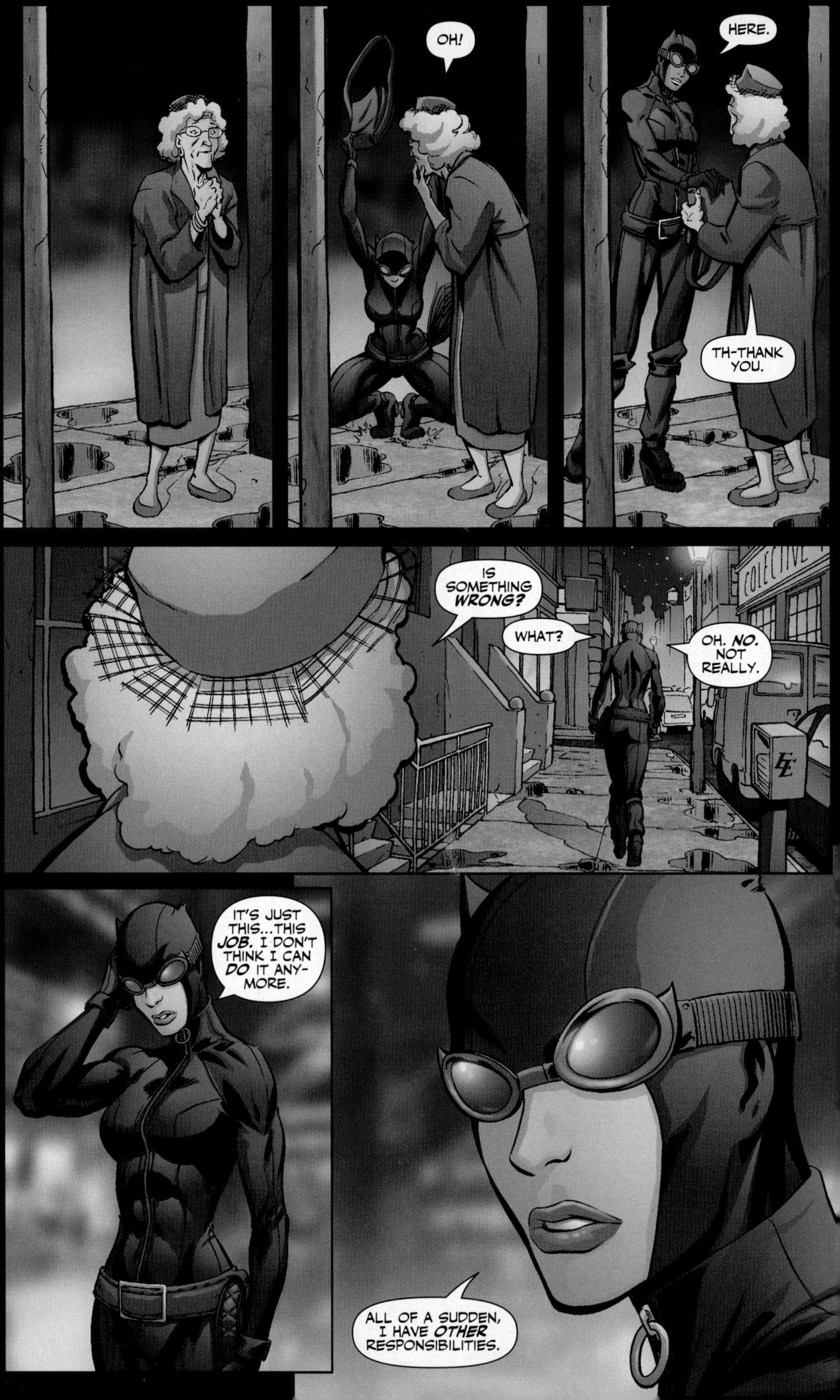
OH!
HERE.
TH-THANK YOU.
IS SOMETHING WRONG?
WHAT?
OH. NO. NOT REALLY.
IT'S JUST THIS...THIS JOB. I DON'T THINK I CAN DO IT ANY-MORE.
ALL OF A SUDDEN, I HAVE OTHER RESPONSIBILITIES.

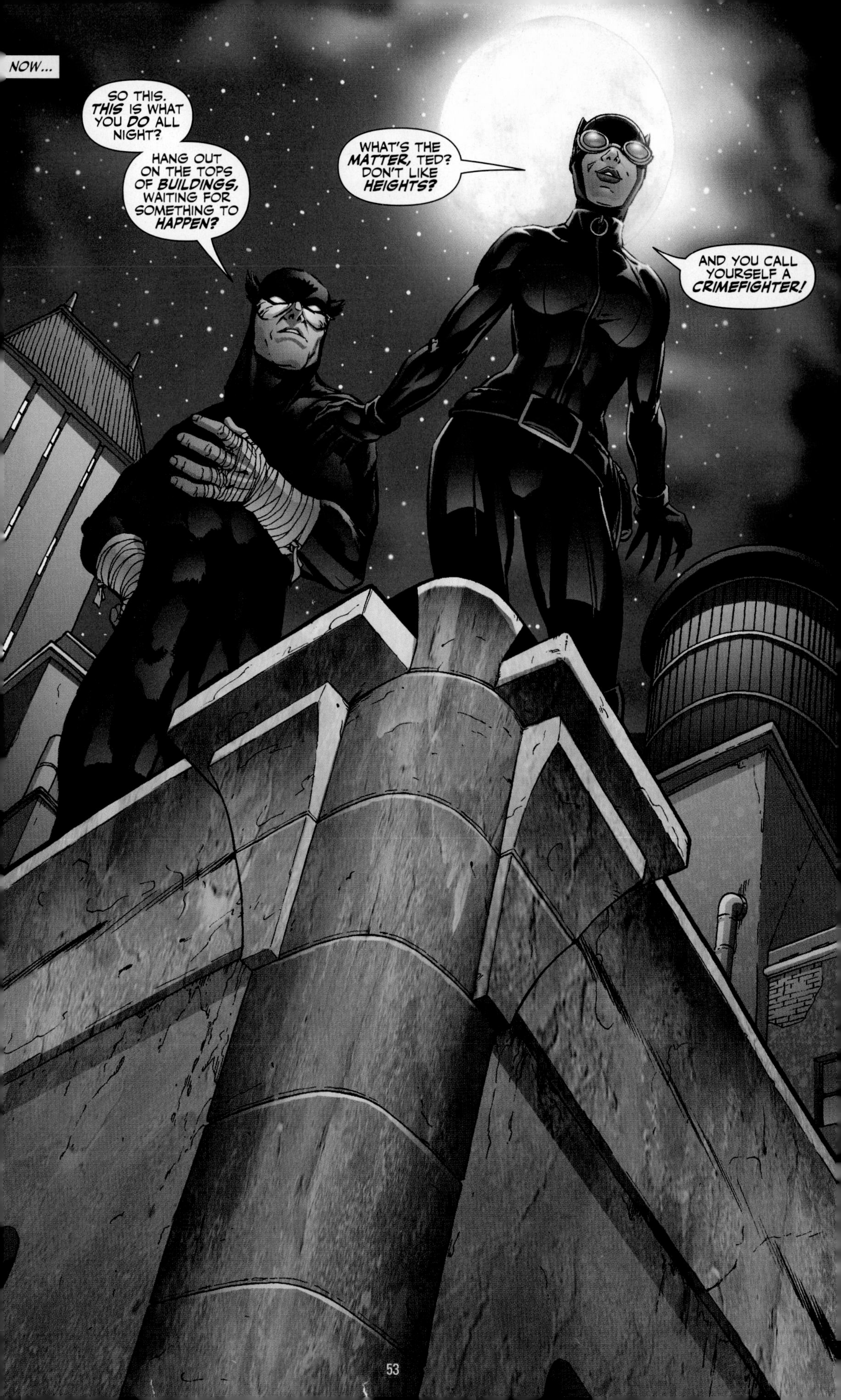
NOW...
SO THIS. THIS IS WHAT YOU DO ALL NIGHT?
HANG OUT ON THE TOPS OF BUILDINGS, WAITING FOR SOMETHING TO HAPPEN?
WHAT'S THE MATTER, TED? DON'T LIKE HEIGHTS?
AND YOU CALL YOURSELF A CRIMEFIGHTER!

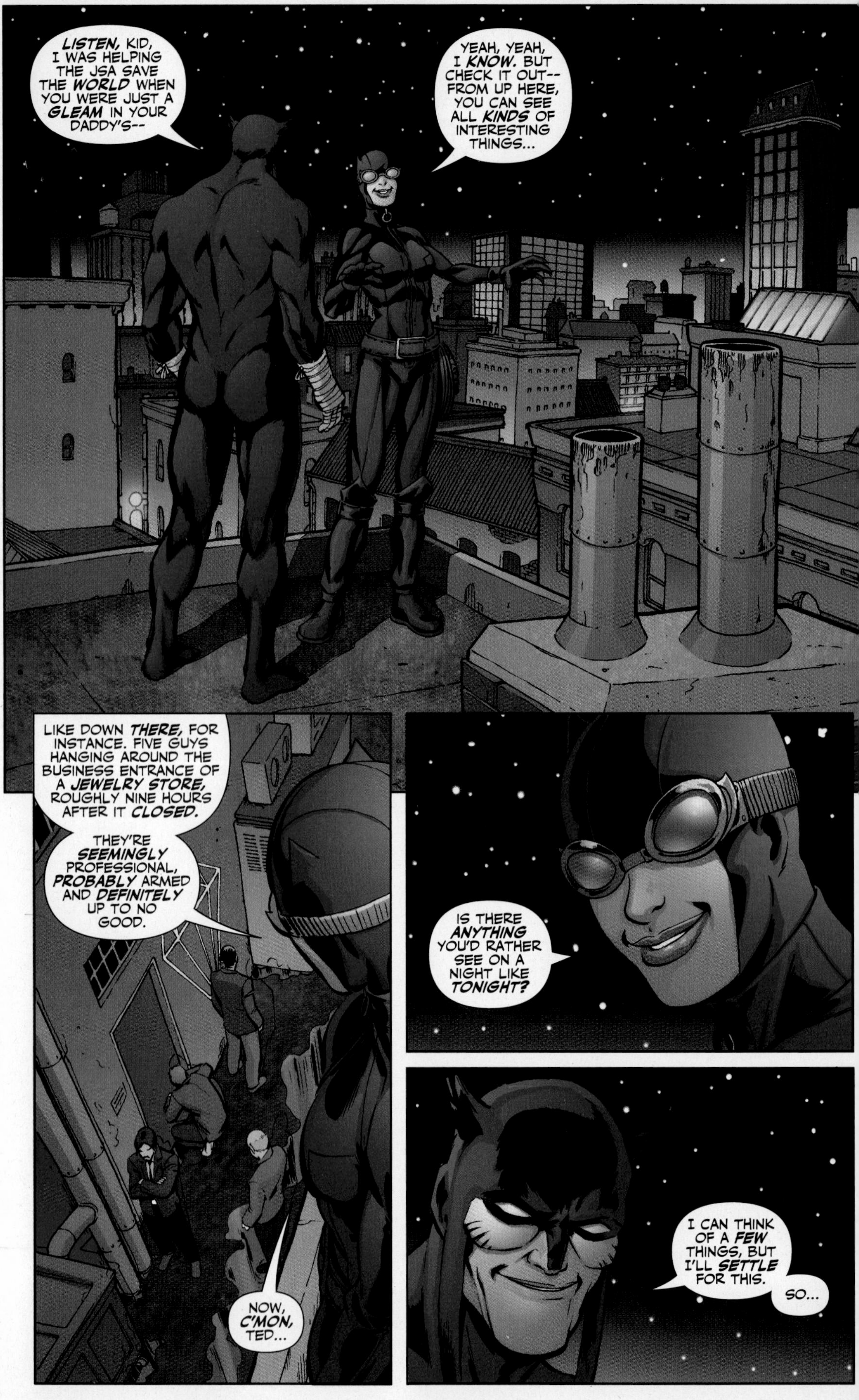
LISTEN, KID, I WAS HELPING THE JSA SAVE THE WORLD WHEN YOU WERE JUST A GLEAM IN YOUR DADDY'S--
YEAH, YEAH, I KNOW. BUT CHECK IT OUT-- FROM UP HERE, YOU CAN SEE ALL KINDS OF INTERESTING THINGS...
LIKE DOWN THERE, FOR INSTANCE. FIVE GUYS HANGING AROUND THE BUSINESS ENTRANCE OF A JEWELRY STORE, ROUGHLY NINE HOURS AFTER IT CLOSED.
THEY'RE SEEMINGLY PROFESSIONAL, PROBABLY ARMED AND DEFINITELY UP TO NO GOOD.
NOW, C'MON, TED...
IS THERE ANYTHING YOU'D RATHER SEE ON A NIGHT LIKE TONIGHT?
I CAN THINK OF A FEW THINGS, BUT I'LL SETTLE FOR THIS.
SO...

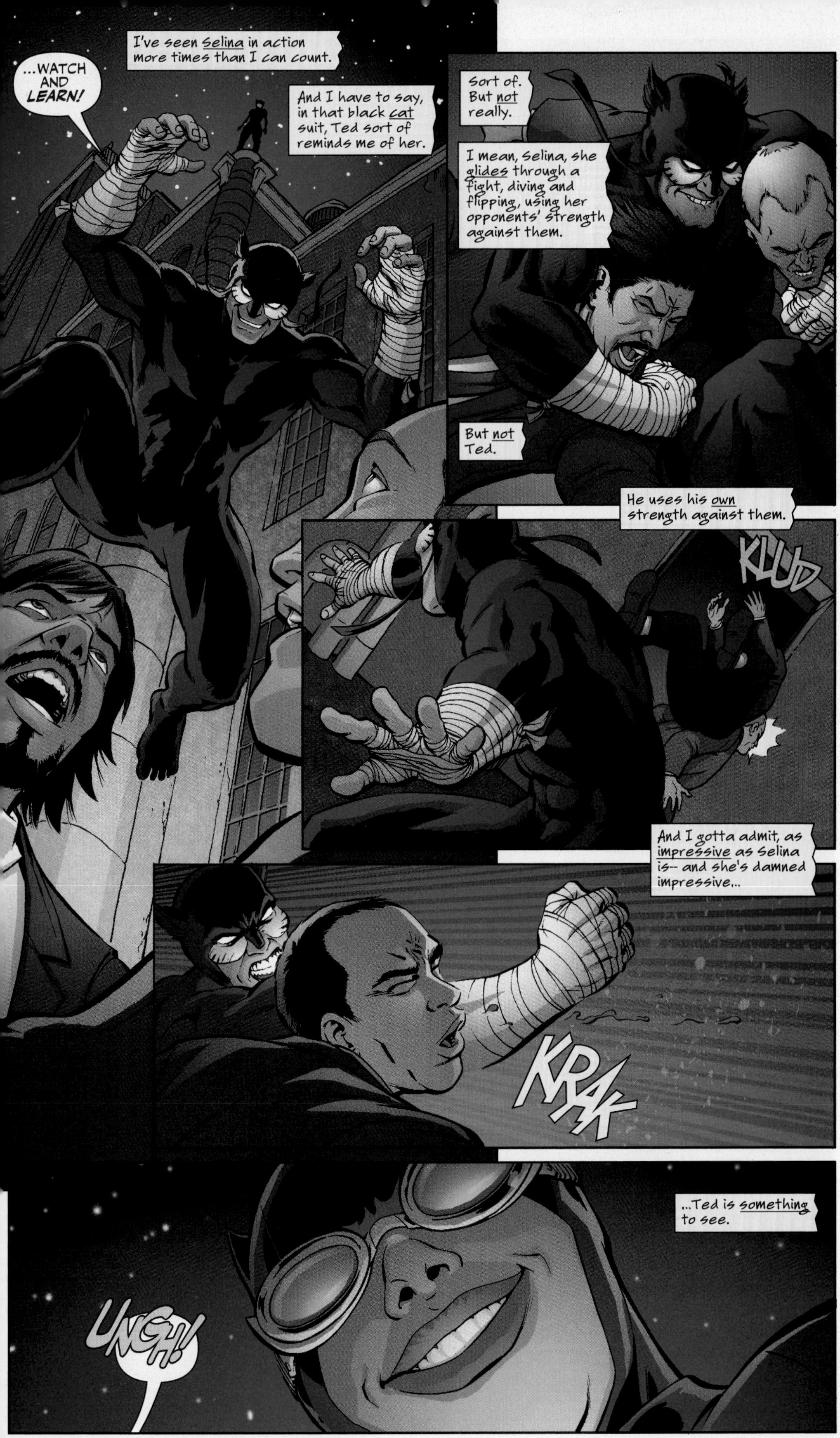

I've seen Selina in action more times than I can count.
...WATCH AND LEARN!
And I have to say, in that black cat suit, Ted sort of reminds me of her.
Sort of. But not really.
I mean, Selina, she glides through a fight, diving and flipping, using her opponents' strength against them.
But not Ted.
He uses his own strength against them.
KLUD
And I gotta admit, as impressive as Selina is-- and she's damned impressive...
KRAK
...Ted is something to see.
UNGH!

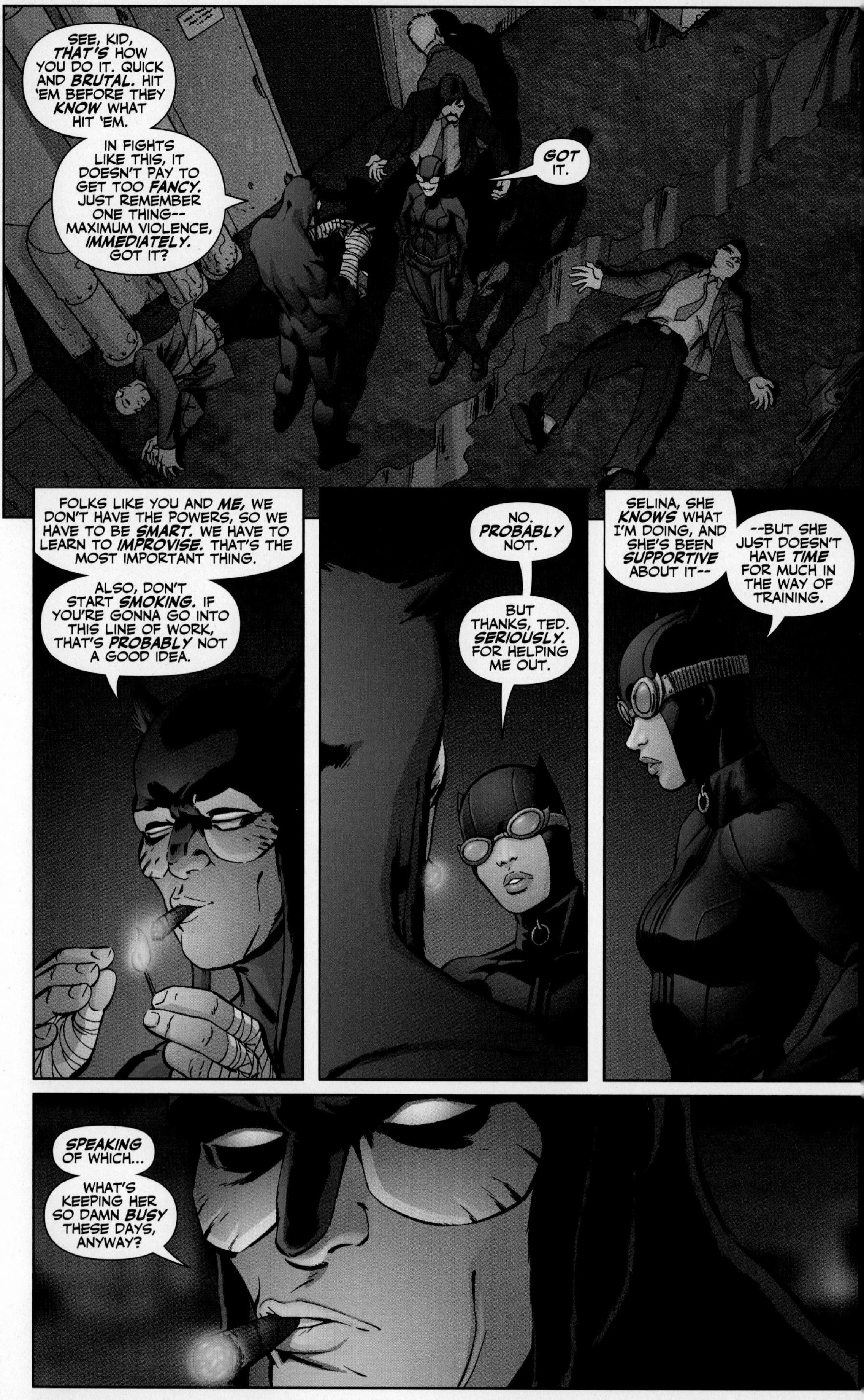
SEE, KID, THAT'S HOW YOU DO IT. QUICK AND BRUTAL. HIT 'EM BEFORE THEY KNOW WHAT HIT 'EM.
IN FIGHTS LIKE THIS, IT DOESN'T PAY TO GET TOO FANCY. JUST REMEMBER ONE THING-- MAXIMUM VIOLENCE, IMMEDIATELY. GOT IT?
GOT IT.
FOLKS LIKE YOU AND ME, WE DON'T HAVE THE POWERS, SO WE HAVE TO BE SMART. WE HAVE TO LEARN TO IMPROVISE. THAT'S THE MOST IMPORTANT THING.
ALSO, DON'T START SMOKING. IF YOU'RE GONNA GO INTO THIS LINE OF WORK, THAT'S PROBABLY NOT A GOOD IDEA.
NO. PROBABLY NOT.
BUT THANKS, TED. SERIOUSLY. FOR HELPING ME OUT.
SELINA, SHE KNOWS WHAT I'M DOING, AND SHE'S BEEN SUPPORTIVE ABOUT IT--
--BUT SHE JUST DOESN'T HAVE TIME FOR MUCH IN THE WAY OF TRAINING.
SPEAKING OF WHICH...
WHAT'S KEEPING HER SO DAMN BUSY THESE DAYS, ANYWAY?

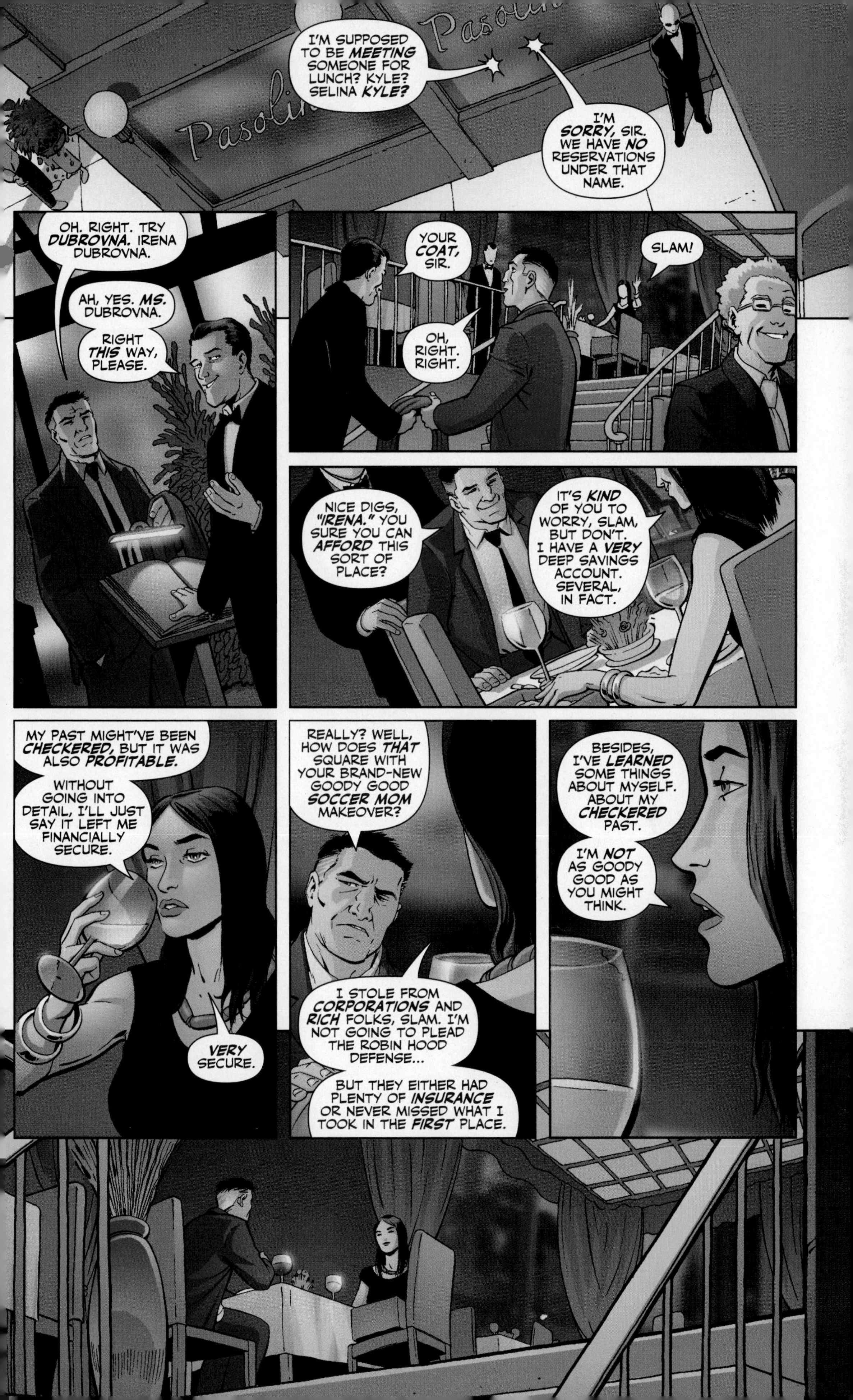
Pasolini
I'M SUPPOSED TO BE MEETING SOMEONE FOR LUNCH? KYLE? SELINA KYLE?
I'M SORRY, SIR. WE HAVE NO RESERVATIONS UNDER THAT NAME.
OH. RIGHT. TRY DUBROVNA. IRENA DUBROVNA.
AH, YES. MS. DUBROVNA.
RIGHT THIS WAY, PLEASE.
YOUR COAT, SIR.
OH, RIGHT. RIGHT.
SLAM!
NICE DIGS, "IRENA." YOU SURE YOU CAN AFFORD THIS SORT OF PLACE?
IT'S KIND OF YOU TO WORRY, SLAM, BUT DON'T. I HAVE A VERY DEEP SAVINGS ACCOUNT. SEVERAL, IN FACT.
MY PAST MIGHT'VE BEEN CHECKERED, BUT IT WAS ALSO PROFITABLE.
WITHOUT GOING INTO DETAIL, I'LL JUST SAY IT LEFT ME FINANCIALLY SECURE.
VERY SECURE.
REALLY? WELL, HOW DOES THAT SQUARE WITH YOUR BRAND-NEW GOODY GOOD SOCCER MOM MAKEOVER?
I STOLE FROM CORPORATIONS AND RICH FOLKS, SLAM. I'M NOT GOING TO PLEAD THE ROBIN HOOD DEFENSE...
BUT THEY EITHER HAD PLENTY OF INSURANCE OR NEVER MISSED WHAT I TOOK IN THE FIRST PLACE.
BESIDES, I'VE LEARNED SOME THINGS ABOUT MYSELF. ABOUT MY CHECKERED PAST.
I'M NOT AS GOODY GOOD AS YOU MIGHT THINK.

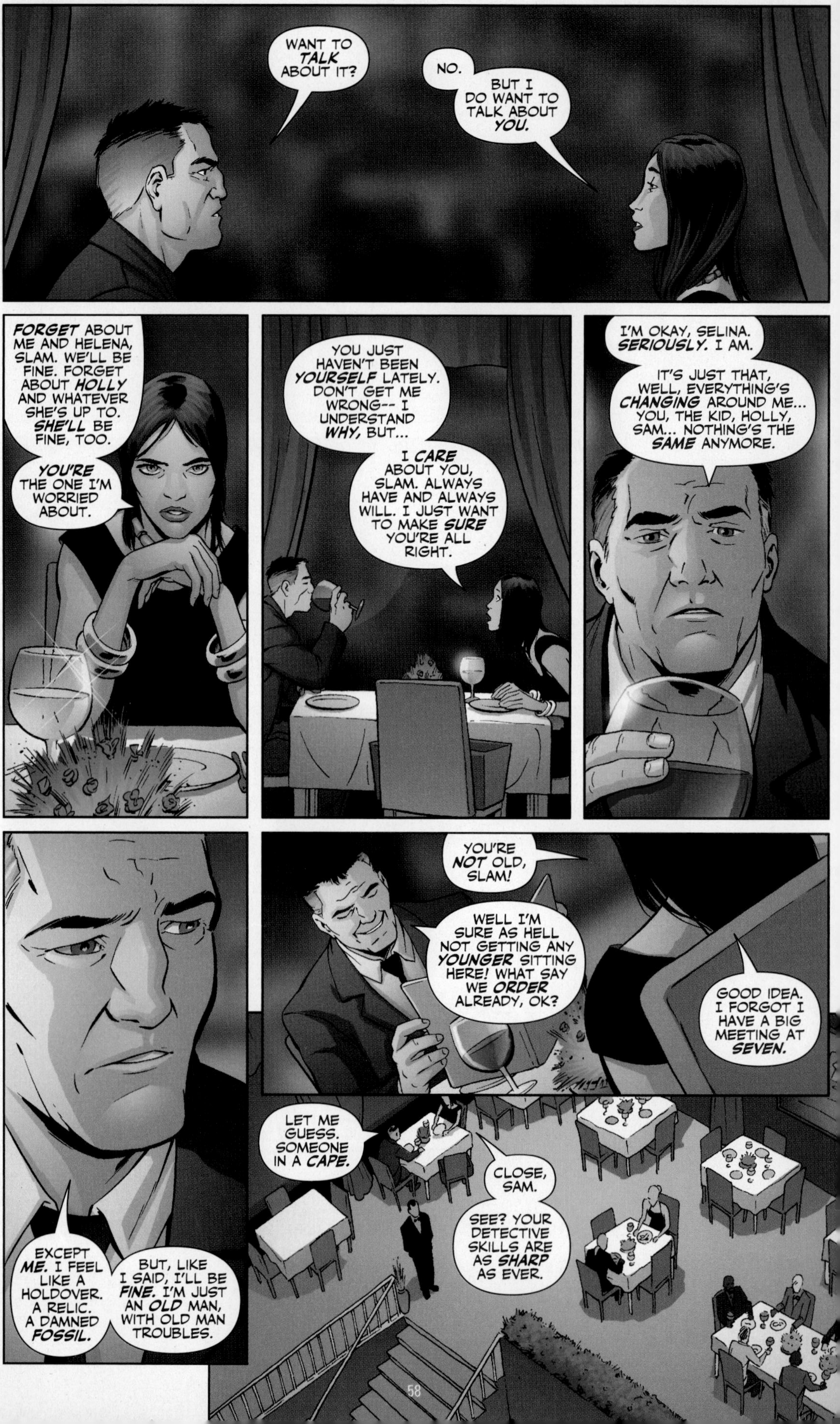
WANT TO TALK ABOUT IT?
NO.
BUT I DO WANT TO TALK ABOUT YOU.
FORGET ABOUT ME AND HELENA, SLAM. WE'LL BE FINE. FORGET ABOUT HOLLY AND WHATEVER SHE'S UP TO. SHE'LL BE FINE, TOO.
YOU'RE THE ONE I'M WORRIED ABOUT.
YOU JUST HAVEN'T BEEN YOURSELF LATELY. DON'T GET ME WRONG-- I UNDERSTAND WHY, BUT...
I CARE ABOUT YOU, SLAM. ALWAYS HAVE AND ALWAYS WILL. I JUST WANT TO MAKE SURE YOU'RE ALL RIGHT.
I'M OKAY, SELINA. SERIOUSLY. I AM.
IT'S JUST THAT, WELL, EVERYTHING'S CHANGING AROUND ME... YOU, THE KID, HOLLY, SAM... NOTHING'S THE SAME ANYMORE.
EXCEPT ME. I FEEL LIKE A HOLDOVER. A RELIC. A DAMNED FOSSIL.
BUT, LIKE I SAID, I'LL BE FINE. I'M JUST AN OLD MAN, WITH OLD MAN TROUBLES.
YOU'RE NOT OLD, SLAM!
WELL I'M SURE AS HELL NOT GETTING ANY YOUNGER SITTING HERE! WHAT SAY WE ORDER ALREADY, OK?
GOOD IDEA. I FORGOT I HAVE A BIG MEETING AT SEVEN.
LET ME GUESS. SOMEONE IN A CAPE.
CLOSE, SAM.
SEE? YOUR DETECTIVE SKILLS ARE AS SHARP AS EVER.

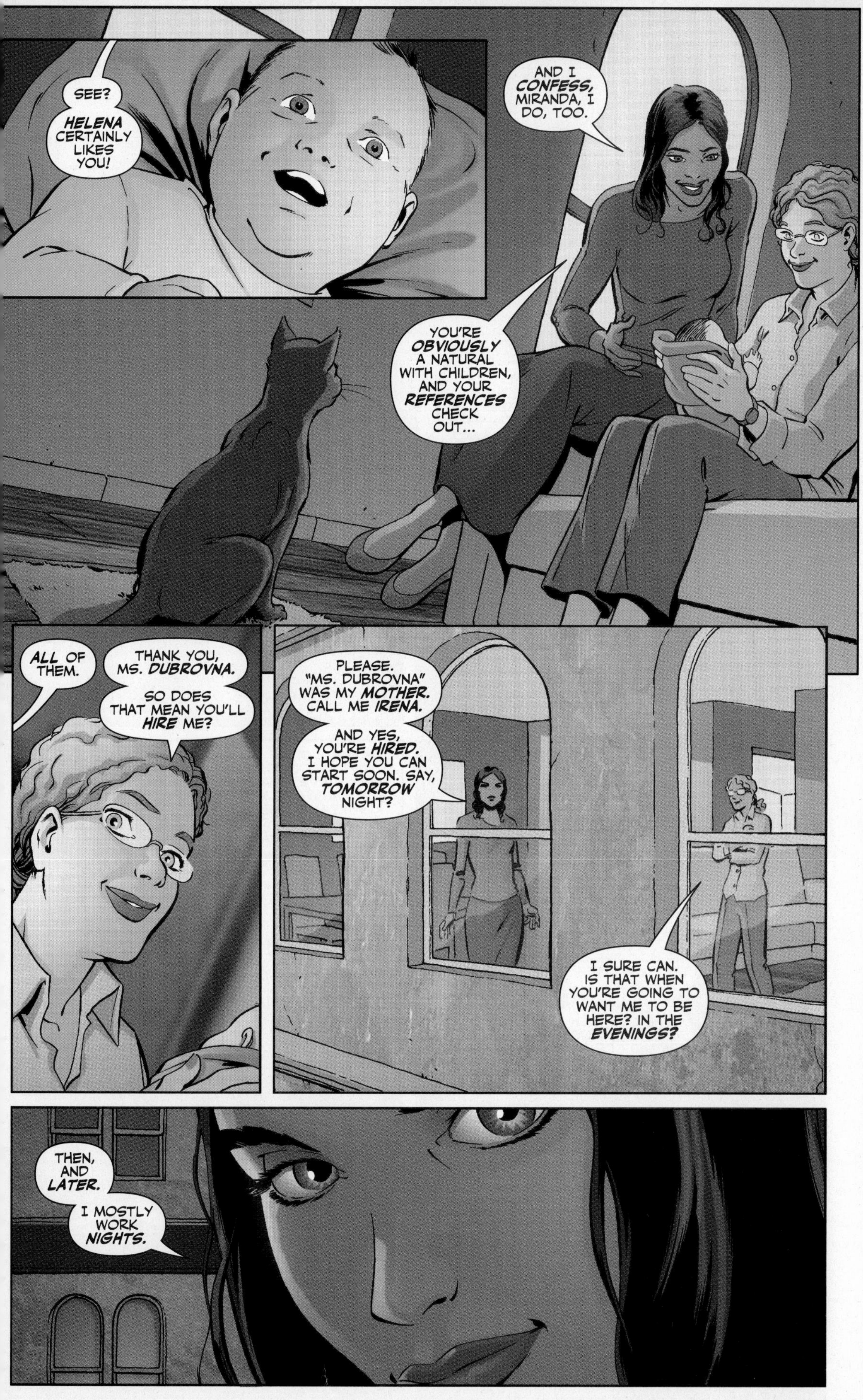
SEE? HELENA CERTAINLY LIKES YOU!
AND I CONFESS, MIRANDA, I DO, TOO.
YOU'RE OBVIOUSLY A NATURAL WITH CHILDREN, AND YOUR REFERENCES CHECK OUT...
ALL OF THEM.
THANK YOU, MS. DUBROVNA.
SO DOES THAT MEAN YOU'LL HIRE ME?
PLEASE. "MS. DUBROVNA" WAS MY MOTHER. CALL ME IRENA.
AND YES, YOU'RE HIRED. I HOPE YOU CAN START SOON. SAY, TOMORROW NIGHT?
I SURE CAN. IS THAT WHEN YOU'RE GOING TO WANT ME TO BE HERE? IN THE EVENINGS?
THEN, AND LATER.
I MOSTLY WORK NIGHTS.

HELLO? I'M LOOKING FOR SOMEONE NAMED *EDISON?*

OVER HERE.

MY NAME'S *LENAHAN.* I'D LIKE A COPY OF THAT *CATWOMAN* CLIP YOU SHOWED A FEW NIGHTS AGO.

YOU AND THE *REST* OF GOTHAM.

WAIT FOR THE *DVD* RELEASE. THE BONUS FEATURES ARE GOING TO BE *CHOICE.*

LET'S START *OVER.*

MY NAME'S *LENAHAN.* I'D LIKE A COPY OF THAT *CATWOMAN* CLIP YOU SHOWED A FEW NIGHTS AGO.

WHY DIDN'T YOU *SAY* SO?

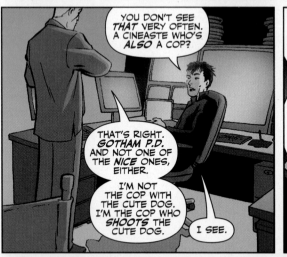

YOU DON'T SEE *THAT* VERY OFTEN. A CINEASTE WHO'S *ALSO* A COP?

THAT'S RIGHT. *GOTHAM P.D.* AND NOT ONE OF THE *NICE* ONES, EITHER.

I'M NOT THE COP WITH THE CUTE DOG. I'M THE COP WHO *SHOOTS* THE CUTE DOG.

I SEE.

THOUGH YOU'RE PROBABLY MORE KIRK DOUGLAS IN *"THE DETECTIVE"* THAN HARVEY KEITEL IN *"BAD LIEUTENANT,"* RIGHT? MORE BREAK-THE-*RULES* THAN OUT-FOR *YOURSELF?*

I MEAN, LIKE GLENN FORD IN *"THE BIG HEAT."* GENE HACKMAN IN *"THE FRENCH CONNECTION."* CHOW YUN FAT IN *"HARD BOILED."* YOU KNOW...

"DIRTY HARRY"...

...NOT DIRTY *COP.*

WHAT THE *HELL...?*

JUST GIVE ME THAT DAMN *CLIP.*

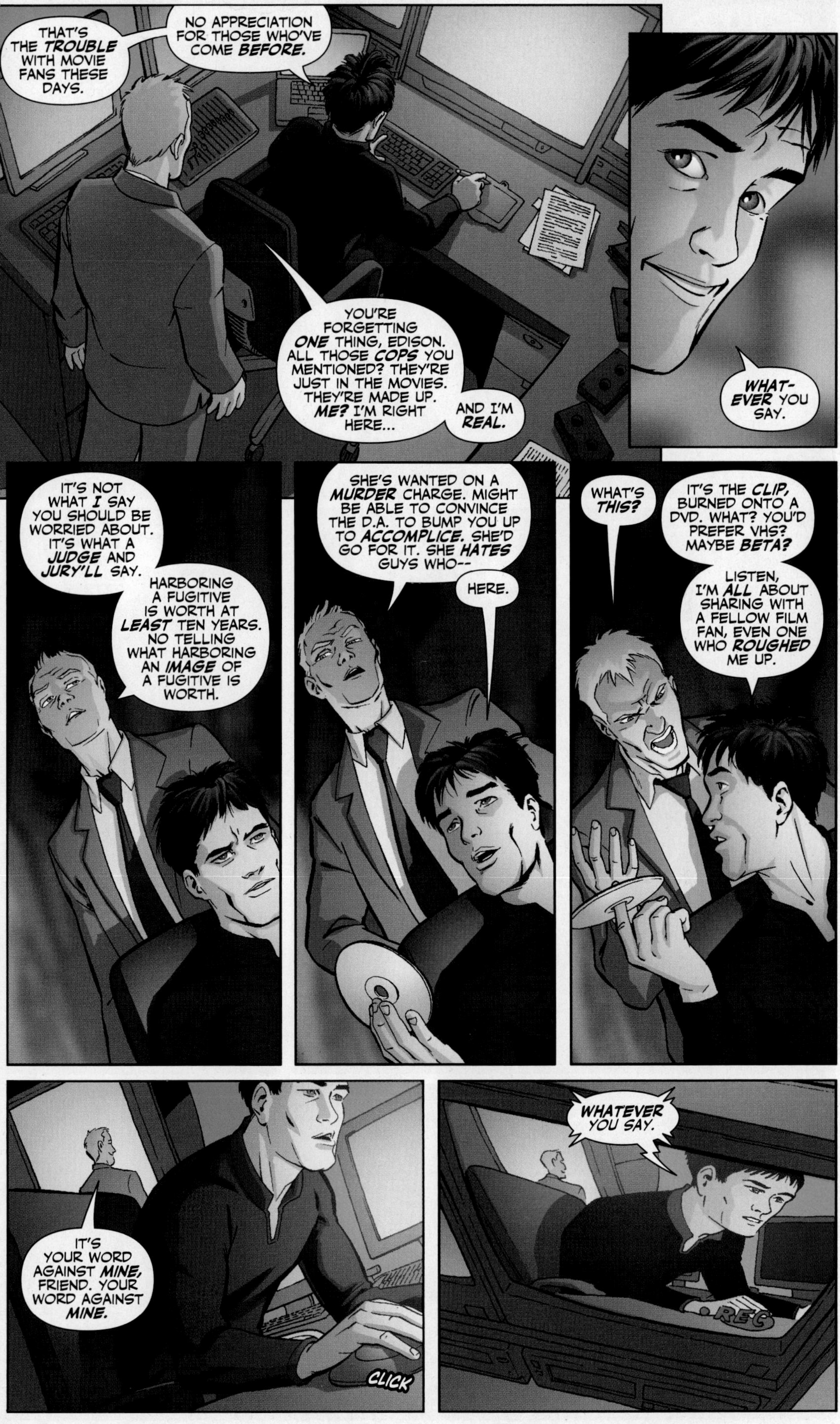
THAT'S THE TROUBLE WITH MOVIE FANS THESE DAYS.
NO APPRECIATION FOR THOSE WHO'VE COME BEFORE.
YOU'RE FORGETTING ONE THING, EDISON. ALL THOSE COPS YOU MENTIONED? THEY'RE JUST IN THE MOVIES. THEY'RE MADE UP. ME? I'M RIGHT HERE...
AND I'M REAL.
WHAT-EVER YOU SAY.
IT'S NOT WHAT I SAY YOU SHOULD BE WORRIED ABOUT. IT'S WHAT A JUDGE AND JURY'LL SAY.
HARBORING A FUGITIVE IS WORTH AT LEAST TEN YEARS. NO TELLING WHAT HARBORING AN IMAGE OF A FUGITIVE IS WORTH.
SHE'S WANTED ON A MURDER CHARGE. MIGHT BE ABLE TO CONVINCE THE D.A. TO BUMP YOU UP TO ACCOMPLICE. SHE'D GO FOR IT. SHE HATES GUYS WHO--
HERE.
WHAT'S THIS?
IT'S THE CLIP, BURNED ONTO A DVD. WHAT? YOU'D PREFER VHS? MAYBE BETA?
LISTEN, I'M ALL ABOUT SHARING WITH A FELLOW FILM FAN, EVEN ONE WHO ROUGHED ME UP.
IT'S YOUR WORD AGAINST MINE, FRIEND. YOUR WORD AGAINST MINE.
CLICK
WHATEVER YOU SAY.
REC

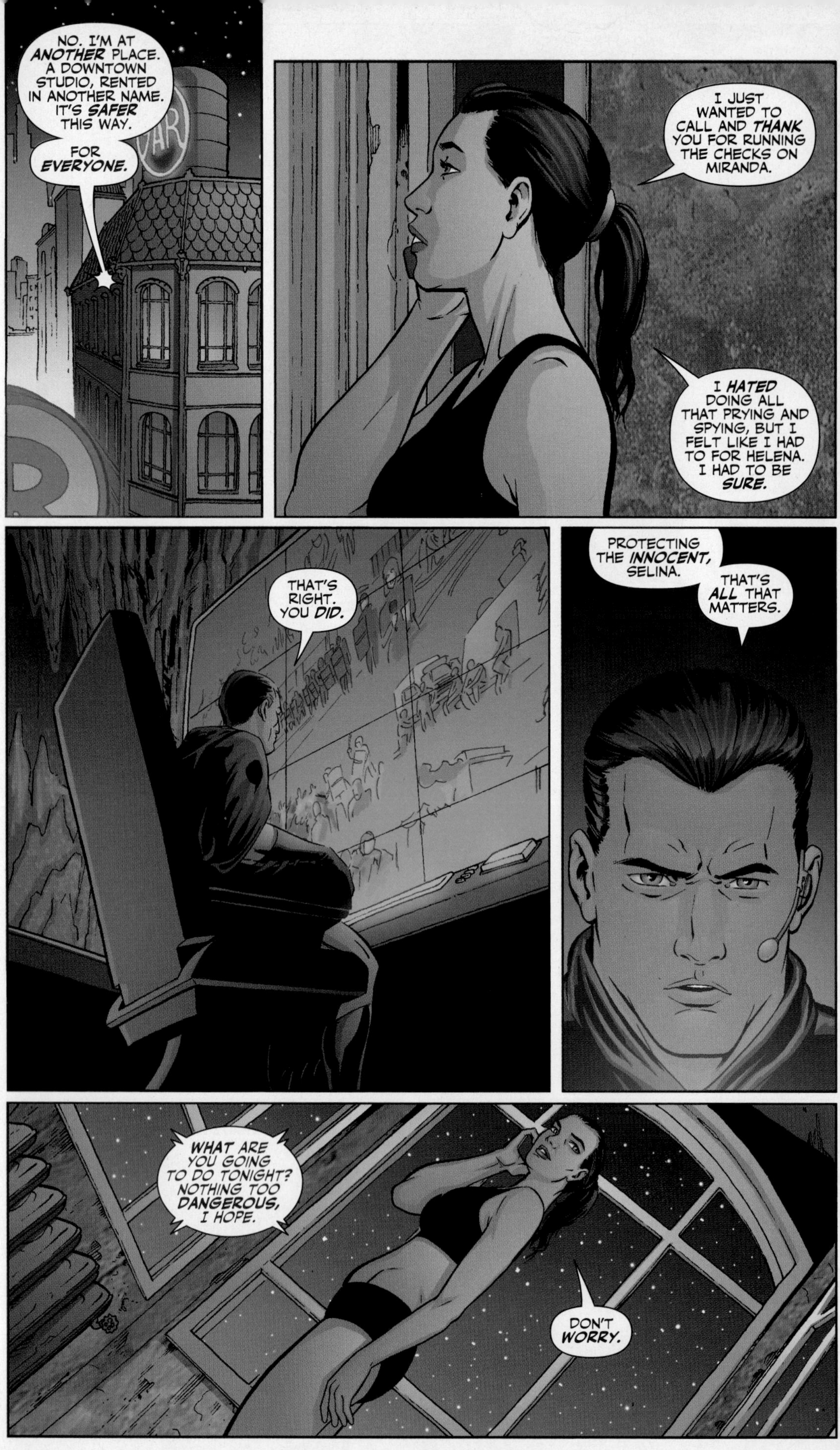

NO. I'M AT ANOTHER PLACE. A DOWNTOWN STUDIO, RENTED IN ANOTHER NAME. IT'S SAFER THIS WAY.
FOR EVERYONE.
I JUST WANTED TO CALL AND THANK YOU FOR RUNNING THE CHECKS ON MIRANDA.
I HATED DOING ALL THAT PRYING AND SPYING, BUT I FELT LIKE I HAD TO FOR HELENA. I HAD TO BE SURE.
THAT'S RIGHT. YOU DID.
PROTECTING THE INNOCENT, SELINA.
THAT'S ALL THAT MATTERS.
WHAT ARE YOU GOING TO DO TONIGHT? NOTHING TOO DANGEROUS, I HOPE.
DON'T WORRY.

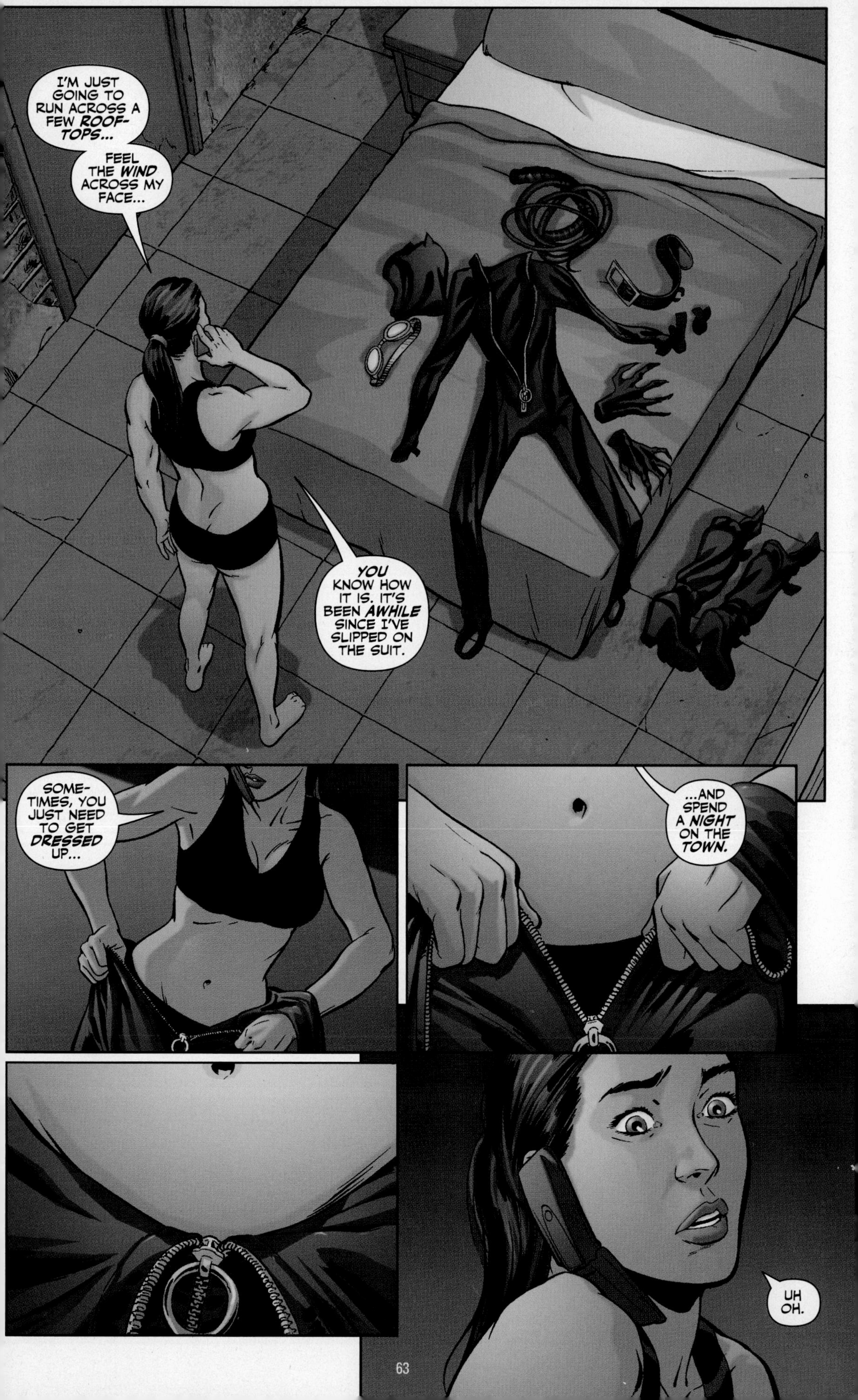
I'M JUST GOING TO RUN ACROSS A FEW ROOF-TOPS...
FEEL THE WIND ACROSS MY FACE...
YOU KNOW HOW IT IS. IT'S BEEN AWHILE SINCE I'VE SLIPPED ON THE SUIT.
SOME-TIMES, YOU JUST NEED TO GET DRESSED UP...
...AND SPEND A NIGHT ON THE TOWN.
UH OH.

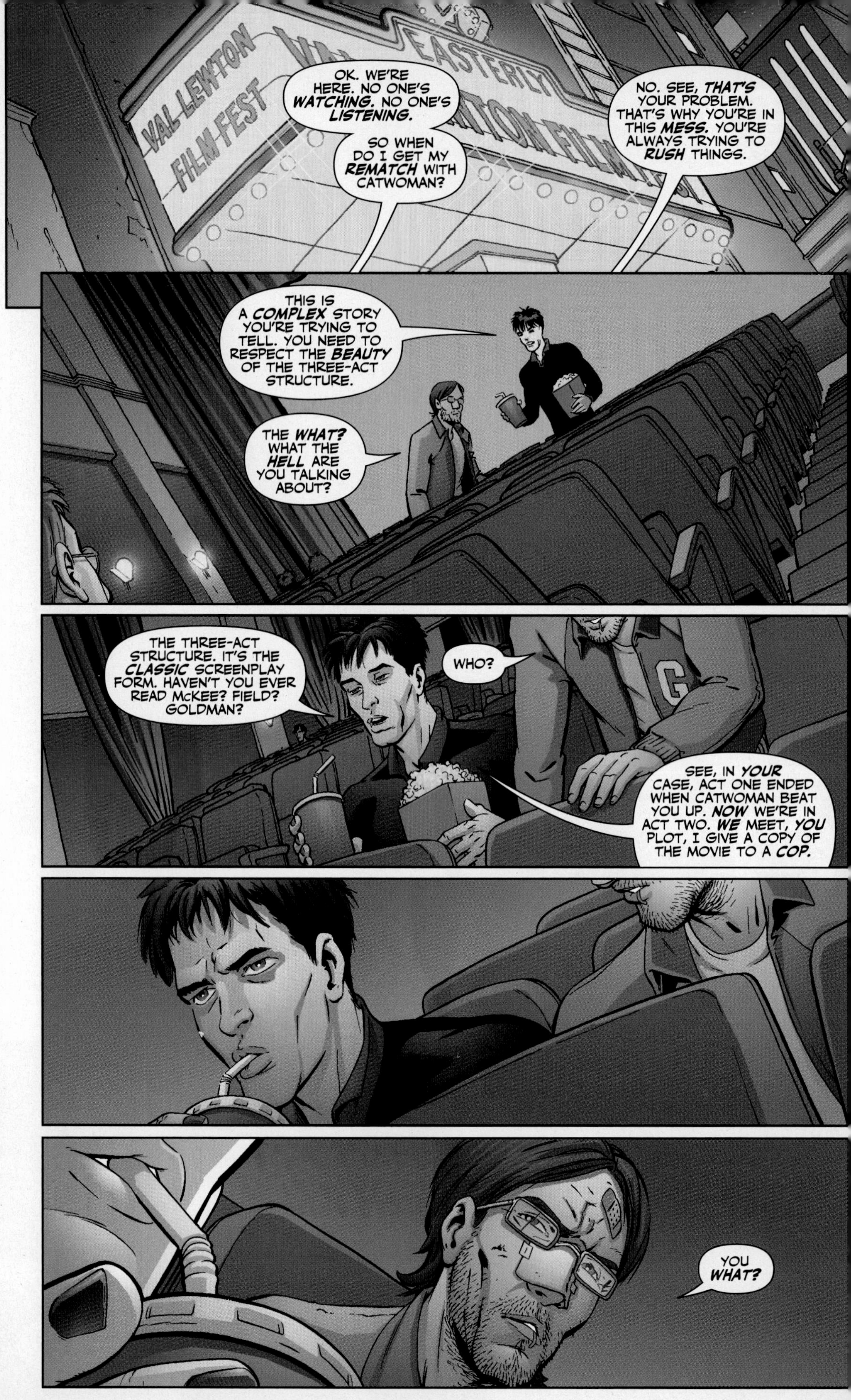
VAL LEWTON FILM FEST
EASTERLY
OK. WE'RE HERE. NO ONE'S WATCHING. NO ONE'S LISTENING.
SO WHEN DO I GET MY REMATCH WITH CATWOMAN?
NO. SEE, THAT'S YOUR PROBLEM. THAT'S WHY YOU'RE IN THIS MESS. YOU'RE ALWAYS TRYING TO RUSH THINGS.
THIS IS A COMPLEX STORY YOU'RE TRYING TO TELL. YOU NEED TO RESPECT THE BEAUTY OF THE THREE-ACT STRUCTURE.
THE WHAT? WHAT THE HELL ARE YOU TALKING ABOUT?
THE THREE-ACT STRUCTURE. IT'S THE CLASSIC SCREENPLAY FORM. HAVEN'T YOU EVER READ McKEE? FIELD? GOLDMAN?
WHO?
SEE, IN YOUR CASE, ACT ONE ENDED WHEN CATWOMAN BEAT YOU UP. NOW WE'RE IN ACT TWO. WE MEET, YOU PLOT, I GIVE A COPY OF THE MOVIE TO A COP.
YOU WHAT?

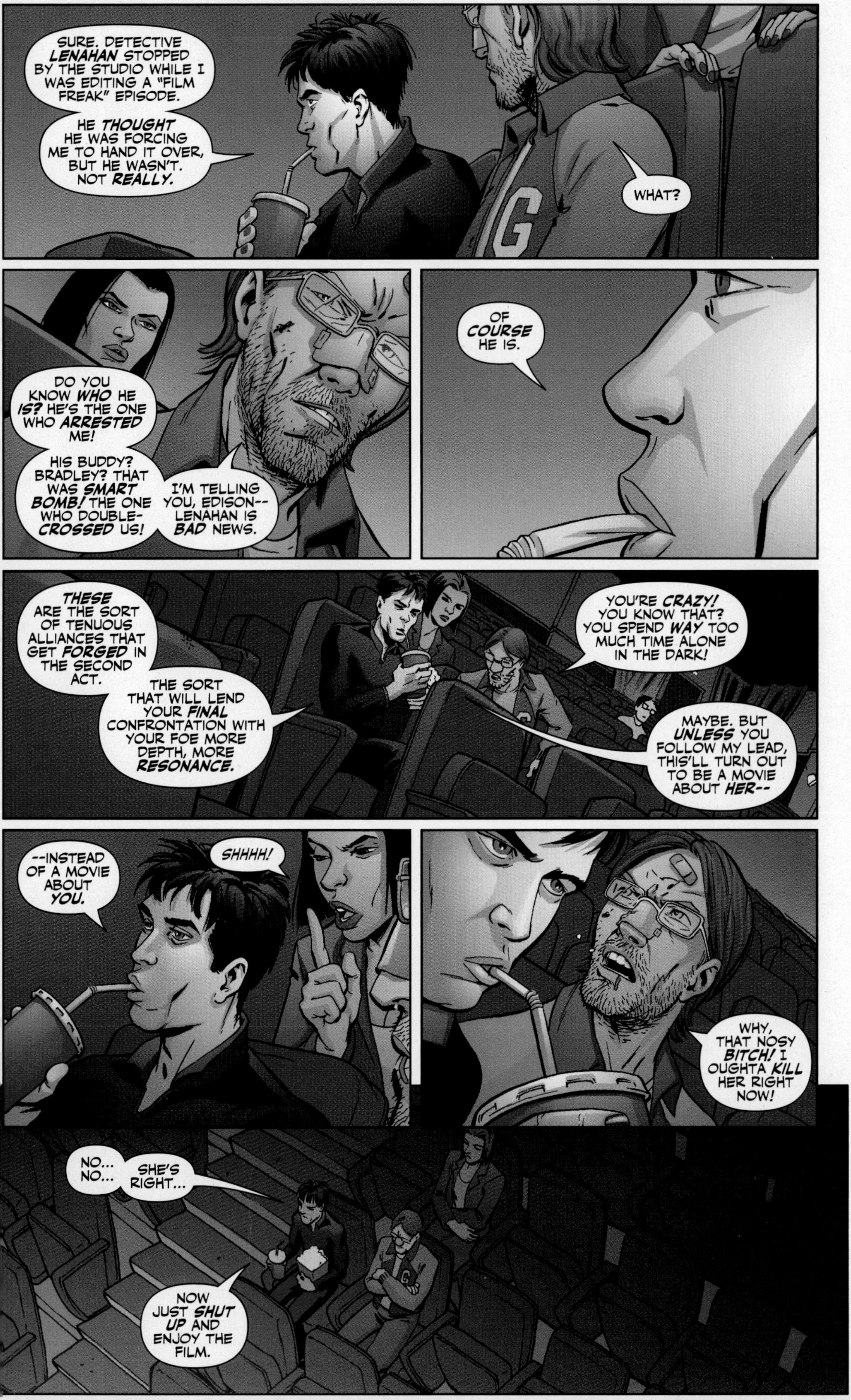
SURE. DETECTIVE LENAHAN STOPPED BY THE STUDIO WHILE I WAS EDITING A "FILM FREAK" EPISODE.
HE THOUGHT HE WAS FORCING ME TO HAND IT OVER, BUT HE WASN'T. NOT REALLY.
WHAT?
DO YOU KNOW WHO HE IS? HE'S THE ONE WHO ARRESTED ME!
HIS BUDDY? BRADLEY? THAT WAS SMART BOMB! THE ONE WHO DOUBLE-CROSSED US!
I'M TELLING YOU, EDISON-- LENAHAN IS BAD NEWS.
OF COURSE HE IS.
THESE ARE THE SORT OF TENUOUS ALLIANCES THAT GET FORGED IN THE SECOND ACT.
THE SORT THAT WILL LEND YOUR FINAL CONFRONTATION WITH YOUR FOE MORE DEPTH, MORE RESONANCE.
YOU'RE CRAZY! YOU KNOW THAT? YOU SPEND WAY TOO MUCH TIME ALONE IN THE DARK!
MAYBE. BUT UNLESS YOU FOLLOW MY LEAD, THIS'LL TURN OUT TO BE A MOVIE ABOUT HER--
--INSTEAD OF A MOVIE ABOUT YOU.
SHHHH!
WHY, THAT NOSY BITCH! I OUGHTA KILL HER RIGHT NOW!
NO... NO...
SHE'S RIGHT...
NOW JUST SHUT UP AND ENJOY THE FILM.

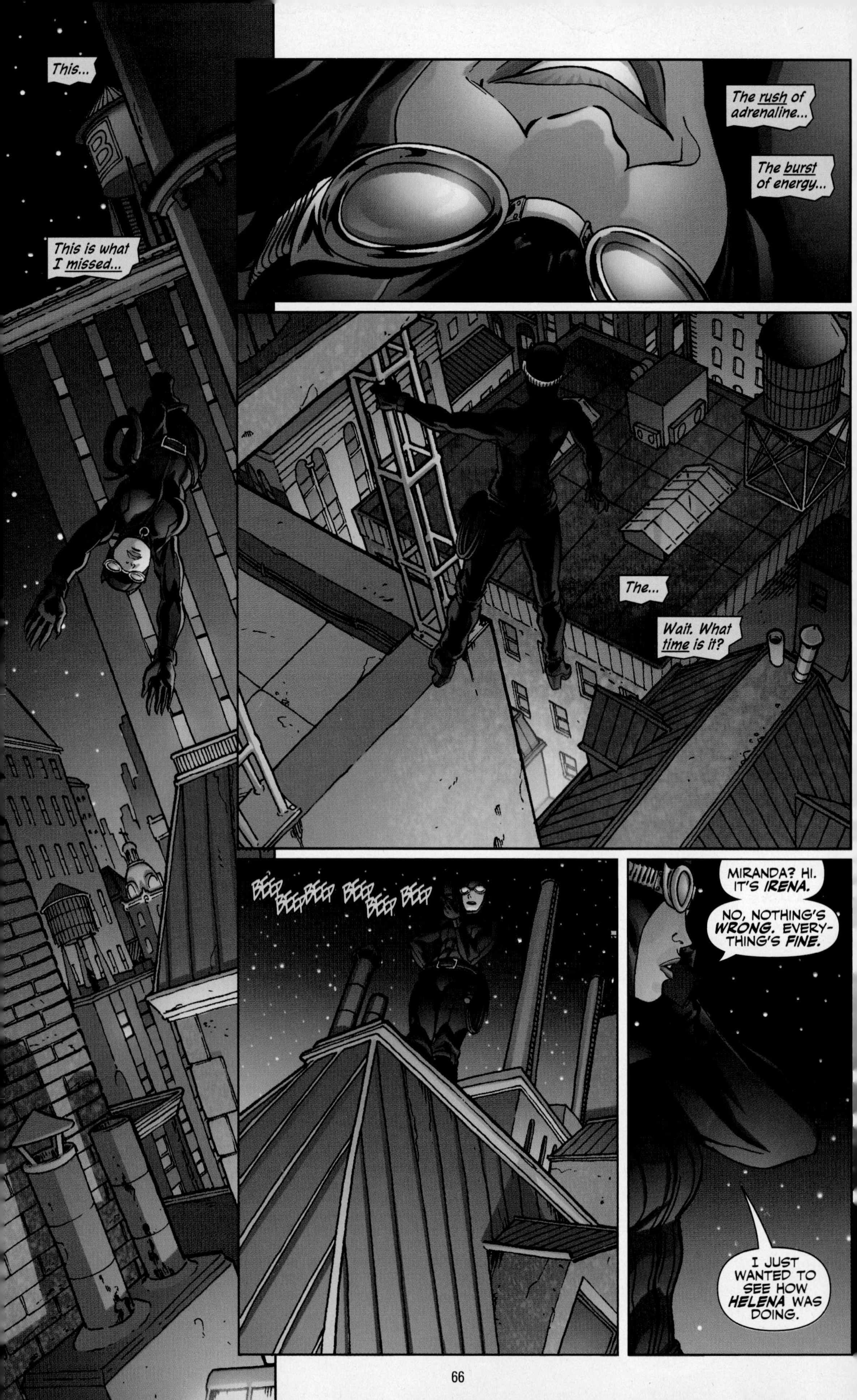

This...
This is what I missed...
The rush of adrenaline...
The burst of energy...
The...
Wait. What time is it?
BEEP BEEP BEEP BEEP BEEP BEEP
MIRANDA? HI. IT'S IRENA.
NO, NOTHING'S WRONG. EVERYTHING'S FINE.
I JUST WANTED TO SEE HOW HELENA WAS DOING.

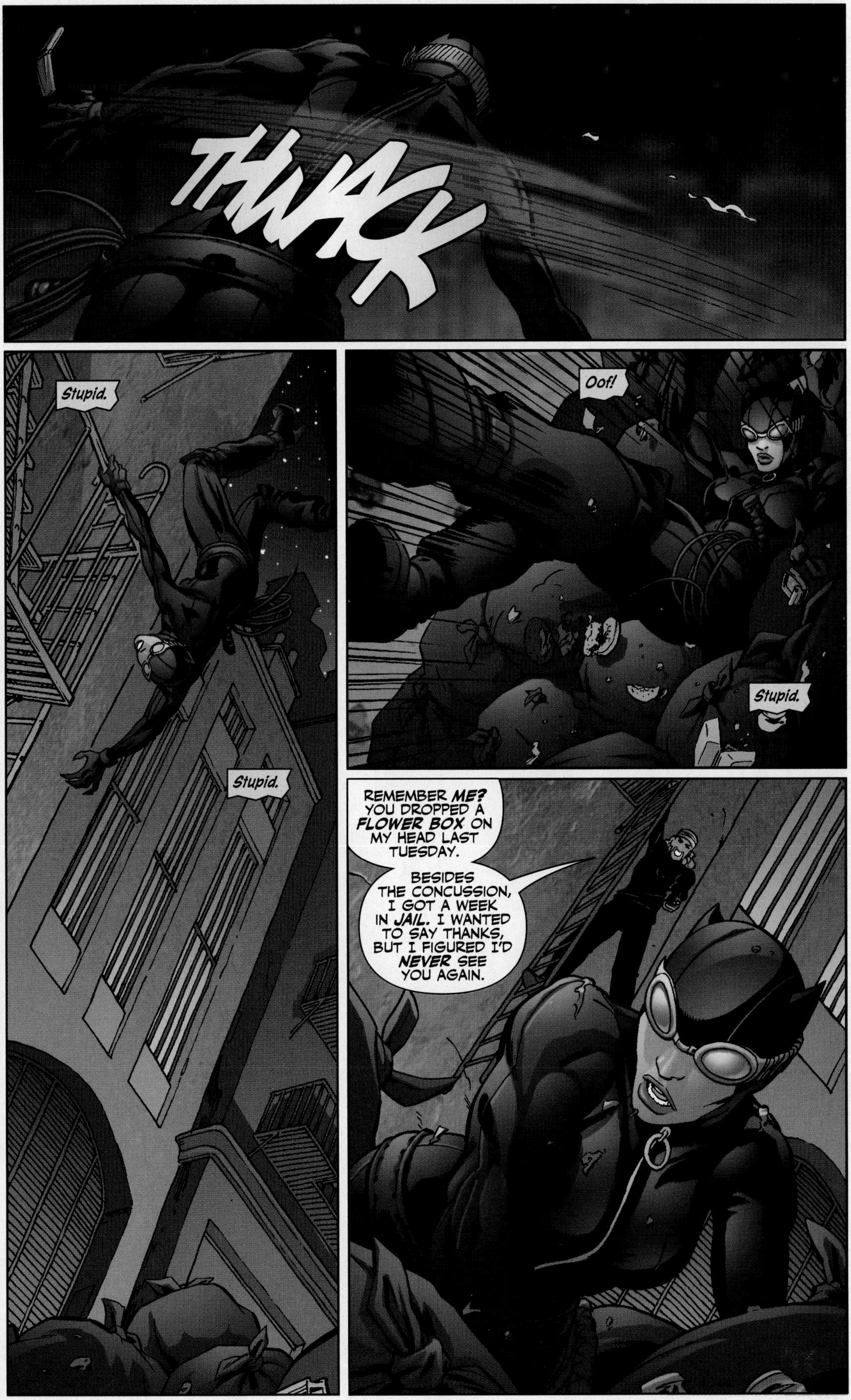
THWACK
Stupid.
Stupid.
Oof!
Stupid.
REMEMBER *ME?* YOU DROPPED A *FLOWER BOX* ON MY HEAD LAST TUESDAY.
BESIDES THE CONCUSSION, I GOT A WEEK IN *JAIL.* I WANTED TO SAY THANKS, BUT I FIGURED I'D *NEVER* SEE YOU AGAIN.

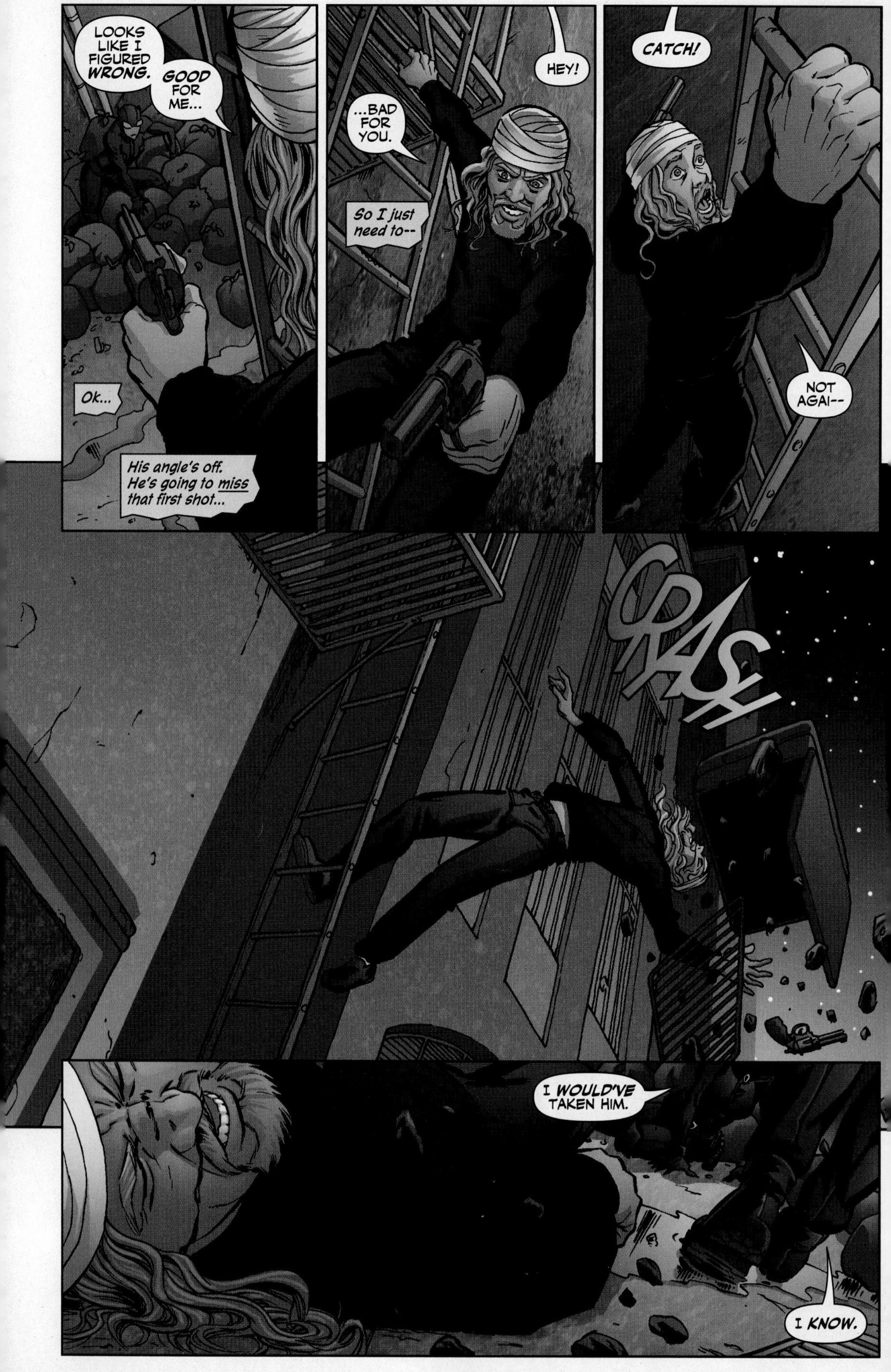

LOOKS LIKE I FIGURED WRONG.
GOOD FOR ME...
Ok...
His angle's off. He's going to miss that first shot...
HEY!
...BAD FOR YOU.
So I just need to--
CATCH!
NOT AGAI--
CRASH
I WOULD'VE TAKEN HIM.
I KNOW.

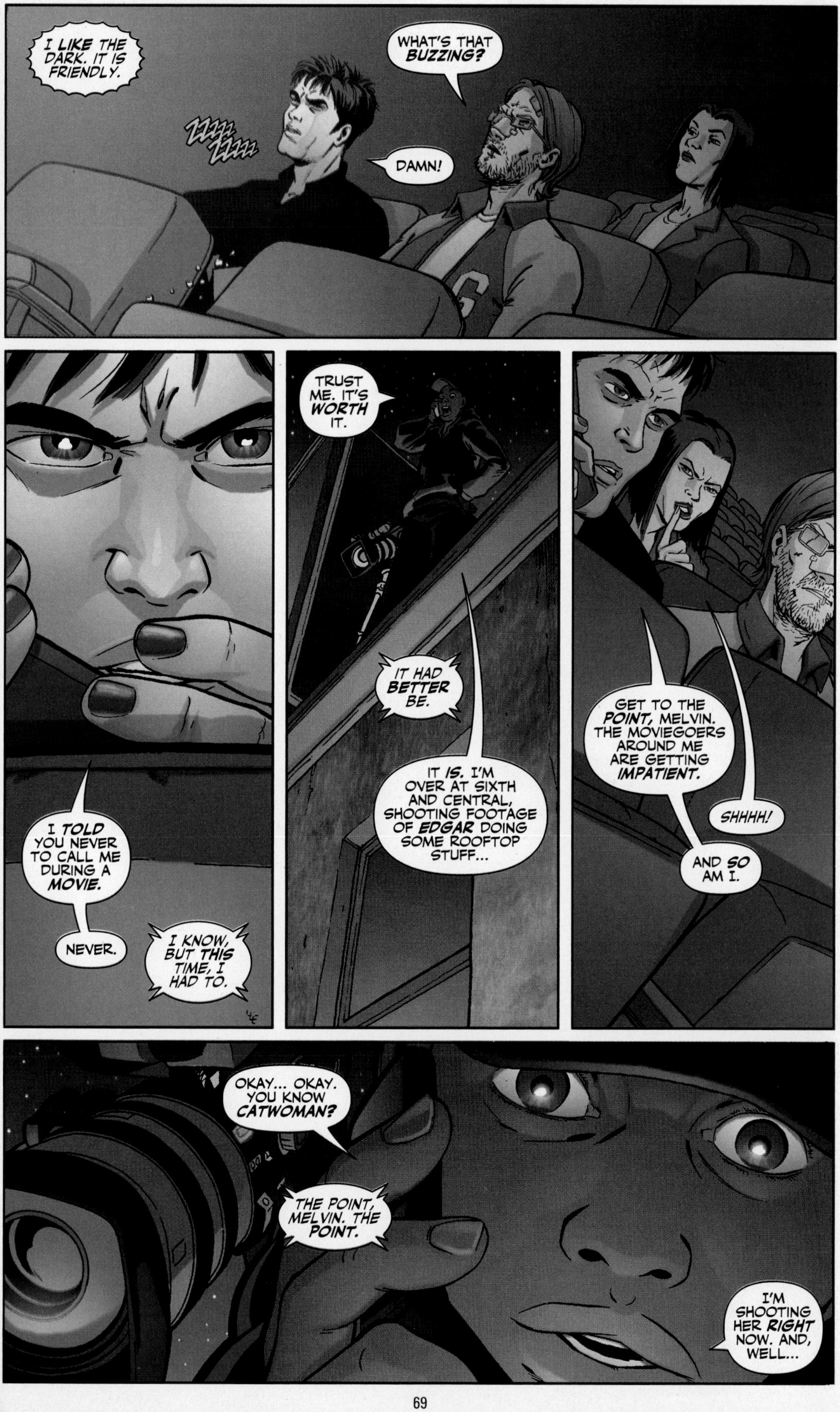
I LIKE THE DARK. IT IS FRIENDLY.
WHAT'S THAT BUZZING?
ZZZZZ ZZZZZ
DAMN!
I TOLD YOU NEVER TO CALL ME DURING A MOVIE.
NEVER.
I KNOW, BUT THIS TIME, I HAD TO.
TRUST ME. IT'S WORTH IT.
IT HAD BETTER BE.
IT IS. I'M OVER AT SIXTH AND CENTRAL, SHOOTING FOOTAGE OF EDGAR DOING SOME ROOFTOP STUFF...
GET TO THE POINT, MELVIN. THE MOVIEGOERS AROUND ME ARE GETTING IMPATIENT.
SHHHH!
AND SO AM I.
OKAY... OKAY. YOU KNOW CATWOMAN?
THE POINT, MELVIN. THE POINT.
I'M SHOOTING HER RIGHT NOW. AND, WELL...

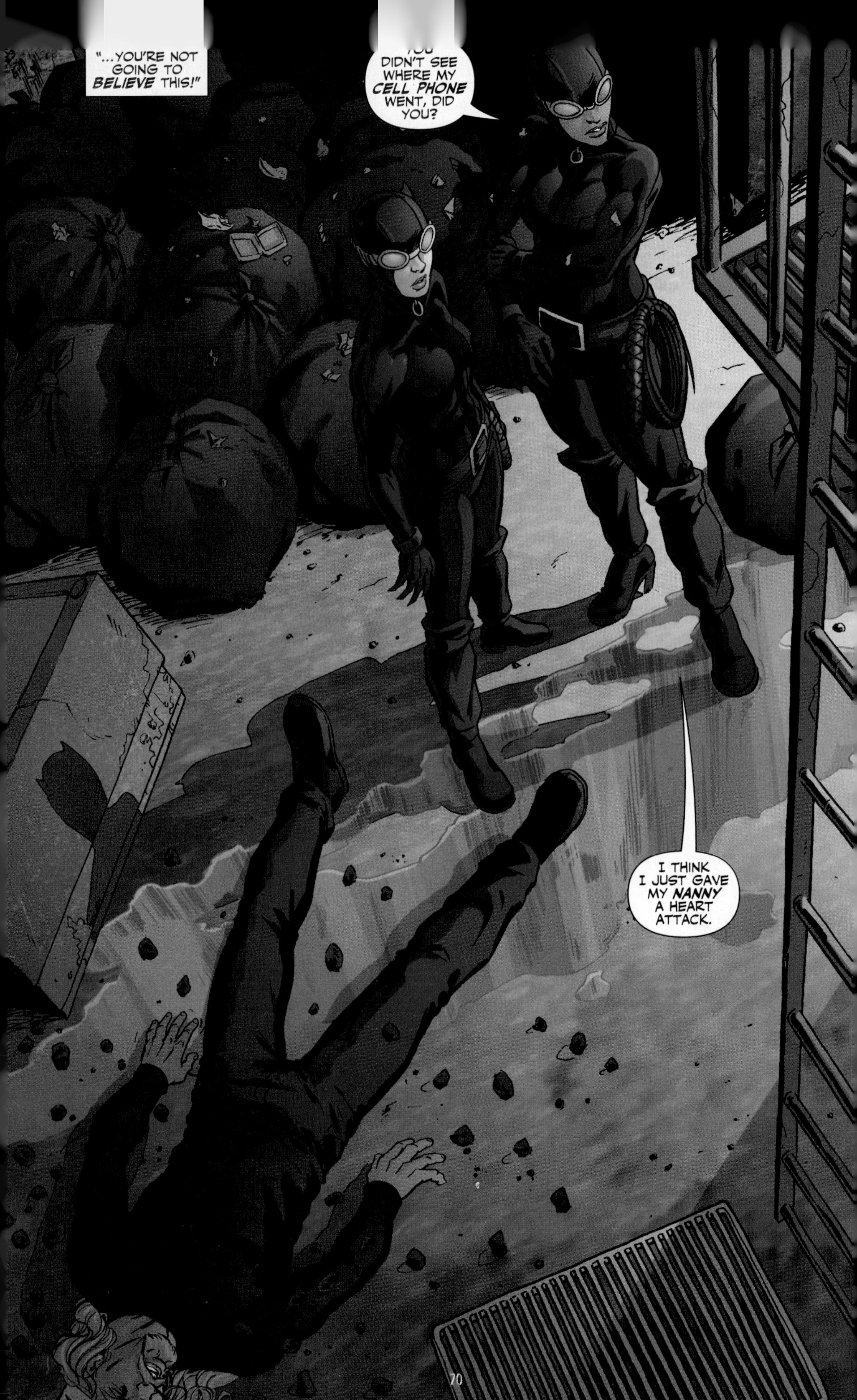
"...YOU'RE NOT GOING TO BELIEVE THIS!"
DIDN'T SEE WHERE MY CELL PHONE WENT, DID YOU?
I THINK I JUST GAVE MY NANNY A HEART ATTACK.

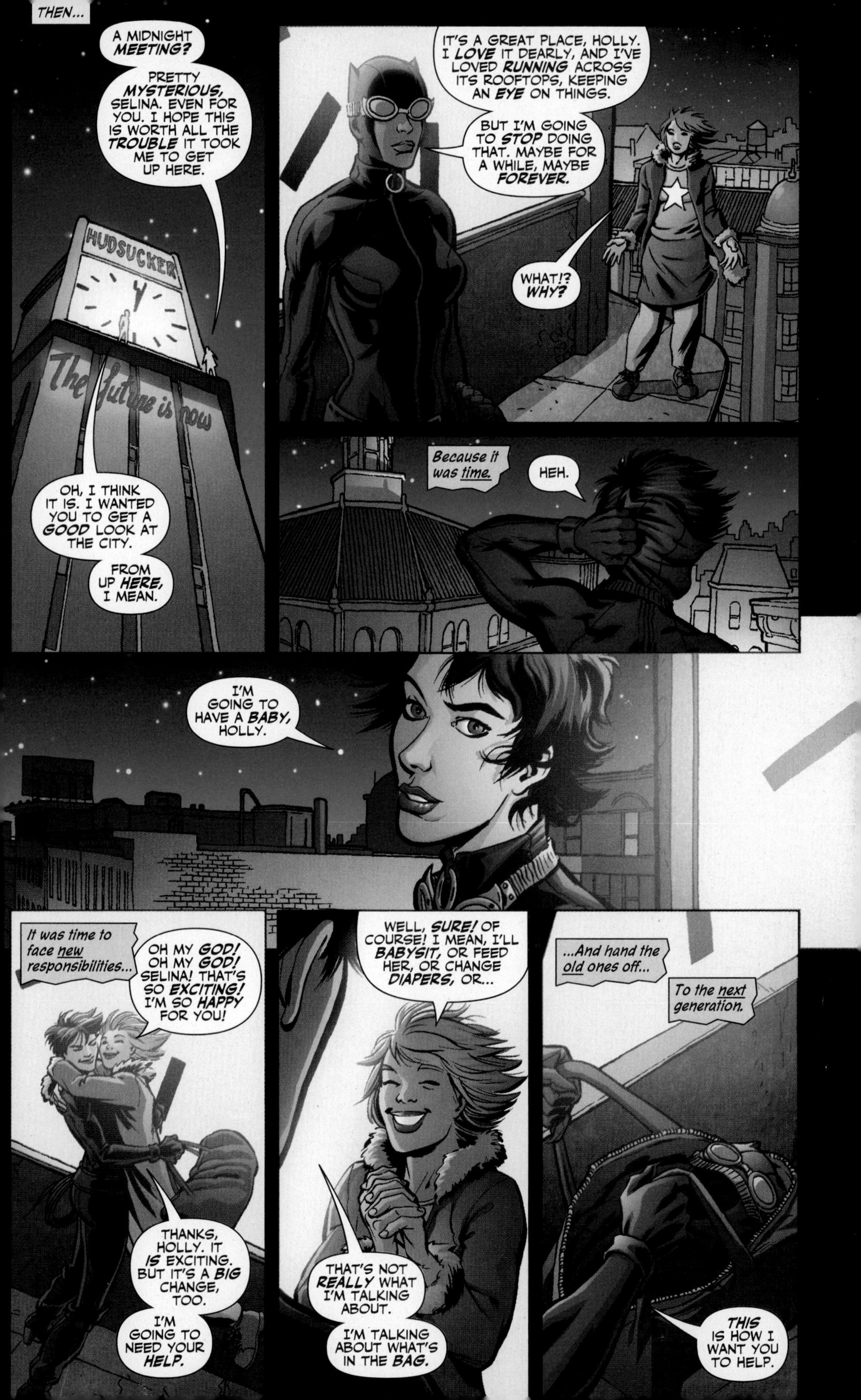
THEN...
A MIDNIGHT MEETING?
PRETTY MYSTERIOUS, SELINA. EVEN FOR YOU. I HOPE THIS IS WORTH ALL THE TROUBLE IT TOOK ME TO GET UP HERE.
HUDSUCKER
The future is now
OH, I THINK IT IS. I WANTED YOU TO GET A GOOD LOOK AT THE CITY.
FROM UP HERE, I MEAN.
IT'S A GREAT PLACE, HOLLY. I LOVE IT DEARLY, AND I'VE LOVED RUNNING ACROSS ITS ROOFTOPS, KEEPING AN EYE ON THINGS.
BUT I'M GOING TO STOP DOING THAT. MAYBE FOR A WHILE, MAYBE FOREVER.
WHAT!? WHY?
Because it was time.
HEH.
I'M GOING TO HAVE A BABY, HOLLY.
It was time to face new responsibilities...
OH MY GOD! OH MY GOD! SELINA! THAT'S SO EXCITING! I'M SO HAPPY FOR YOU!
THANKS, HOLLY. IT IS EXCITING. BUT IT'S A BIG CHANGE, TOO.
I'M GOING TO NEED YOUR HELP.
WELL, SURE! OF COURSE! I MEAN, I'LL BABYSIT, OR FEED HER, OR CHANGE DIAPERS, OR...
THAT'S NOT REALLY WHAT I'M TALKING ABOUT.
I'M TALKING ABOUT WHAT'S IN THE BAG.
...And hand the old ones off...
To the next generation.
THIS IS HOW I WANT YOU TO HELP.

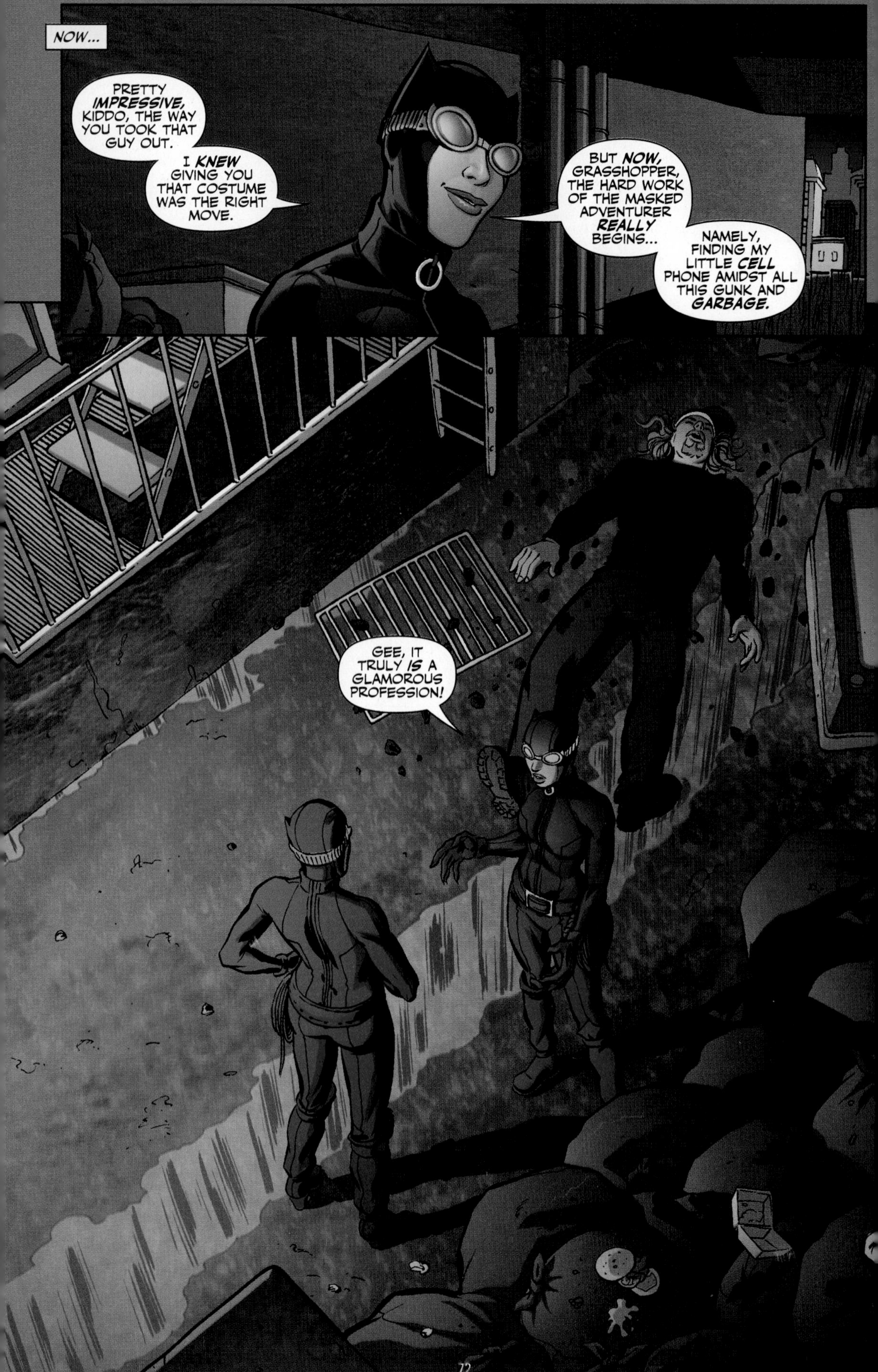
NOW...
PRETTY IMPRESSIVE, KIDDO, THE WAY YOU TOOK THAT GUY OUT.
I KNEW GIVING YOU THAT COSTUME WAS THE RIGHT MOVE.
BUT NOW, GRASSHOPPER, THE HARD WORK OF THE MASKED ADVENTURER REALLY BEGINS...
NAMELY, FINDING MY LITTLE CELL PHONE AMIDST ALL THIS GUNK AND GARBAGE.
GEE, IT TRULY IS A GLAMOROUS PROFESSION!

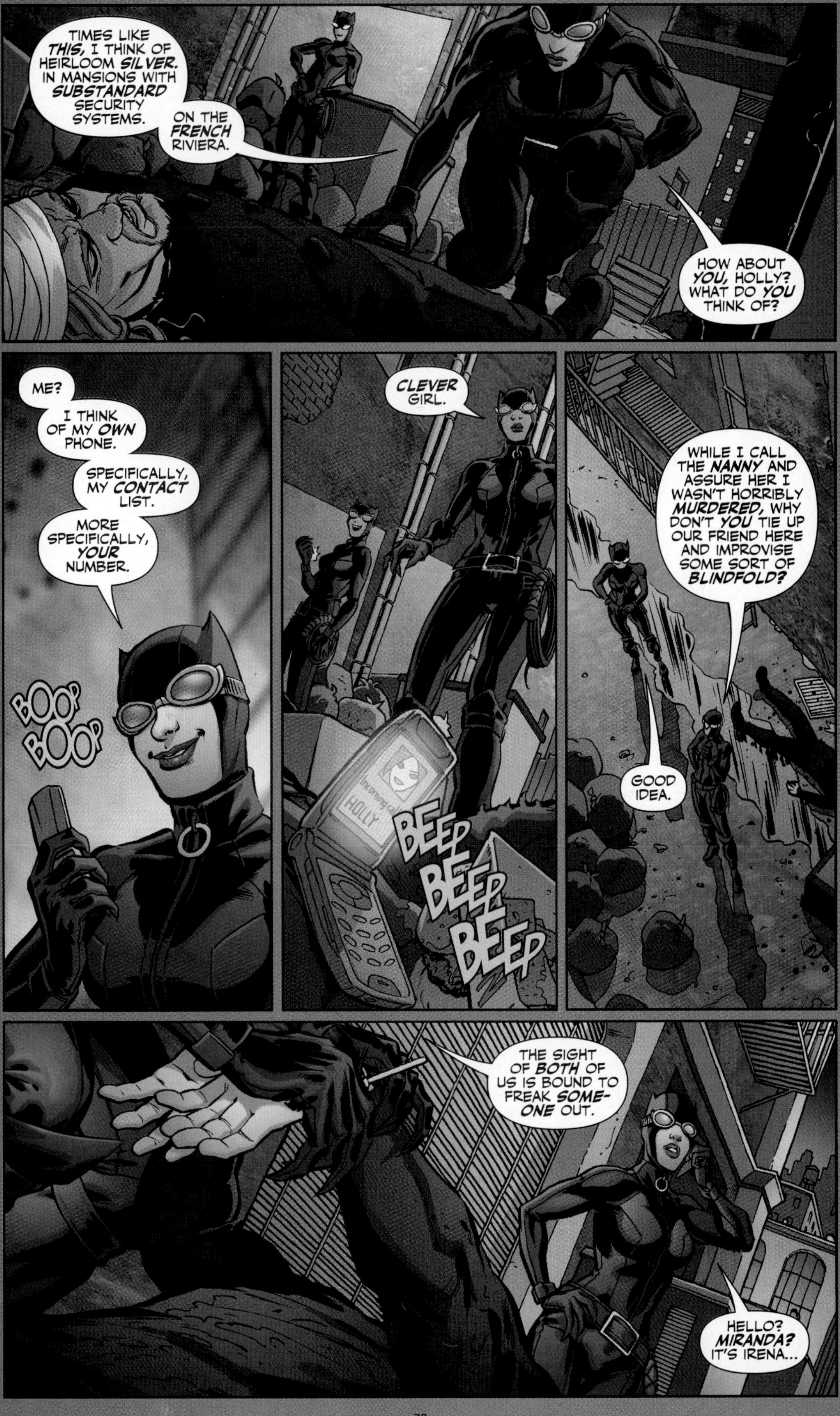

TIMES LIKE THIS, I THINK OF HEIRLOOM SILVER. IN MANSIONS WITH SUBSTANDARD SECURITY SYSTEMS.
ON THE FRENCH RIVIERA.
HOW ABOUT YOU, HOLLY? WHAT DO YOU THINK OF?
ME?
I THINK OF MY OWN PHONE.
SPECIFICALLY, MY CONTACT LIST.
MORE SPECIFICALLY, YOUR NUMBER.
BOOP BOOP
CLEVER GIRL.
Incoming call
HOLLY
BEEP BEEP BEEP
WHILE I CALL THE NANNY AND ASSURE HER I WASN'T HORRIBLY MURDERED, WHY DON'T YOU TIE UP OUR FRIEND HERE AND IMPROVISE SOME SORT OF BLINDFOLD?
GOOD IDEA.
THE SIGHT OF BOTH OF US IS BOUND TO FREAK SOME-ONE OUT.
HELLO? MIRANDA? IT'S IRENA...

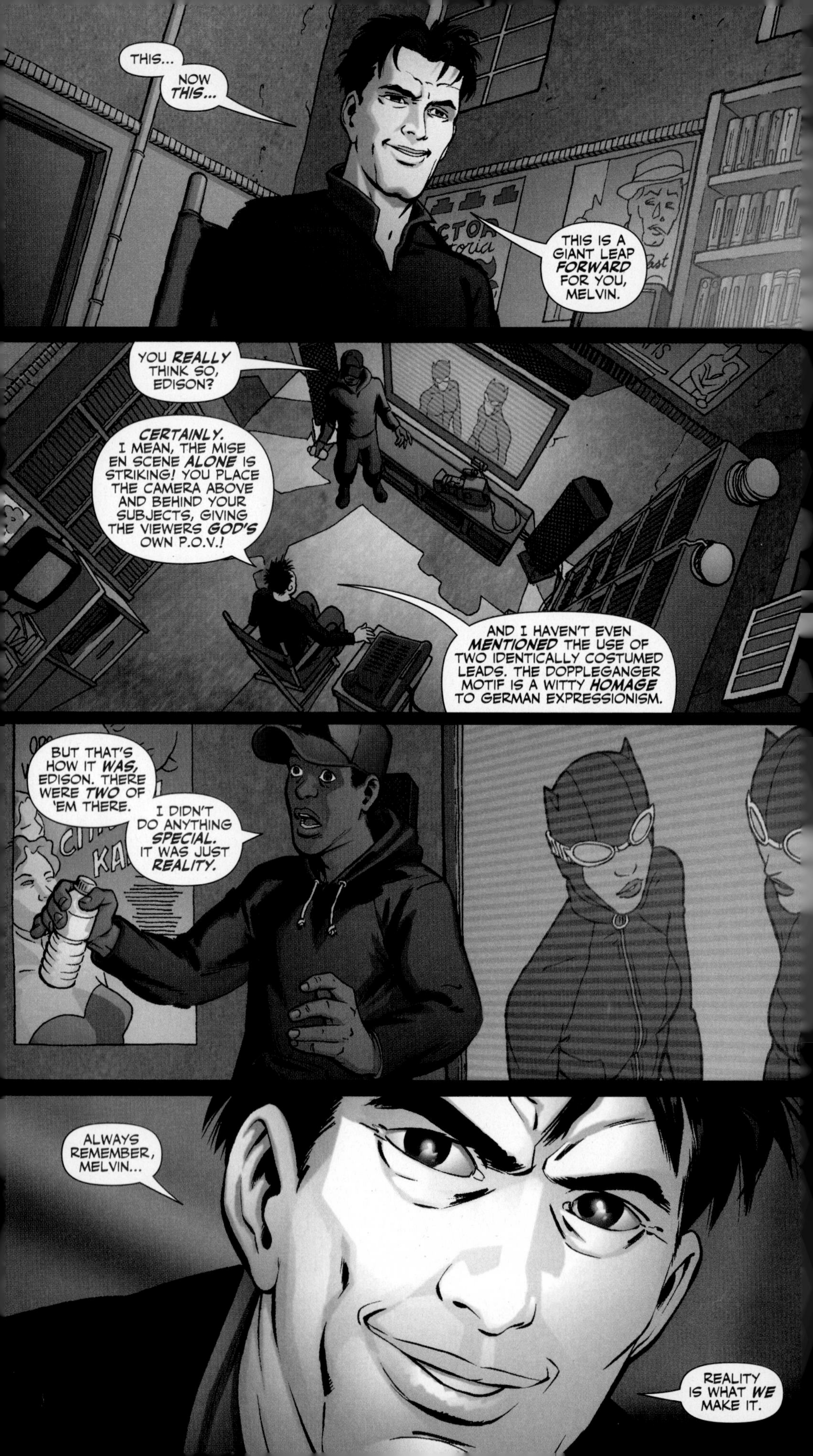
THIS... NOW THIS...
THIS IS A GIANT LEAP FORWARD FOR YOU, MELVIN.
YOU REALLY THINK SO, EDISON?
CERTAINLY. I MEAN, THE MISE EN SCENE ALONE IS STRIKING! YOU PLACE THE CAMERA ABOVE AND BEHIND YOUR SUBJECTS, GIVING THE VIEWERS GOD'S OWN P.O.V.!
AND I HAVEN'T EVEN MENTIONED THE USE OF TWO IDENTICALLY COSTUMED LEADS. THE DOPPLEGANGER MOTIF IS A WITTY HOMAGE TO GERMAN EXPRESSIONISM.
BUT THAT'S HOW IT WAS, EDISON. THERE WERE TWO OF 'EM THERE.
I DIDN'T DO ANYTHING SPECIAL. IT WAS JUST REALITY.
ALWAYS REMEMBER, MELVIN...
REALITY IS WHAT WE MAKE IT.

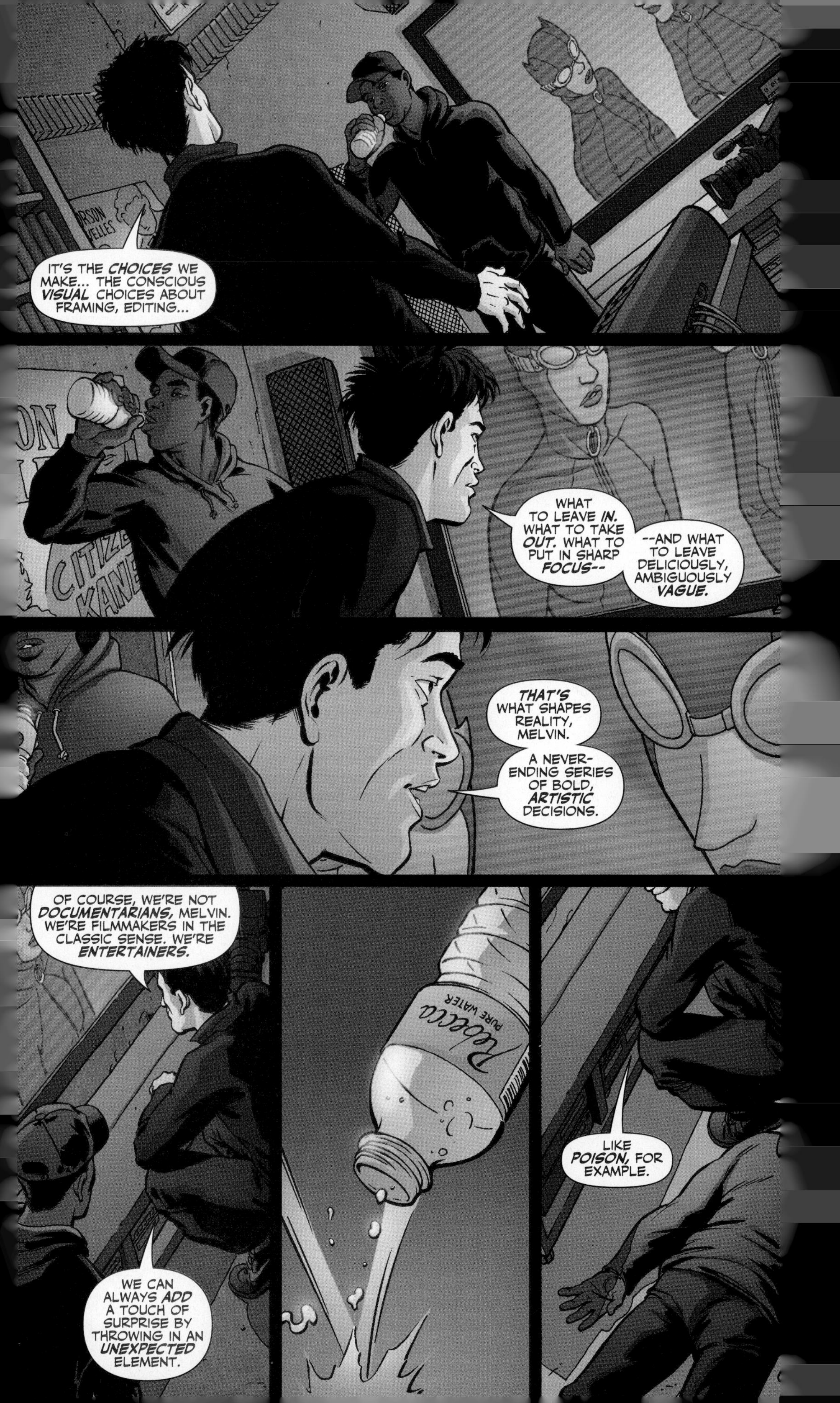
ORSON WELLES
IT'S THE CHOICES WE MAKE... THE CONSCIOUS VISUAL CHOICES ABOUT FRAMING, EDITING...
CITIZEN KANE
WHAT TO LEAVE IN. WHAT TO TAKE OUT. WHAT TO PUT IN SHARP FOCUS--
--AND WHAT TO LEAVE DELICIOUSLY, AMBIGUOUSLY VAGUE.
THAT'S WHAT SHAPES REALITY, MELVIN.
A NEVER-ENDING SERIES OF BOLD, ARTISTIC DECISIONS.
OF COURSE, WE'RE NOT DOCUMENTARIANS, MELVIN. WE'RE FILMMAKERS IN THE CLASSIC SENSE. WE'RE ENTERTAINERS.
WE CAN ALWAYS ADD A TOUCH OF SURPRISE BY THROWING IN AN UNEXPECTED ELEMENT.
Rebecca
PURE WATER
LIKE POISON, FOR EXAMPLE.

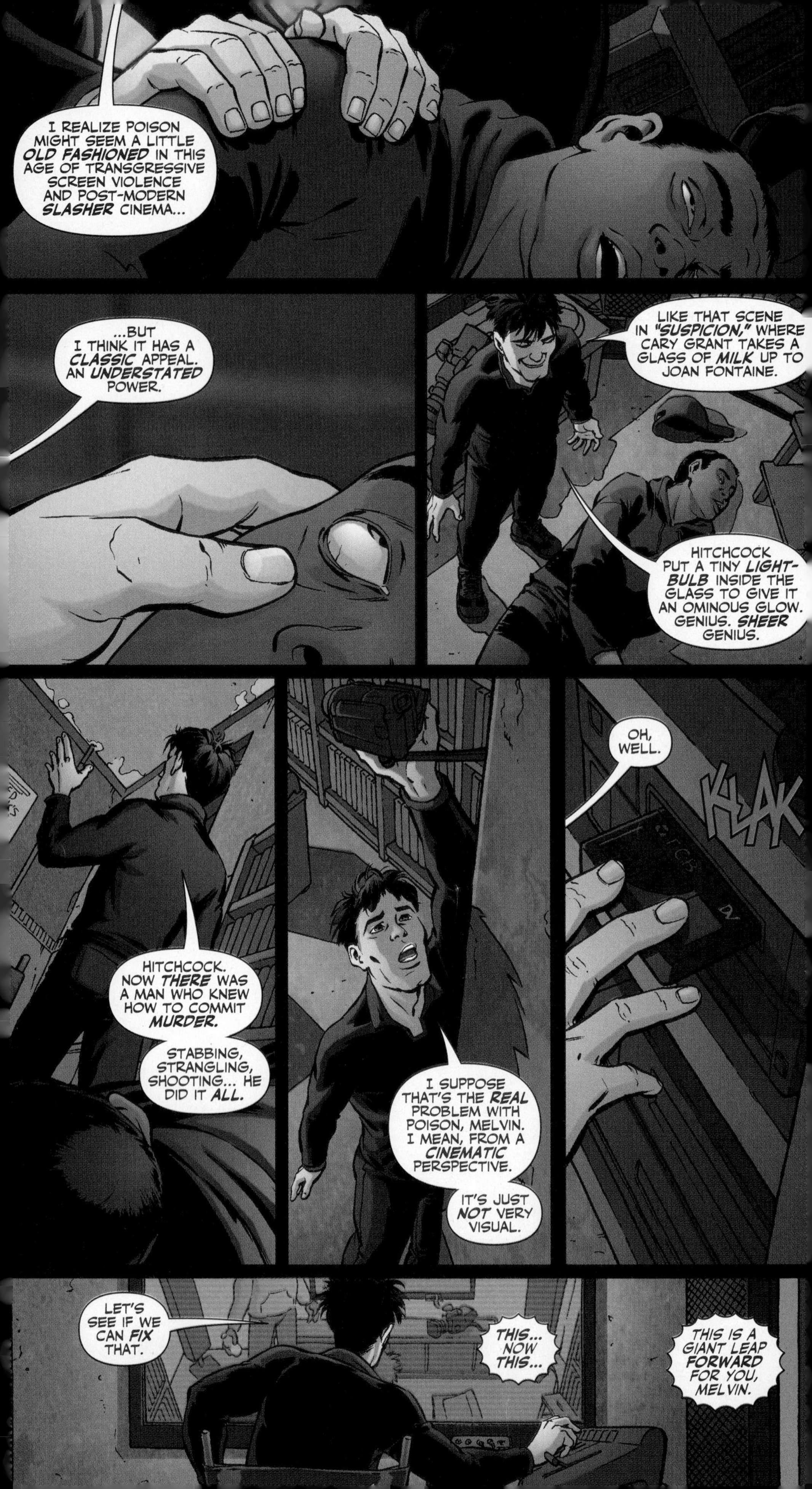
I REALIZE POISON MIGHT SEEM A LITTLE OLD FASHIONED IN THIS AGE OF TRANSGRESSIVE SCREEN VIOLENCE AND POST-MODERN SLASHER CINEMA...
...BUT I THINK IT HAS A CLASSIC APPEAL. AN UNDERSTATED POWER.
LIKE THAT SCENE IN "SUSPICION," WHERE CARY GRANT TAKES A GLASS OF MILK UP TO JOAN FONTAINE.
HITCHCOCK PUT A TINY LIGHT-BULB INSIDE THE GLASS TO GIVE IT AN OMINOUS GLOW. GENIUS. SHEER GENIUS.
HITCHCOCK. NOW THERE WAS A MAN WHO KNEW HOW TO COMMIT MURDER.
STABBING, STRANGLING, SHOOTING... HE DID IT ALL.
I SUPPOSE THAT'S THE REAL PROBLEM WITH POISON, MELVIN. I MEAN, FROM A CINEMATIC PERSPECTIVE.
IT'S JUST NOT VERY VISUAL.
OH, WELL.
KLAK
LET'S SEE IF WE CAN FIX THAT.
THIS... NOW THIS...
THIS IS A GIANT LEAP FORWARD FOR YOU, MELVIN.

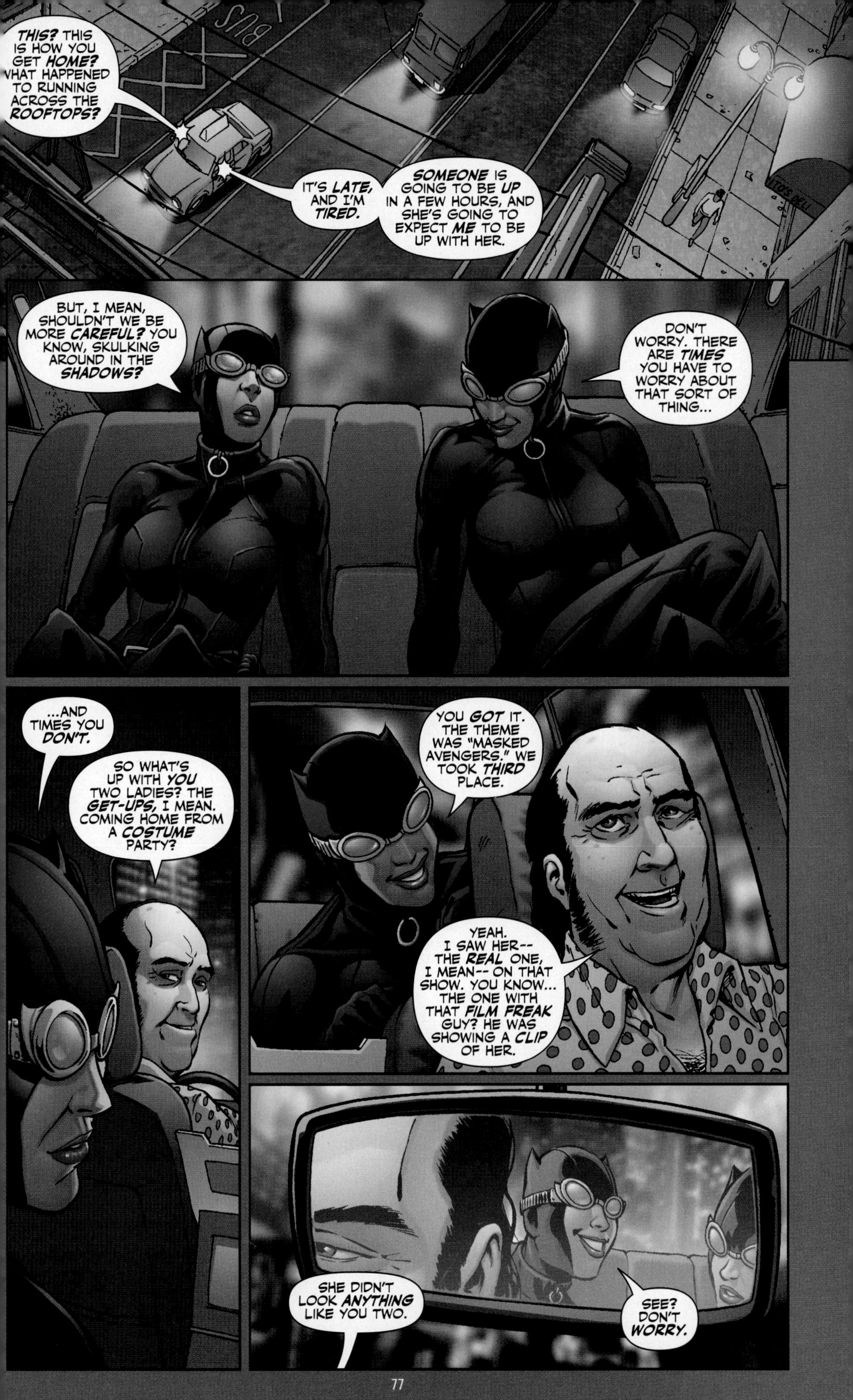
THIS? THIS IS HOW YOU GET HOME? WHAT HAPPENED TO RUNNING ACROSS THE ROOFTOPS?
IT'S LATE, AND I'M TIRED.
SOMEONE IS GOING TO BE UP IN A FEW HOURS, AND SHE'S GOING TO EXPECT ME TO BE UP WITH HER.
BUS
BUT, I MEAN, SHOULDN'T WE BE MORE CAREFUL? YOU KNOW, SKULKING AROUND IN THE SHADOWS?
DON'T WORRY. THERE ARE TIMES YOU HAVE TO WORRY ABOUT THAT SORT OF THING...
...AND TIMES YOU DON'T.
SO WHAT'S UP WITH YOU TWO LADIES? THE GET-UPS, I MEAN. COMING HOME FROM A COSTUME PARTY?
YOU GOT IT. THE THEME WAS "MASKED AVENGERS." WE TOOK THIRD PLACE.
YEAH. I SAW HER-- THE REAL ONE, I MEAN-- ON THAT SHOW. YOU KNOW... THE ONE WITH THAT FILM FREAK GUY? HE WAS SHOWING A CLIP OF HER.
SHE DIDN'T LOOK ANYTHING LIKE YOU TWO.
SEE? DON'T WORRY.

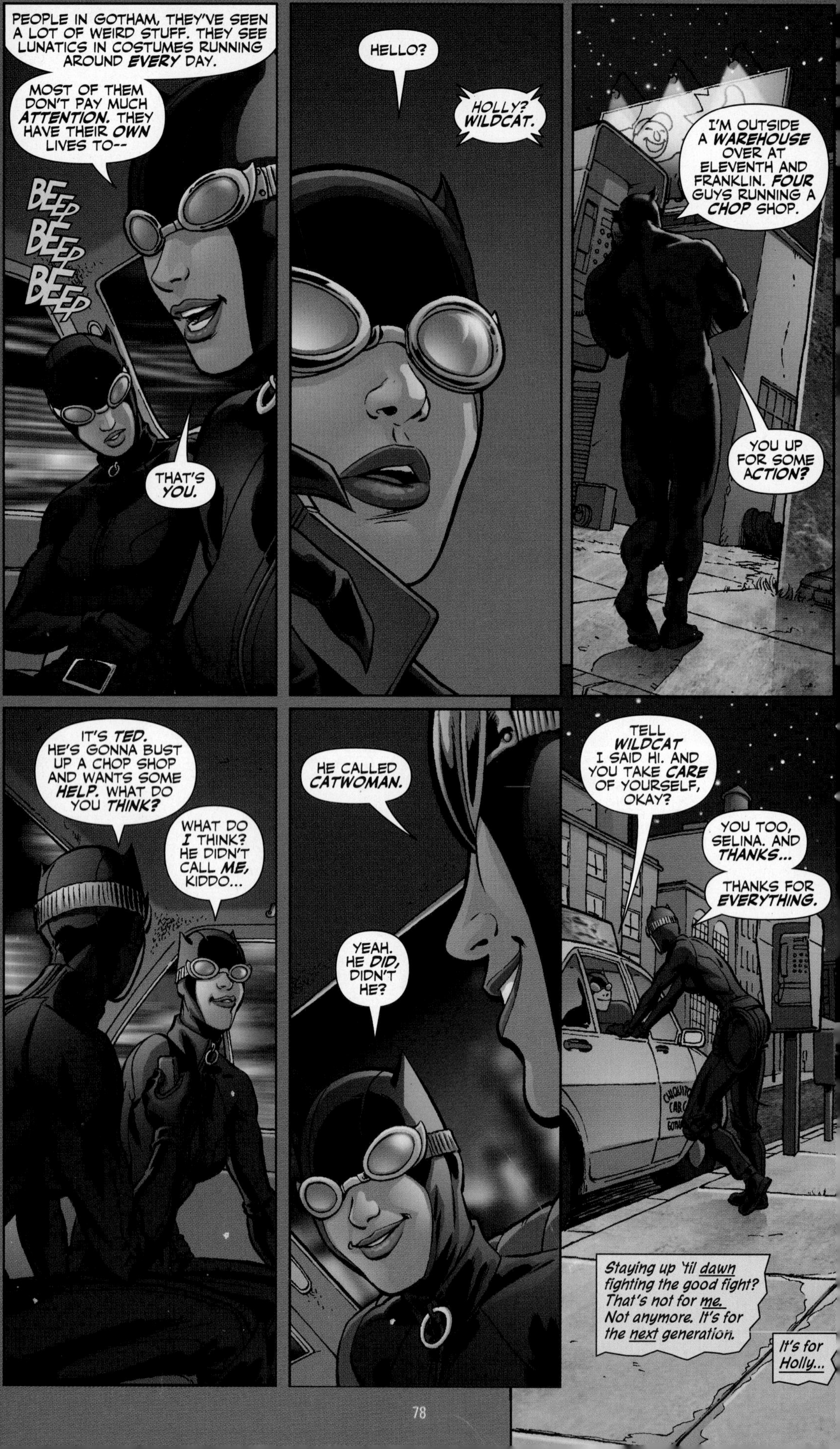
PEOPLE IN GOTHAM, THEY'VE SEEN A LOT OF WEIRD STUFF. THEY SEE LUNATICS IN COSTUMES RUNNING AROUND EVERY DAY.
MOST OF THEM DON'T PAY MUCH ATTENTION. THEY HAVE THEIR OWN LIVES TO--
BEEP BEEP BEEP
THAT'S YOU.
HELLO?
HOLLY? WILDCAT.
I'M OUTSIDE A WAREHOUSE OVER AT ELEVENTH AND FRANKLIN. FOUR GUYS RUNNING A CHOP SHOP.
YOU UP FOR SOME ACTION?
IT'S TED. HE'S GONNA BUST UP A CHOP SHOP AND WANTS SOME HELP. WHAT DO YOU THINK?
WHAT DO I THINK? HE DIDN'T CALL ME, KIDDO...
HE CALLED CATWOMAN.
YEAH. HE DID, DIDN'T HE?
TELL WILDCAT I SAID HI. AND YOU TAKE CARE OF YOURSELF, OKAY?
YOU TOO, SELINA. AND THANKS...
THANKS FOR EVERYTHING.
Staying up 'til dawn fighting the good fight? That's not for me. Not anymore. It's for the next generation.
It's for Holly...

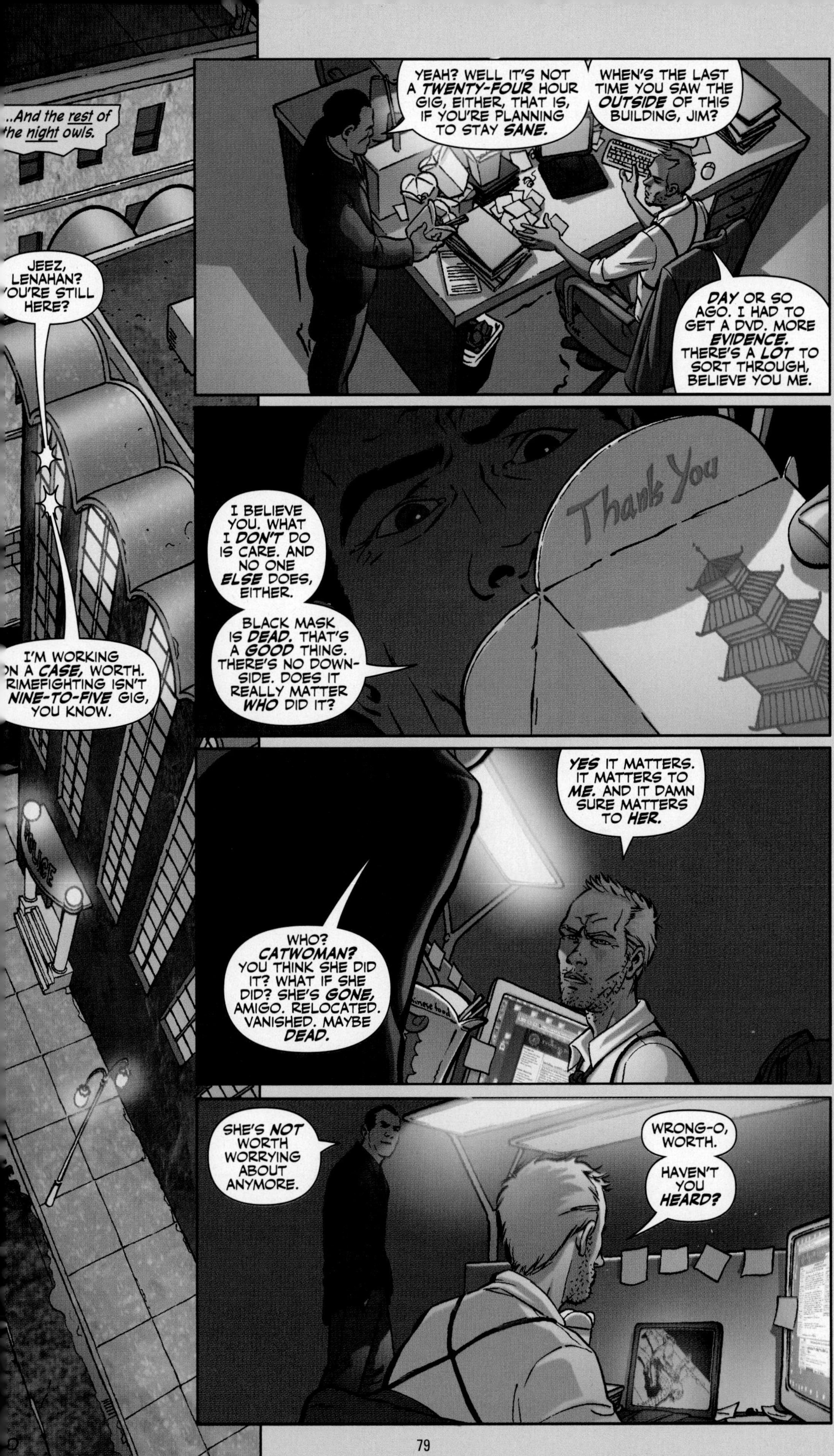
..And the rest of the night owls.
JEEZ, LENAHAN? YOU'RE STILL HERE?
I'M WORKING ON A CASE, WORTH. CRIMEFIGHTING ISN'T A NINE-TO-FIVE GIG, YOU KNOW.
YEAH? WELL IT'S NOT A TWENTY-FOUR HOUR GIG, EITHER, THAT IS, IF YOU'RE PLANNING TO STAY SANE.
WHEN'S THE LAST TIME YOU SAW THE OUTSIDE OF THIS BUILDING, JIM?
DAY OR SO AGO. I HAD TO GET A DVD. MORE EVIDENCE. THERE'S A LOT TO SORT THROUGH, BELIEVE YOU ME.
Thank You
I BELIEVE YOU. WHAT I DON'T DO IS CARE. AND NO ONE ELSE DOES, EITHER.
BLACK MASK IS DEAD. THAT'S A GOOD THING. THERE'S NO DOWN-SIDE. DOES IT REALLY MATTER WHO DID IT?
YES IT MATTERS. IT MATTERS TO ME. AND IT DAMN SURE MATTERS TO HER.
WHO? CATWOMAN? YOU THINK SHE DID IT? WHAT IF SHE DID? SHE'S GONE, AMIGO. RELOCATED. VANISHED. MAYBE DEAD.
SHE'S NOT WORTH WORRYING ABOUT ANYMORE.
WRONG-O, WORTH.
HAVEN'T YOU HEARD?

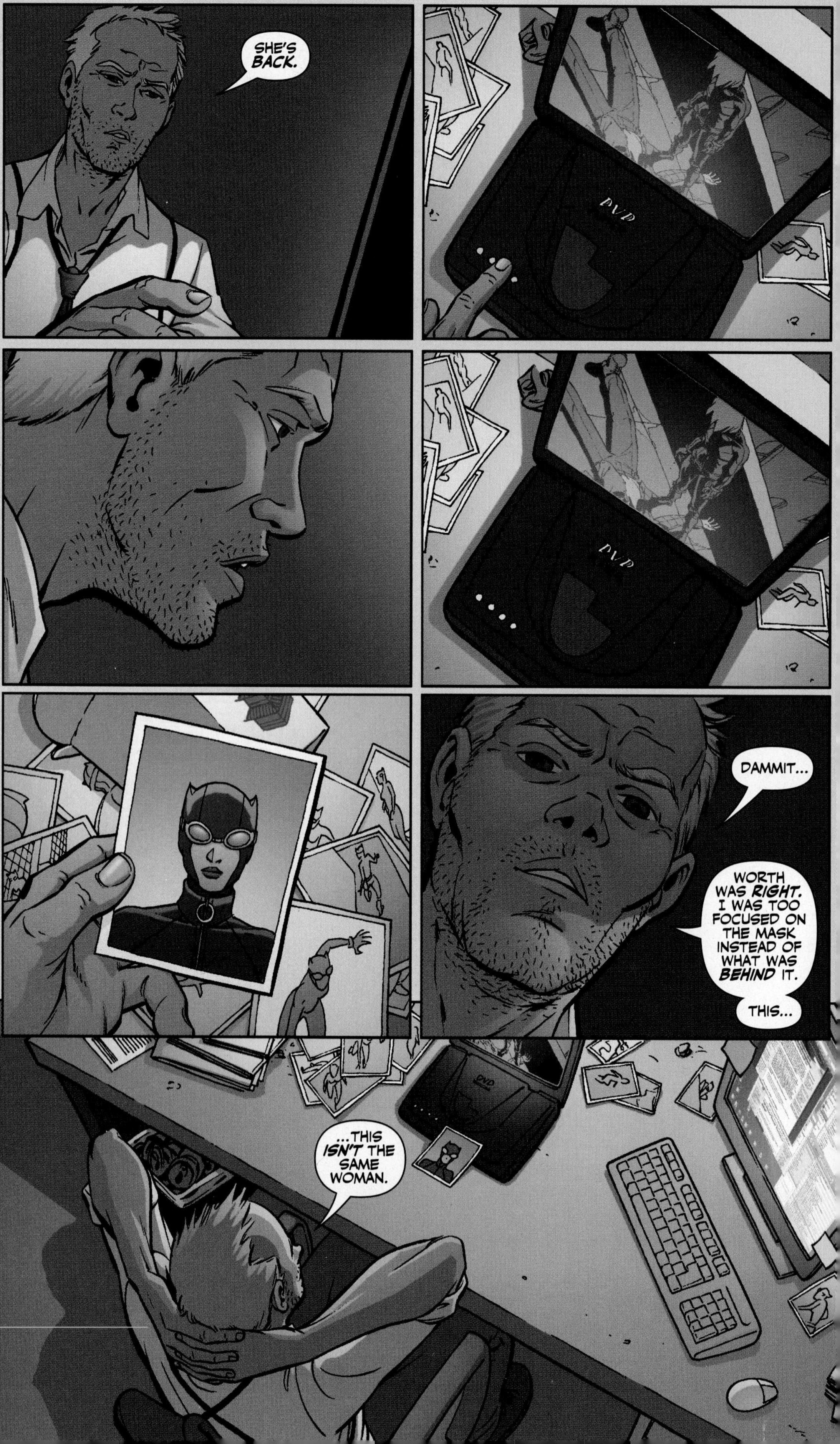
SHE'S BACK.
DVD
DVD
DAMMIT...
WORTH WAS RIGHT. I WAS TOO FOCUSED ON THE MASK INSTEAD OF WHAT WAS BEHIND IT.
THIS...
...THIS ISN'T THE SAME WOMAN.

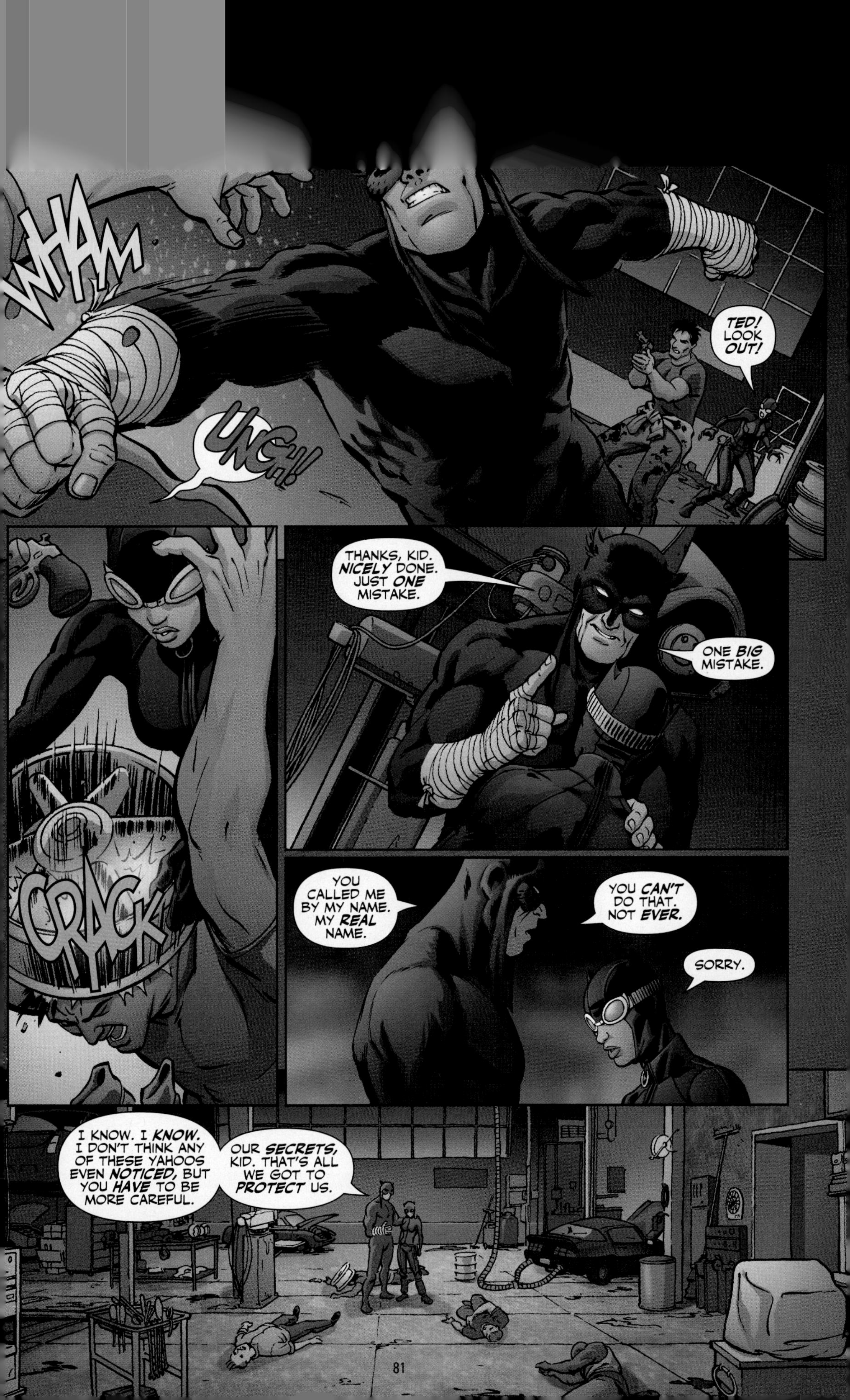

WHAM
UNGH!!
TED! LOOK OUT!
CRACK
THANKS, KID. NICELY DONE. JUST ONE MISTAKE.
ONE BIG MISTAKE.
YOU CALLED ME BY MY NAME. MY REAL NAME.
YOU CAN'T DO THAT. NOT EVER.
SORRY.
I KNOW. I KNOW. I DON'T THINK ANY OF THESE YAHOOS EVEN NOTICED, BUT YOU HAVE TO BE MORE CAREFUL.
OUR SECRETS, KID. THAT'S ALL WE GOT TO PROTECT US.

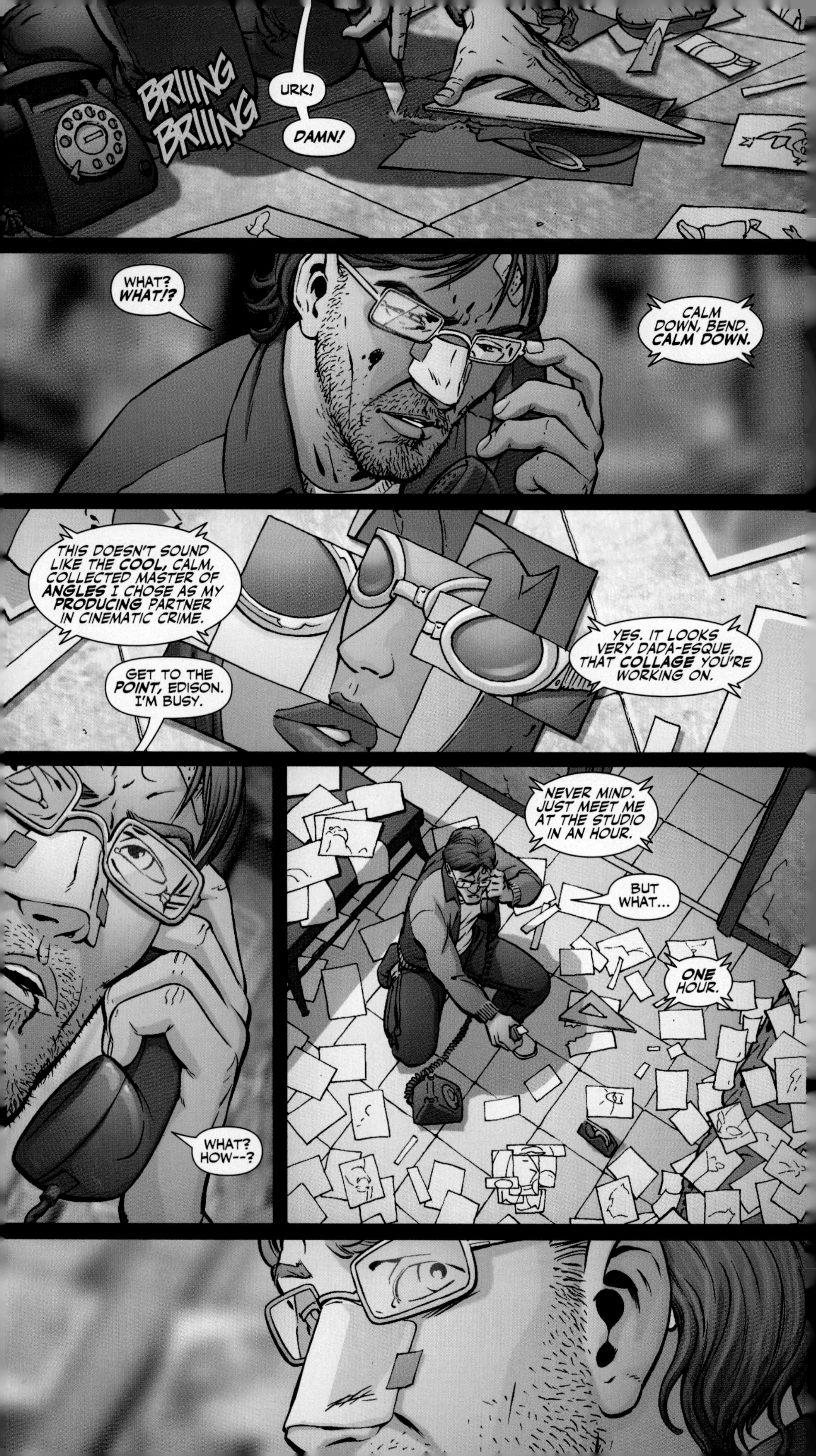
BRIIING BRIIING
URK!
DAMN!
WHAT? WHAT!?
CALM DOWN, BEND. CALM DOWN.
THIS DOESN'T SOUND LIKE THE COOL, CALM, COLLECTED MASTER OF ANGLES I CHOSE AS MY PRODUCING PARTNER IN CINEMATIC CRIME.
GET TO THE POINT, EDISON. I'M BUSY.
YES. IT LOOKS VERY DADA-ESQUE, THAT COLLAGE YOU'RE WORKING ON.
WHAT? HOW--?
NEVER MIND. JUST MEET ME AT THE STUDIO IN AN HOUR.
BUT WHAT...
ONE HOUR.

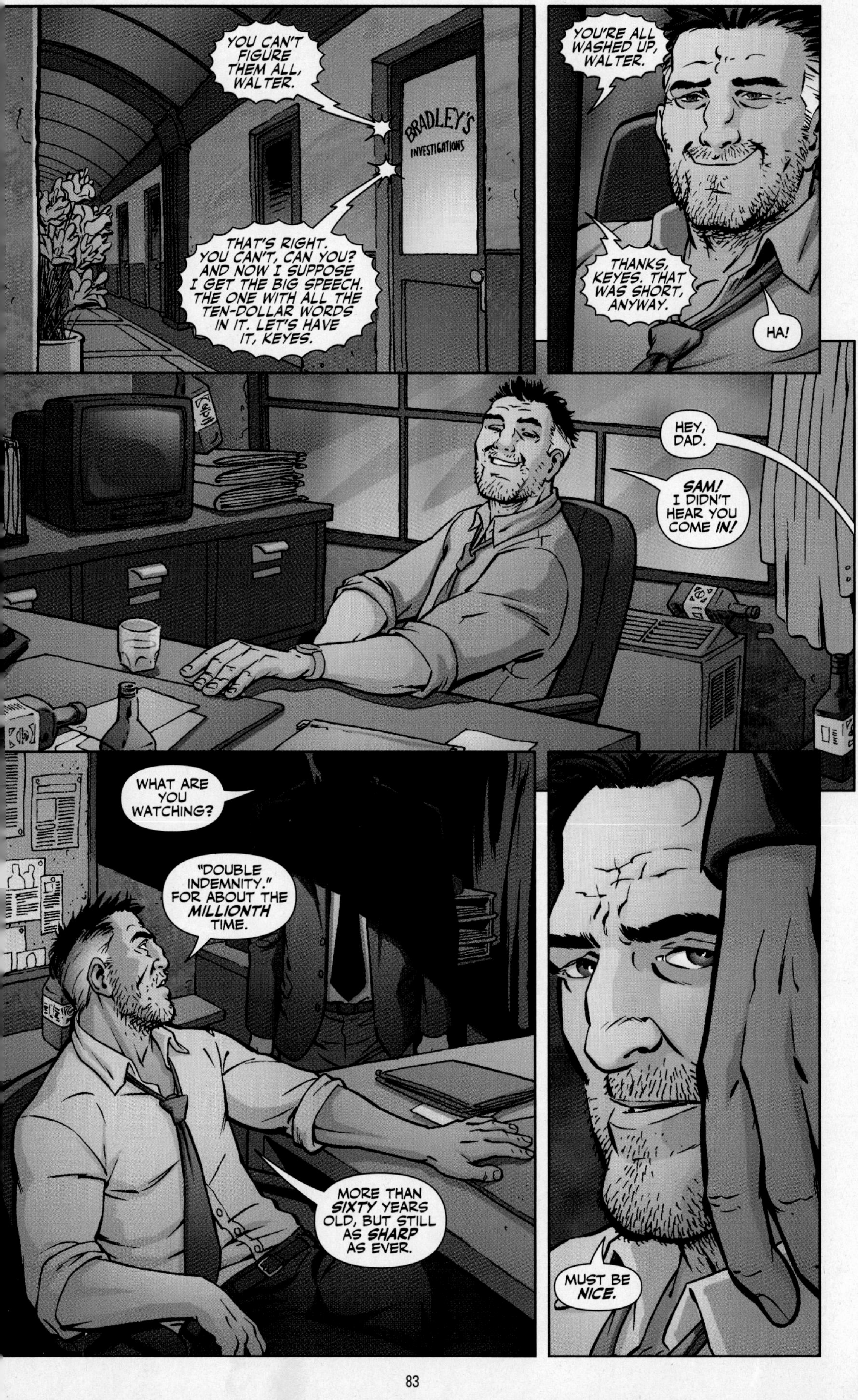
YOU CAN'T FIGURE THEM ALL, WALTER.
BRADLEY'S INVESTIGATIONS
THAT'S RIGHT. YOU CAN'T, CAN YOU? AND NOW I SUPPOSE I GET THE BIG SPEECH. THE ONE WITH ALL THE TEN-DOLLAR WORDS IN IT. LET'S HAVE IT, KEYES.
YOU'RE ALL WASHED UP, WALTER.
THANKS, KEYES. THAT WAS SHORT, ANYWAY.
HA!
HEY, DAD.
SAM! I DIDN'T HEAR YOU COME IN!
WHAT ARE YOU WATCHING?
"DOUBLE INDEMNITY." FOR ABOUT THE MILLIONTH TIME.
MORE THAN SIXTY YEARS OLD, BUT STILL AS SHARP AS EVER.
MUST BE NICE.

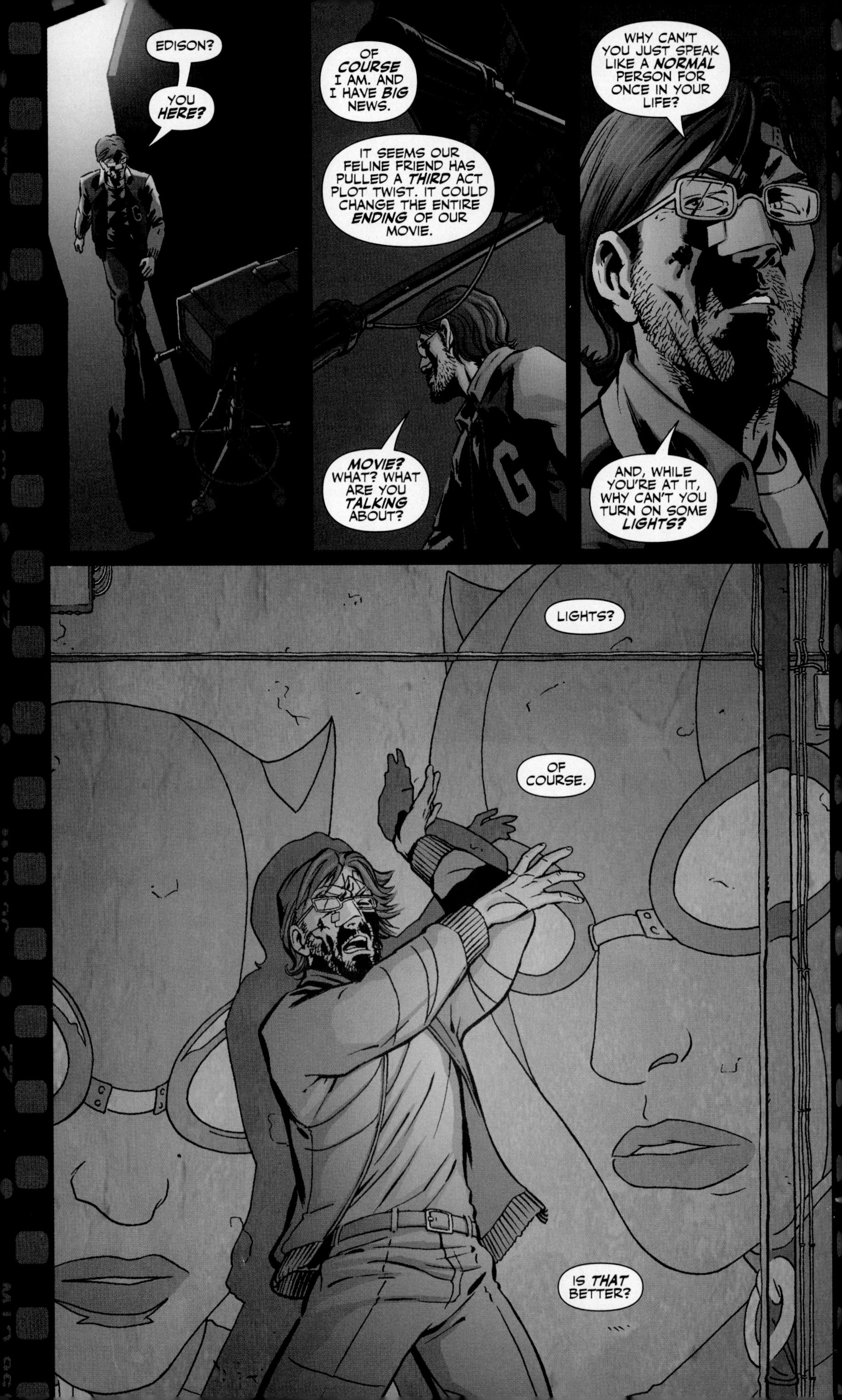
EDISON?
YOU *HERE?*
OF *COURSE* I AM. AND I HAVE *BIG* NEWS.
IT SEEMS OUR FELINE FRIEND HAS PULLED A *THIRD* ACT PLOT TWIST. IT COULD CHANGE THE ENTIRE *ENDING* OF OUR MOVIE.
MOVIE? WHAT? WHAT ARE YOU *TALKING* ABOUT?
WHY CAN'T YOU JUST SPEAK LIKE A *NORMAL* PERSON FOR ONCE IN YOUR LIFE?
AND, WHILE YOU'RE AT IT, WHY CAN'T YOU TURN ON SOME *LIGHTS?*
LIGHTS?
OF COURSE.
IS *THAT* BETTER?

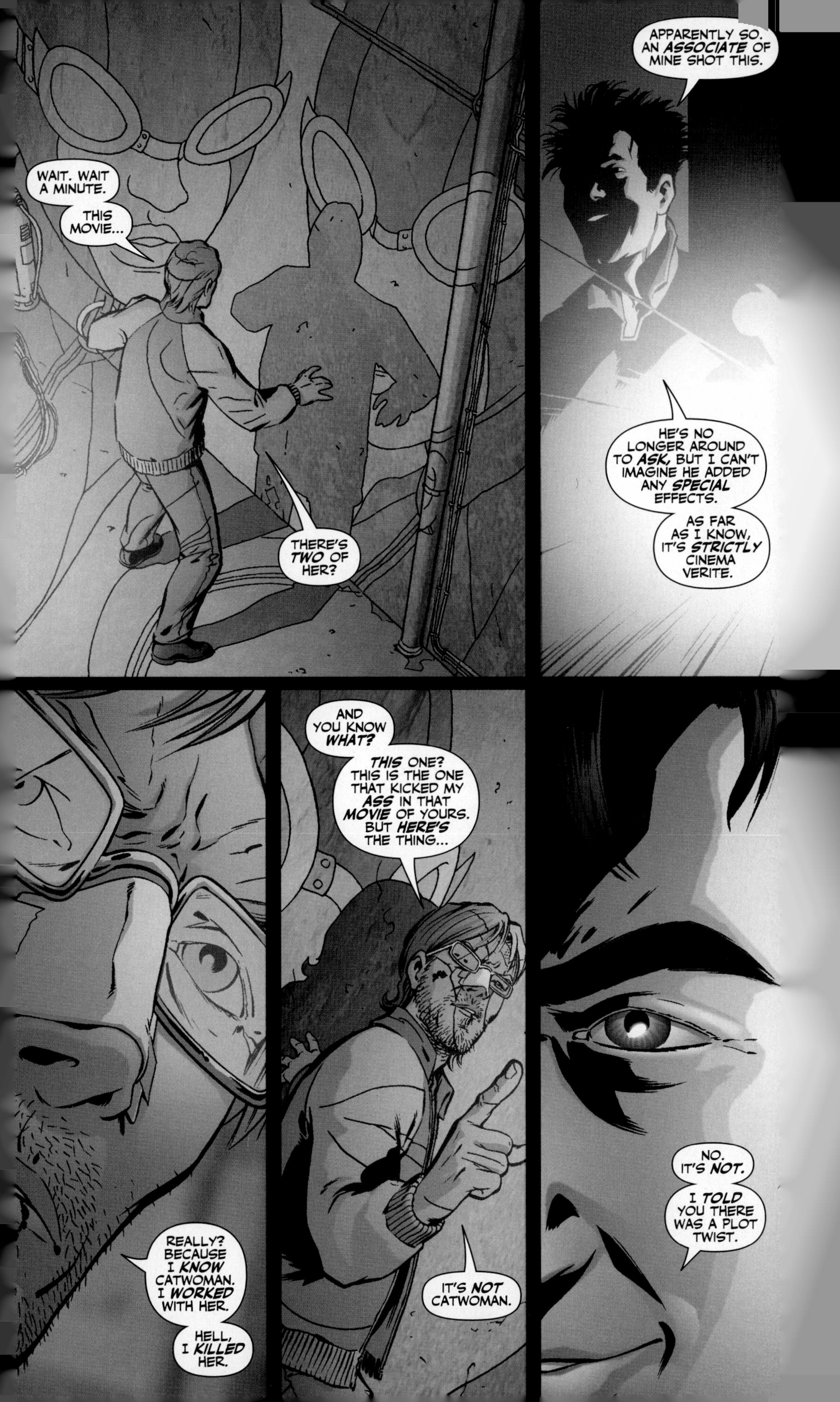
WAIT. WAIT A MINUTE.
THIS MOVIE...
THERE'S *TWO* OF HER?
APPARENTLY SO. AN *ASSOCIATE* OF MINE SHOT THIS.
HE'S NO LONGER AROUND TO *ASK,* BUT I CAN'T IMAGINE HE ADDED ANY *SPECIAL* EFFECTS.
AS FAR AS I KNOW, IT'S *STRICTLY* CINEMA VERITE.
REALLY? BECAUSE I *KNOW* CATWOMAN. I *WORKED* WITH HER.
HELL, I *KILLED* HER.
AND YOU KNOW *WHAT?*
THIS ONE? THIS IS THE ONE THAT KICKED MY *ASS* IN THAT *MOVIE* OF YOURS. BUT *HERE'S* THE THING...
IT'S *NOT* CATWOMAN.
NO. IT'S *NOT.*
I *TOLD* YOU THERE WAS A PLOT TWIST.

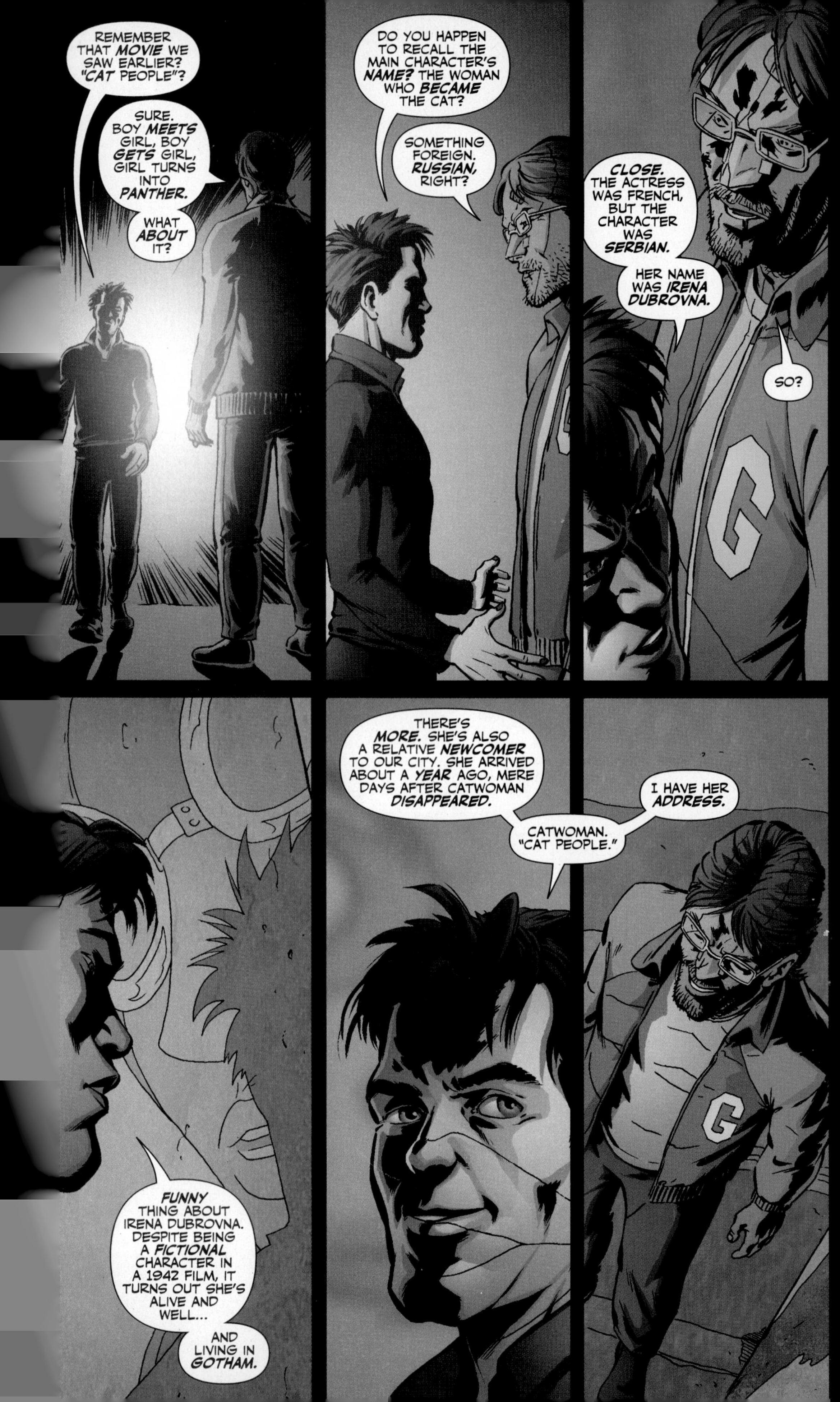

REMEMBER THAT *MOVIE* WE SAW EARLIER? "*CAT* PEOPLE"?
SURE. BOY *MEETS* GIRL, BOY *GETS* GIRL, GIRL TURNS INTO *PANTHER.*
WHAT *ABOUT* IT?
DO YOU HAPPEN TO RECALL THE MAIN CHARACTER'S *NAME?* THE WOMAN WHO *BECAME* THE CAT?
SOMETHING FOREIGN. *RUSSIAN,* RIGHT?
CLOSE. THE ACTRESS WAS FRENCH, BUT THE CHARACTER WAS *SERBIAN.*
HER NAME WAS *IRENA DUBROVNA.*
SO?
FUNNY THING ABOUT IRENA DUBROVNA. DESPITE BEING A *FICTIONAL* CHARACTER IN A 1942 FILM, IT TURNS OUT SHE'S ALIVE AND WELL...
AND LIVING IN *GOTHAM.*
THERE'S *MORE.* SHE'S ALSO A RELATIVE *NEWCOMER* TO OUR CITY. SHE ARRIVED ABOUT A *YEAR* AGO, MERE DAYS AFTER CATWOMAN *DISAPPEARED.*
CATWOMAN. "CAT PEOPLE."
I HAVE HER *ADDRESS.*

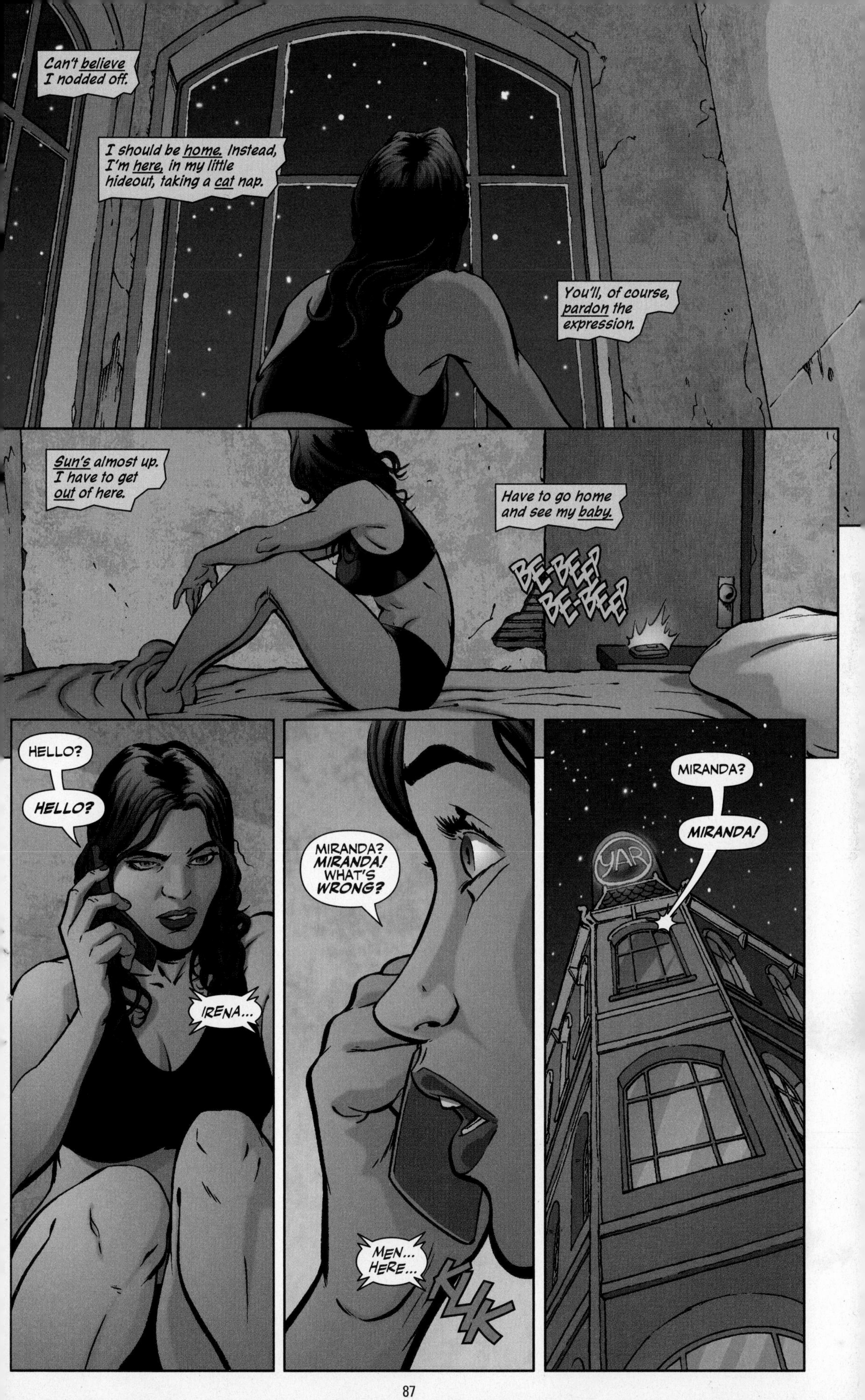

Can't believe I nodded off.
I should be home. Instead, I'm here, in my little hideout, taking a cat nap.
You'll, of course, pardon the expression.
Sun's almost up. I have to get out of here.
Have to go home and see my baby.
BE-BEEP BE-BEEP
HELLO?
HELLO?
IRENA...
MIRANDA? MIRANDA! WHAT'S WRONG?
MEN... HERE...
KLIK
MIRANDA?
MIRANDA!

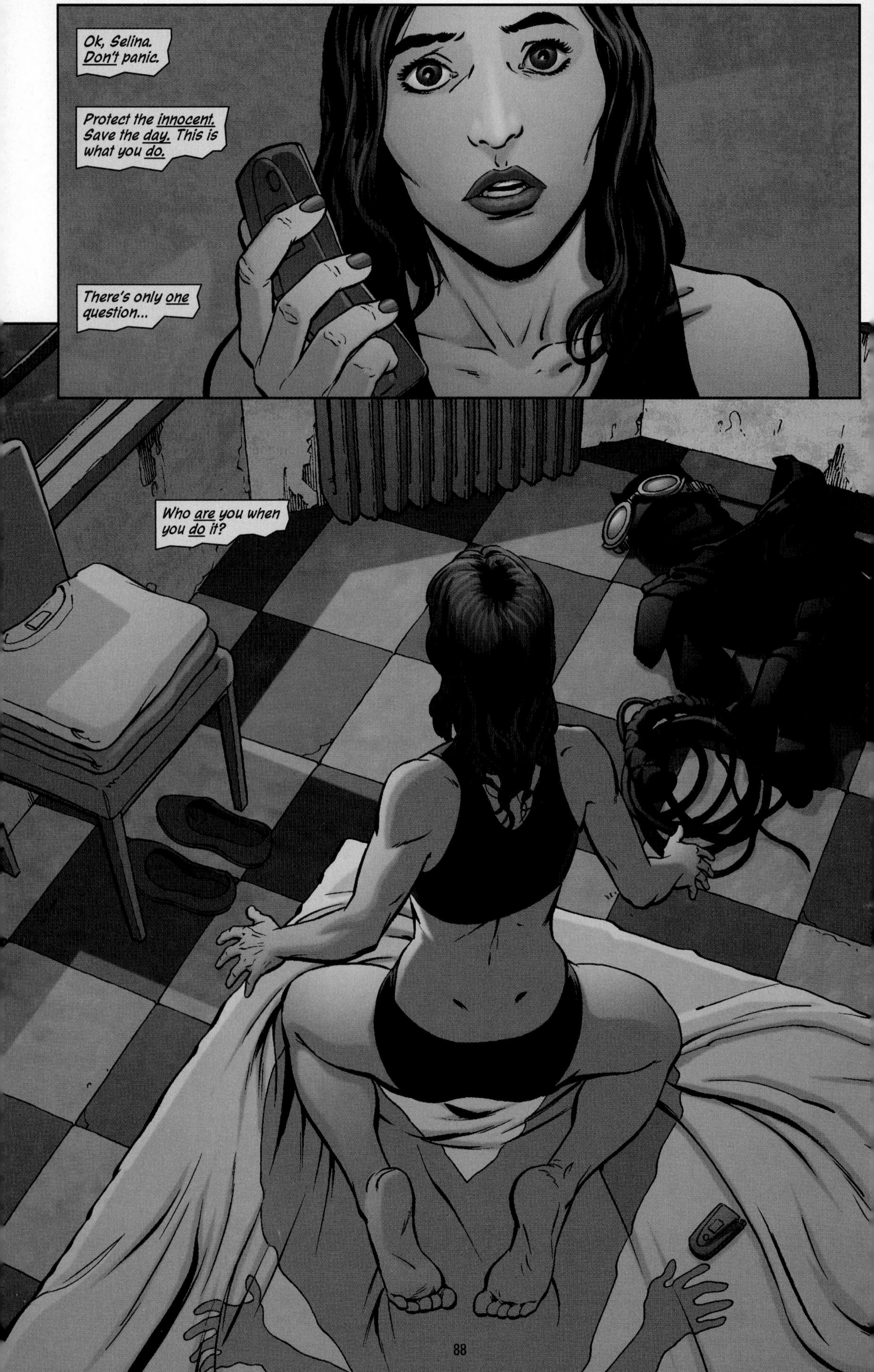

Ok, Selina. Don't panic.
Protect the innocent. Save the day. This is what you do.
There's only one question...
Who are you when you do it?

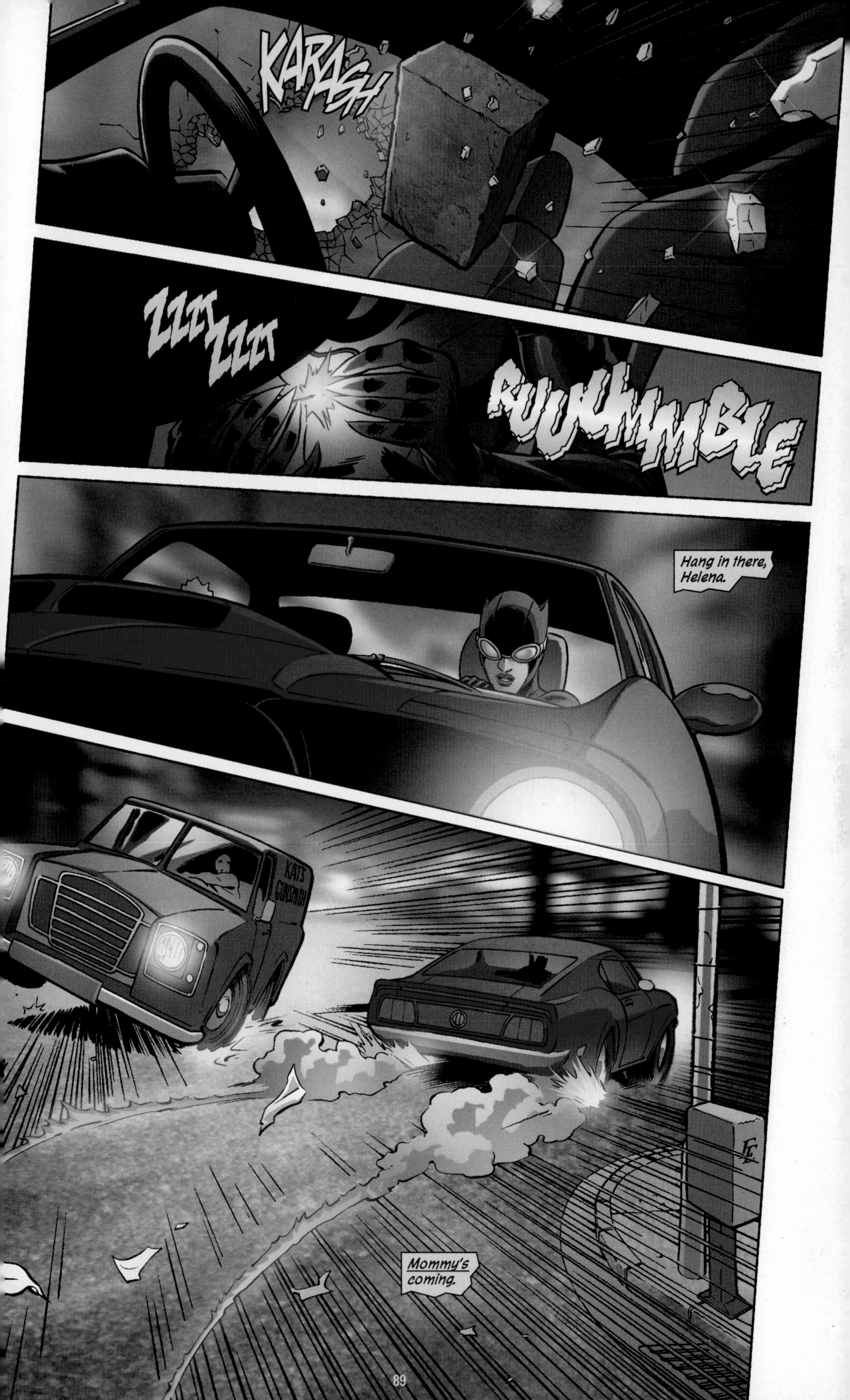
KARASH
ZZZT
ZZZT
RUUMMBLE
Hang in there, Helena.
KAT'S
Mommy's coming.

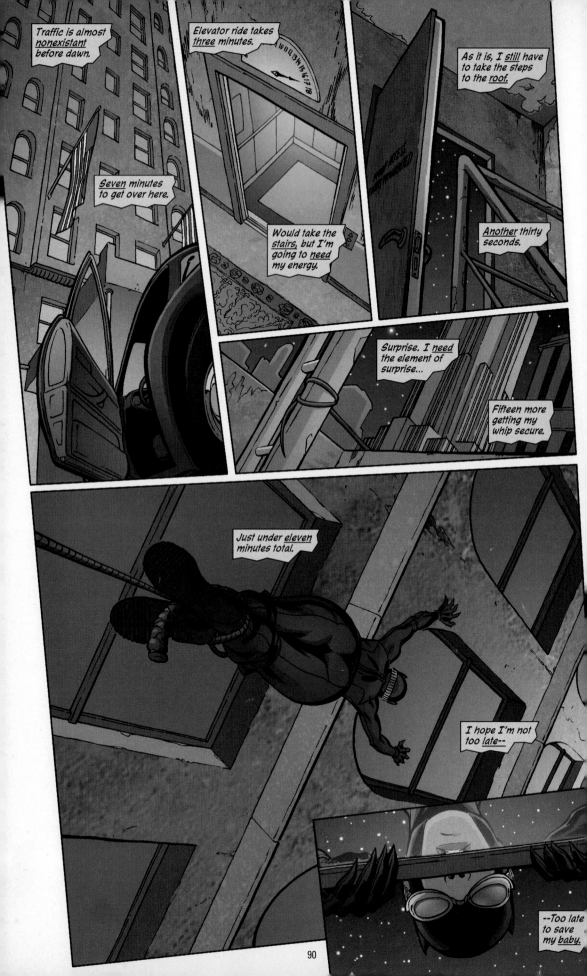

Traffic is almost _nonexistant_ before dawn.

Elevator ride takes _three_ minutes.

As it is, I _still_ have to take the steps to the _roof._

Seven minutes to get over here.

Would take the _stairs,_ but I'm going to _need_ my energy.

Another thirty seconds.

Surprise. I _need_ the element of surprise...

Fifteen more getting my whip secure.

Just under _eleven_ minutes total.

I hope I'm not too _late_--

--Too late to save my _baby._

90

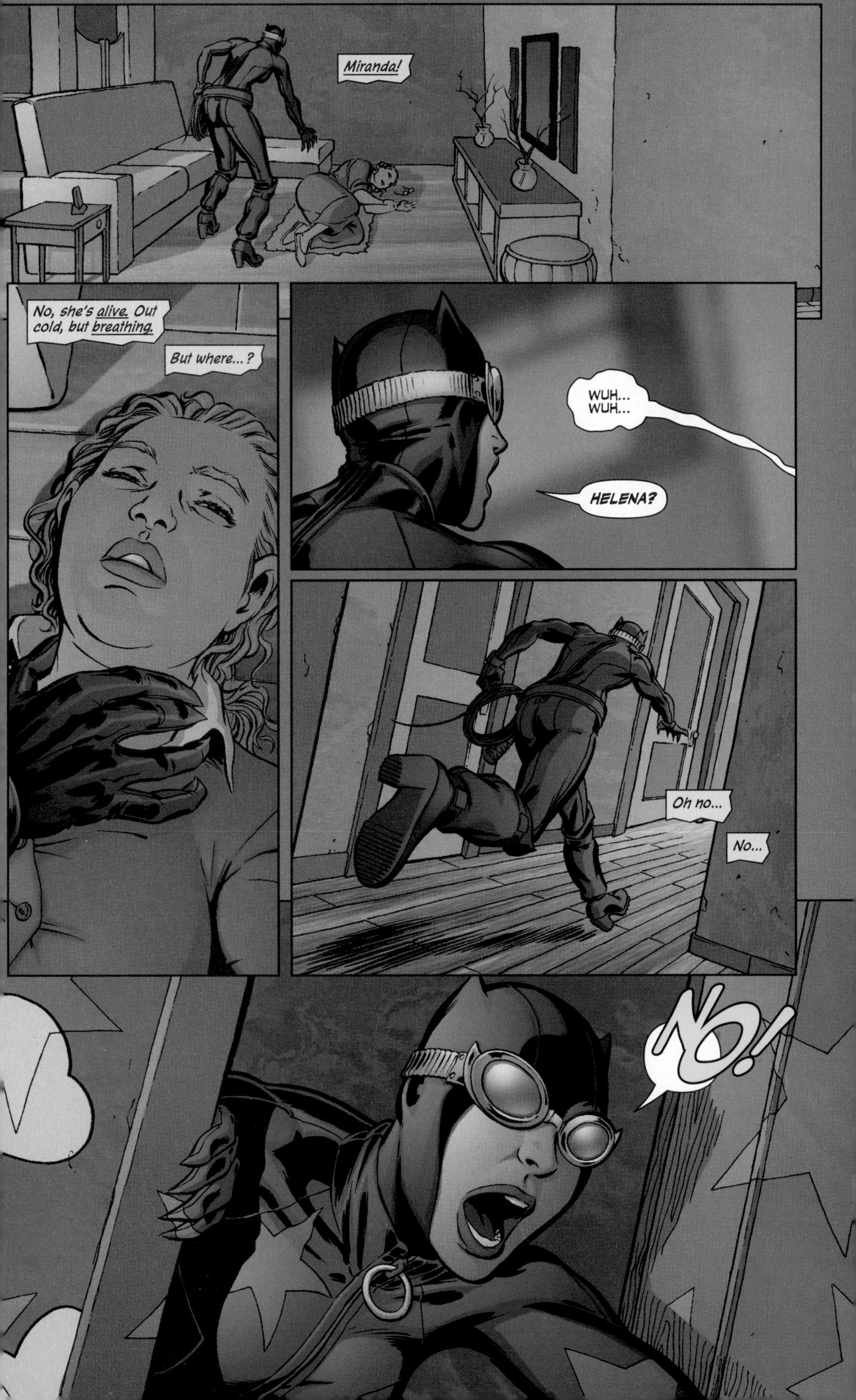
Miranda!
No, she's alive. Out cold, but breathing.
But where...?
WUH... WUH...
HELENA?
Oh no...
No...
NO!

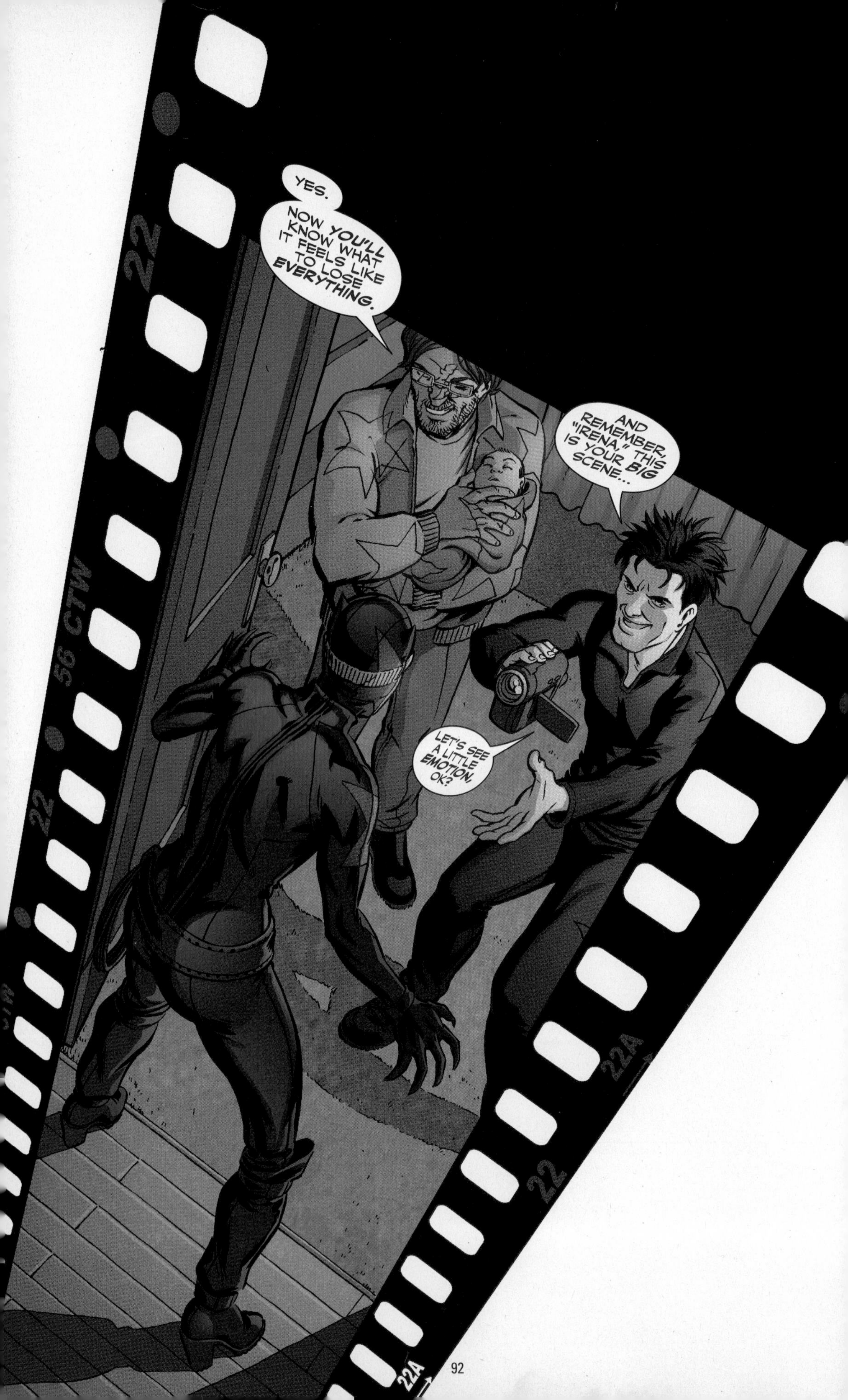
YES.
NOW YOU'LL KNOW WHAT IT FEELS LIKE TO LOSE EVERYTHING.
AND REMEMBER, "IRENA," THIS IS YOUR BIG SCENE...
LET'S SEE A LITTLE EMOTION, OK?
22
56 CTW
22A

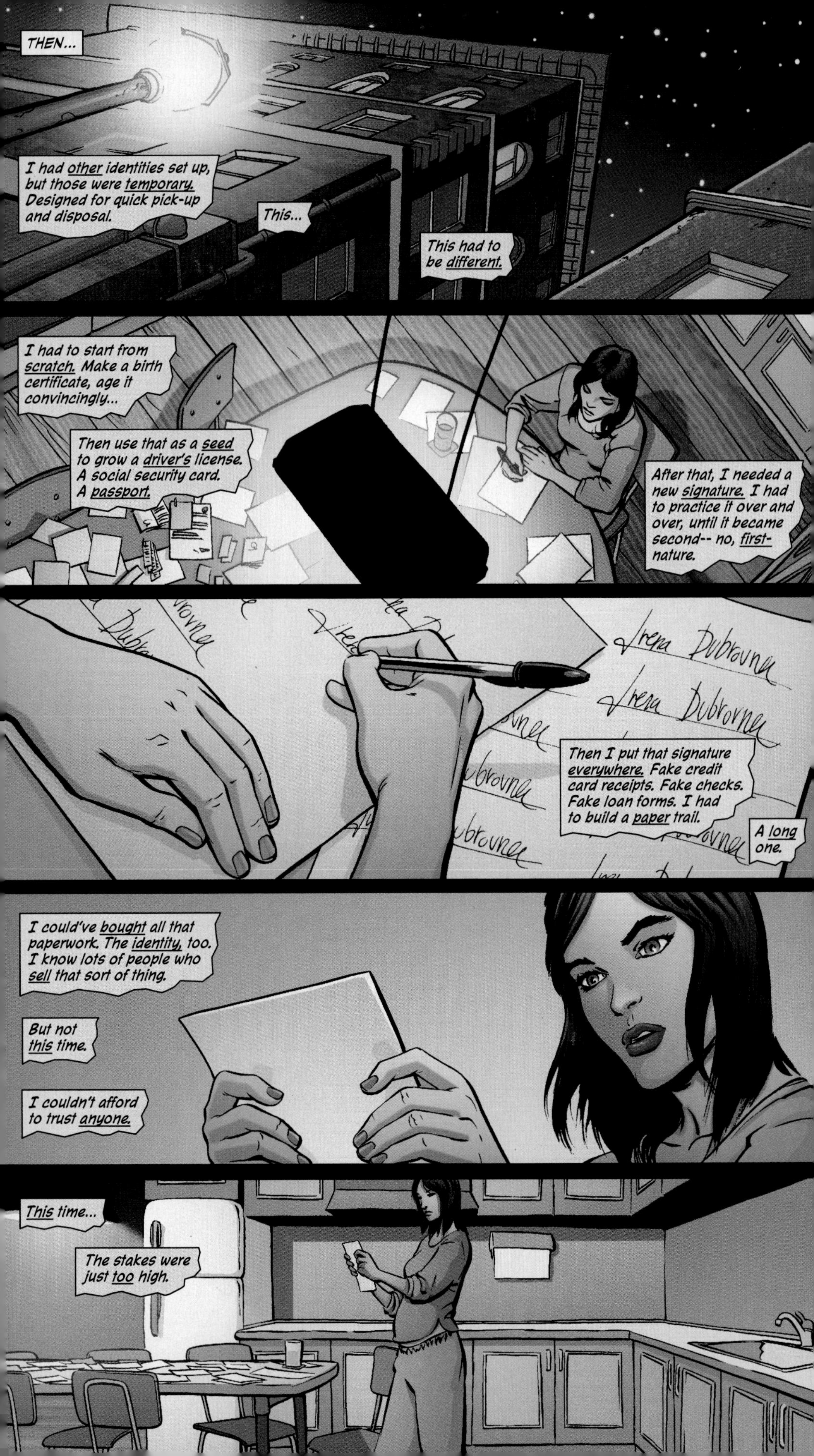
THEN...
I had other identities set up, but those were temporary. Designed for quick pick-up and disposal.
This...
This had to be different.
I had to start from scratch. Make a birth certificate, age it convincingly...
Then use that as a seed to grow a driver's license. A social security card. A passport.
After that, I needed a new signature. I had to practice it over and over, until it became second-- no, first-nature.
Then I put that signature everywhere. Fake credit card receipts. Fake checks. Fake loan forms. I had to build a paper trail.
A long one.
I could've bought all that paperwork. The identity, too. I know lots of people who sell that sort of thing.
But not this time.
I couldn't afford to trust anyone.
This time...
The stakes were just too high.

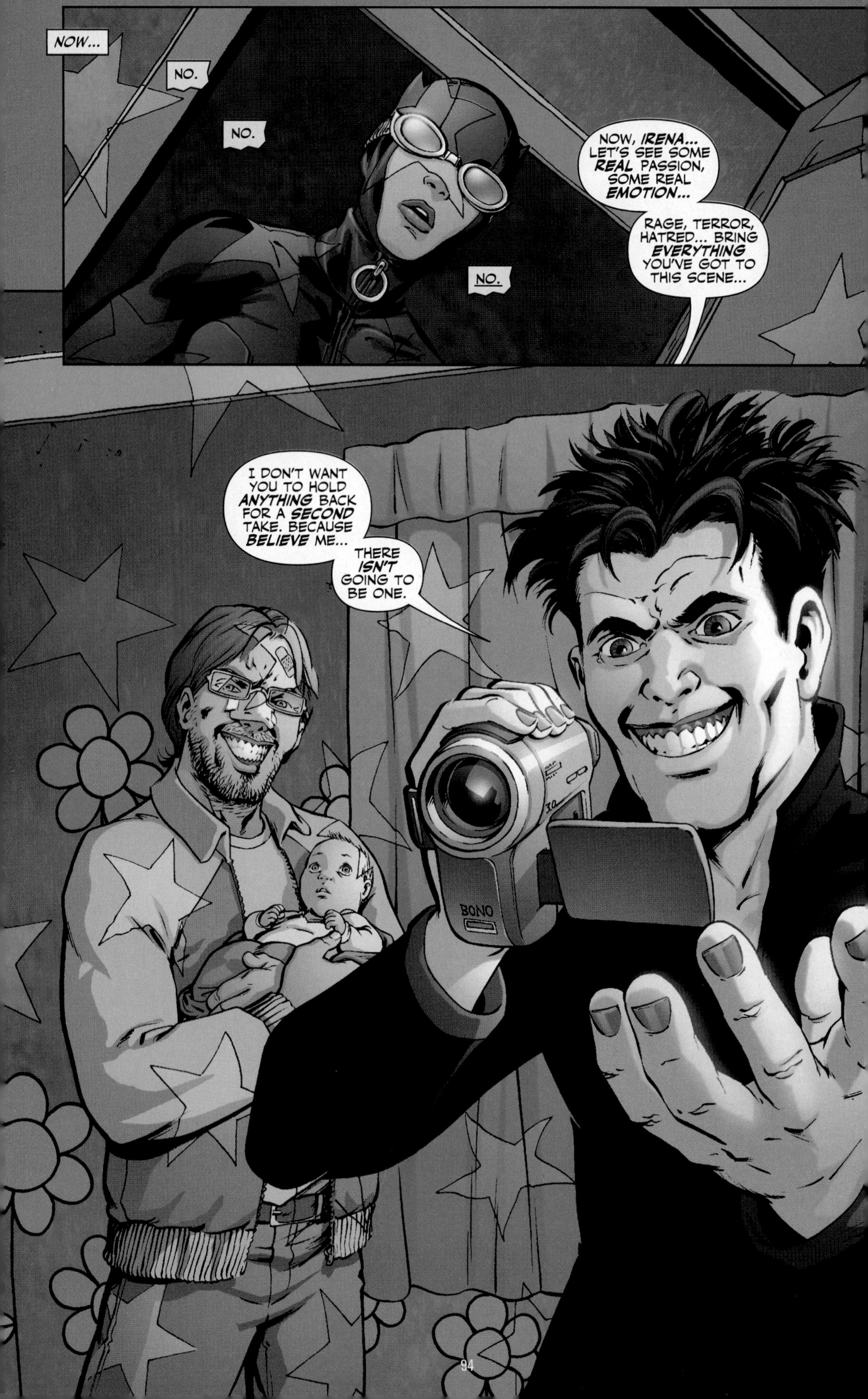
NOW...
NO.
NO.
NO.
NOW, IRENA... LET'S SEE SOME REAL PASSION, SOME REAL EMOTION...
RAGE, TERROR, HATRED... BRING EVERYTHING YOU'VE GOT TO THIS SCENE...
I DON'T WANT YOU TO HOLD ANYTHING BACK FOR A SECOND TAKE. BECAUSE BELIEVE ME...
THERE ISN'T GOING TO BE ONE.
BONO

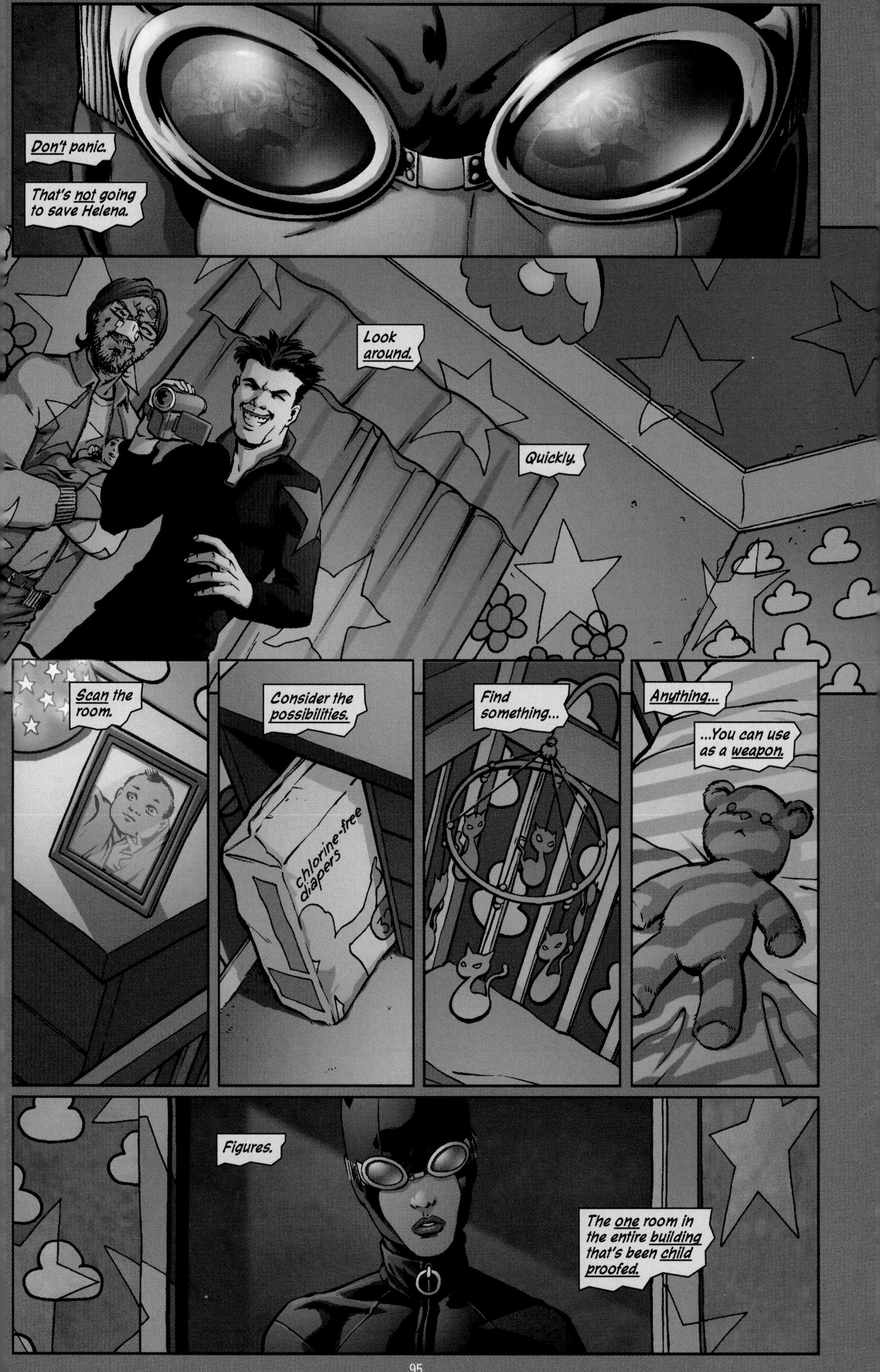
Don't panic.
That's not going to save Helena.
Look around.
Quickly.
Scan the room.
Consider the possibilities.
chlorine-free diapers
Find something...
Anything...
...You can use as a weapon.
Figures.
The one room in the entire building that's been child proofed.

WHAT'S THE *MATTER,* DUBROVNA? *CAT* GOT YOUR TONGUE?

PLEASE, BEND. THAT'S *NOT* THE KIND OF HUMOR WE WANT IN THIS FILM.

I'M TRYING TO DO SOMETHING *SOPHISTICATED* HERE. THINK WILDER. THINK LUBITSCH.

RELAX, EDISON. WE CAN ALWAYS DUB SOME *OTHER* SOUND OVER IT IN POST-PRODUCTION.

SOMETHING *DRAMATIC.* SOMETHING THAT WILL *GRAB* THE AUDIENCE'S ATTENTION.

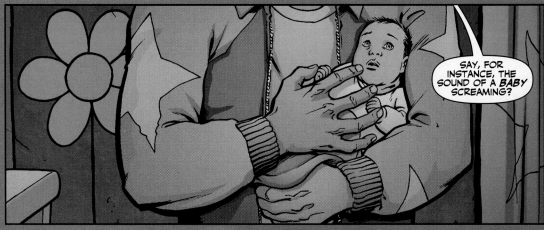

SAY, FOR INSTANCE, THE SOUND OF A *BABY* SCREAMING?

That's it.

THE EAST END...

LENAHAN, AT *FIRST* I THOUGHT YOU JUST NEEDED TO STEP OUT AND GET A LITTLE FRESH *AIR*...

BUT NOW, LOOKING AT *THIS*, I'M THINKING YOU NEED TO GET OUT OF GOTHAM *COMPLETELY*... AND GET A GIRL...

ANY GIRL...

...EXCEPT, OF COURSE, *HER.*

YOU MEAN *"THEM,"* WORTH.

TAKE A *CLOSER* LOOK...

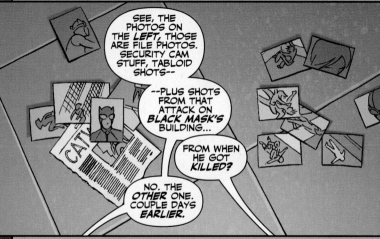

SEE, THE PHOTOS ON THE *LEFT,* THOSE ARE FILE PHOTOS. SECURITY CAM STUFF, TABLOID SHOTS--

--PLUS SHOTS FROM THAT ATTACK ON *BLACK MASK'S* BUILDING...

FROM WHEN HE GOT *KILLED?*

NO. THE *OTHER* ONE. COUPLE DAYS *EARLIER.*

BUT THESE, *THESE* WERE TAKEN OFF A DVD OF THAT PUBLIC ACCESS SHOW. YOU KNOW? THE *FILM FREAK* GUY?

YEAH. I'VE HEARD OF IT. *SO?*

SO? ISN'T IT *OBVIOUS?*

WE'RE NOT LOOKING FOR *ONE* CATWOMAN...

WE'RE LOOKING FOR *TWO.*

BRIIING BRIIING

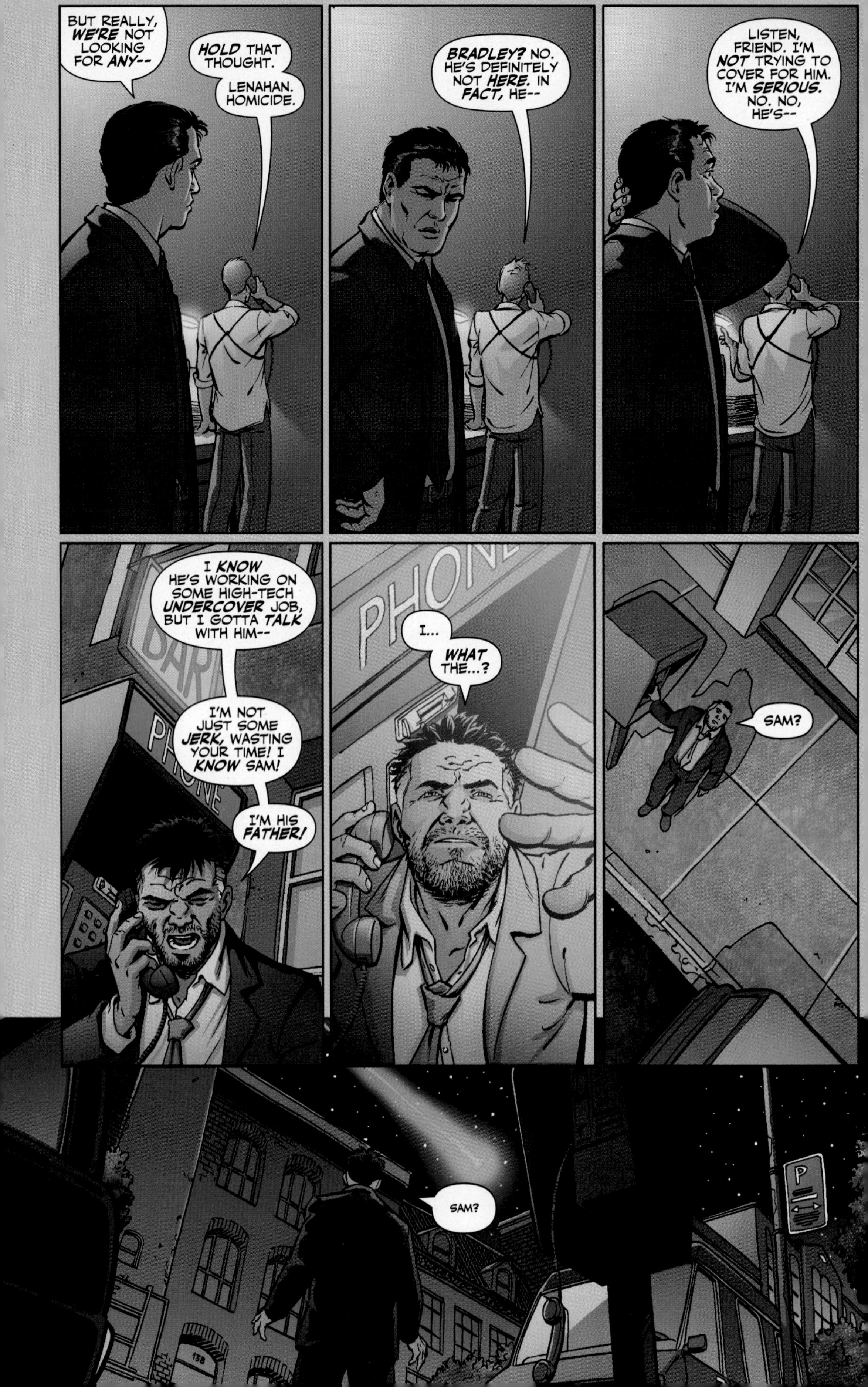

BUT REALLY, WE'RE NOT LOOKING FOR ANY--
HOLD THAT THOUGHT.
LENAHAN. HOMICIDE.
BRADLEY? NO. HE'S DEFINITELY NOT HERE. IN FACT, HE--
LISTEN, FRIEND. I'M NOT TRYING TO COVER FOR HIM. I'M SERIOUS. NO. NO, HE'S--
I KNOW HE'S WORKING ON SOME HIGH-TECH UNDERCOVER JOB, BUT I GOTTA TALK WITH HIM--
I'M NOT JUST SOME JERK, WASTING YOUR TIME! I KNOW SAM!
I'M HIS FATHER!
PHONE
I... WHAT THE...?
SAM?
SAM?

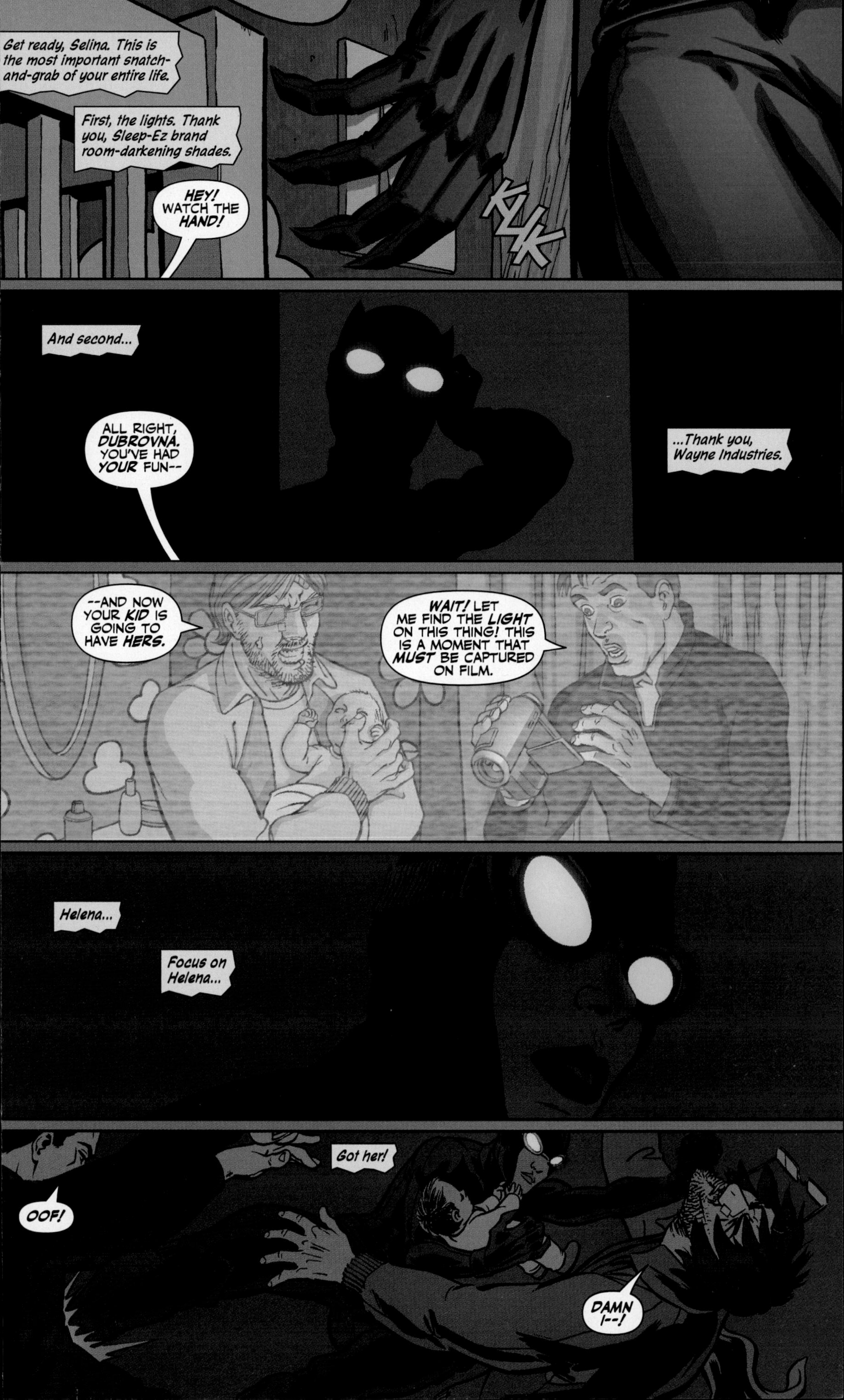

Get ready, Selina. This is the most important snatch-and-grab of your entire life.
First, the lights. Thank you, Sleep-Ez brand room-darkening shades.
HEY! WATCH THE HAND!
KLIK
And second...
ALL RIGHT, DUBROVNA. YOU'VE HAD YOUR FUN--
...Thank you, Wayne Industries.
--AND NOW YOUR KID IS GOING TO HAVE HERS.
WAIT! LET ME FIND THE LIGHT ON THIS THING! THIS IS A MOMENT THAT MUST BE CAPTURED ON FILM.
Helena...
Focus on Helena...
Got her!
OOF!
DAMN I--!

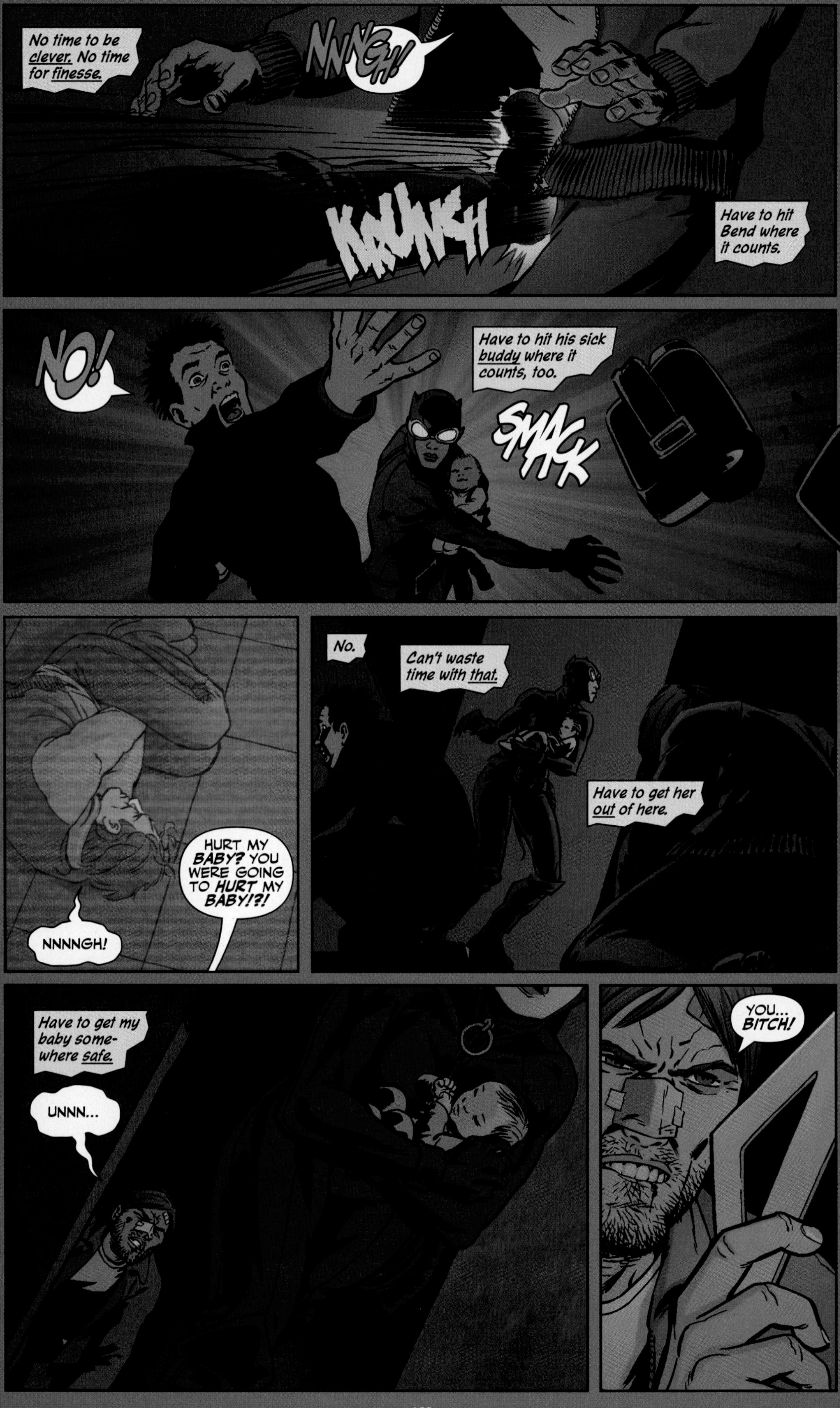
No time to be clever. No time for finesse.
NNNGH!
KRUNCH
Have to hit Bend where it counts.
NO!
Have to hit his sick buddy where it counts, too.
SMACK
HURT MY BABY? YOU WERE GOING TO HURT MY BABY!?!
NNNNGH!
No.
Can't waste time with that.
Have to get her out of here.
Have to get my baby somewhere safe.
UNNN...
YOU... BITCH!

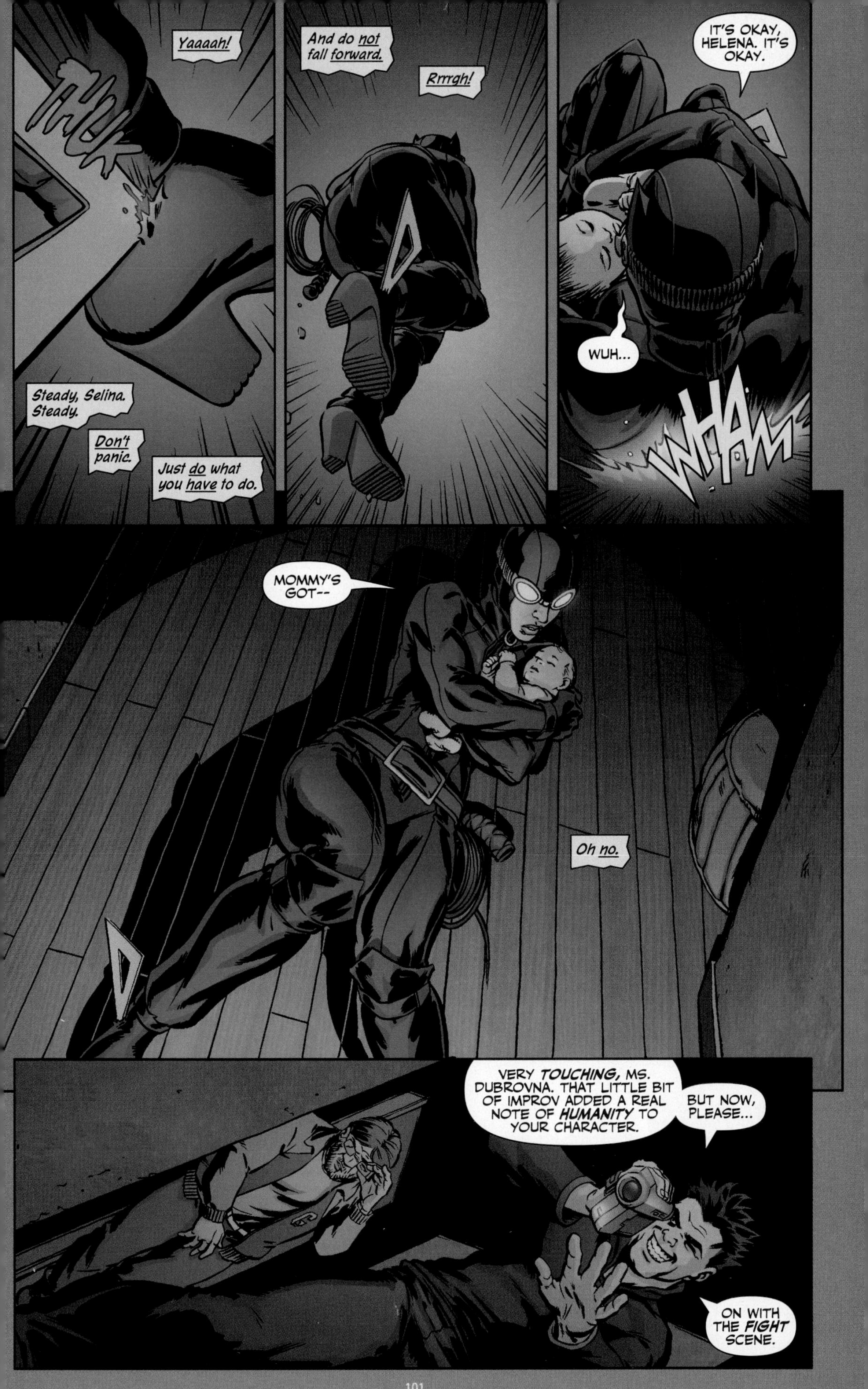
Yaaaah!
THUK
Steady, Selina. Steady.
Don't panic.
Just do what you have to do.
And do not fall forward.
Rrrgh!
IT'S OKAY, HELENA. IT'S OKAY.
WUH...
WHAM
MOMMY'S GOT--
Oh no.
VERY TOUCHING, MS. DUBROVNA. THAT LITTLE BIT OF IMPROV ADDED A REAL NOTE OF HUMANITY TO YOUR CHARACTER.
BUT NOW, PLEASE...
ON WITH THE FIGHT SCENE.

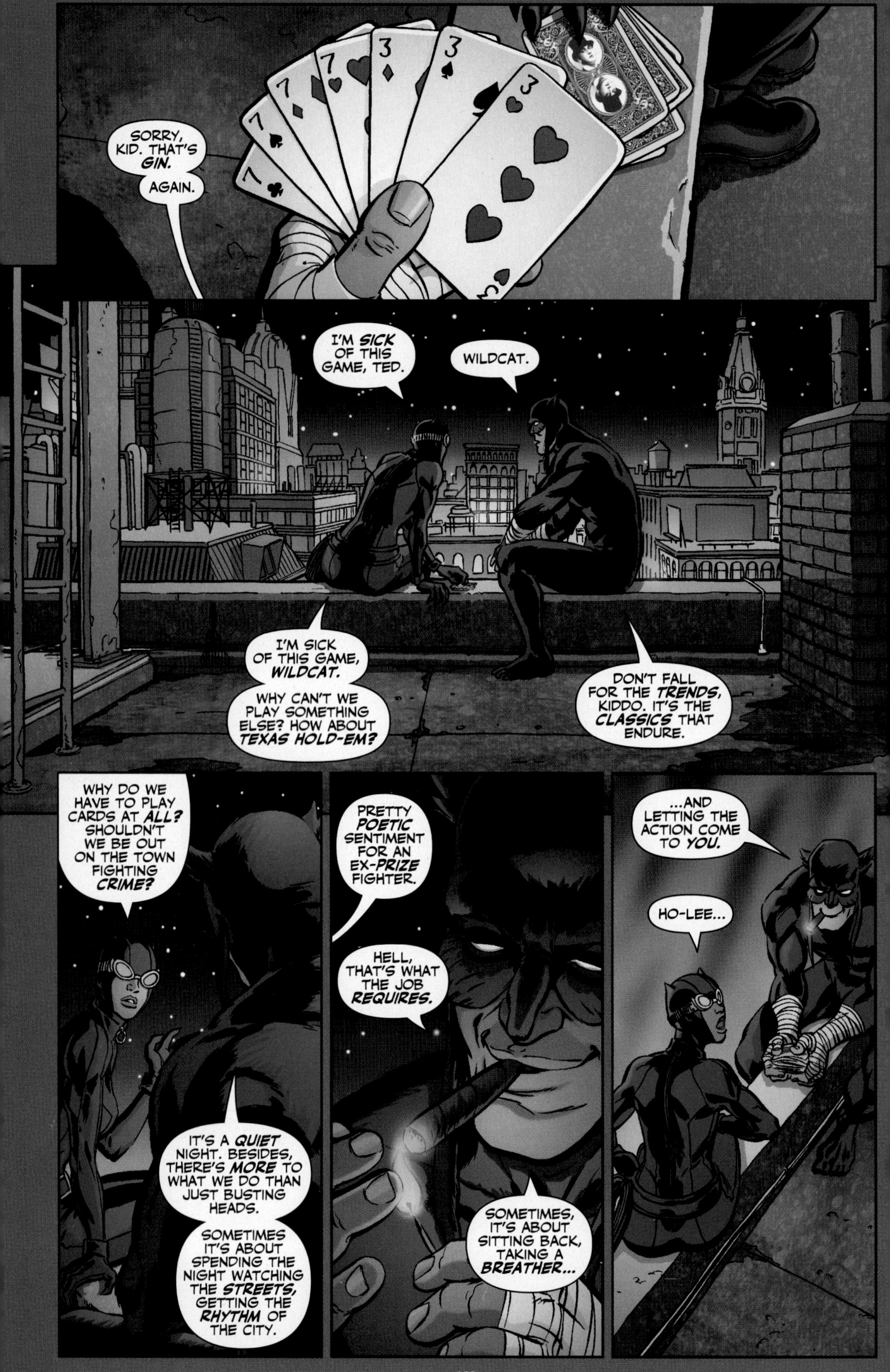
SORRY, KID. THAT'S GIN.
AGAIN.
I'M SICK OF THIS GAME, TED.
WILDCAT.
I'M SICK OF THIS GAME, WILDCAT.
WHY CAN'T WE PLAY SOMETHING ELSE? HOW ABOUT TEXAS HOLD-EM?
DON'T FALL FOR THE TRENDS, KIDDO. IT'S THE CLASSICS THAT ENDURE.
WHY DO WE HAVE TO PLAY CARDS AT ALL? SHOULDN'T WE BE OUT ON THE TOWN FIGHTING CRIME?
IT'S A QUIET NIGHT. BESIDES, THERE'S MORE TO WHAT WE DO THAN JUST BUSTING HEADS.
SOMETIMES IT'S ABOUT SPENDING THE NIGHT WATCHING THE STREETS, GETTING THE RHYTHM OF THE CITY.
PRETTY POETIC SENTIMENT FOR AN EX-PRIZE FIGHTER.
HELL, THAT'S WHAT THE JOB REQUIRES.
SOMETIMES, IT'S ABOUT SITTING BACK, TAKING A BREATHER...
...AND LETTING THE ACTION COME TO YOU.
HO-LEE...

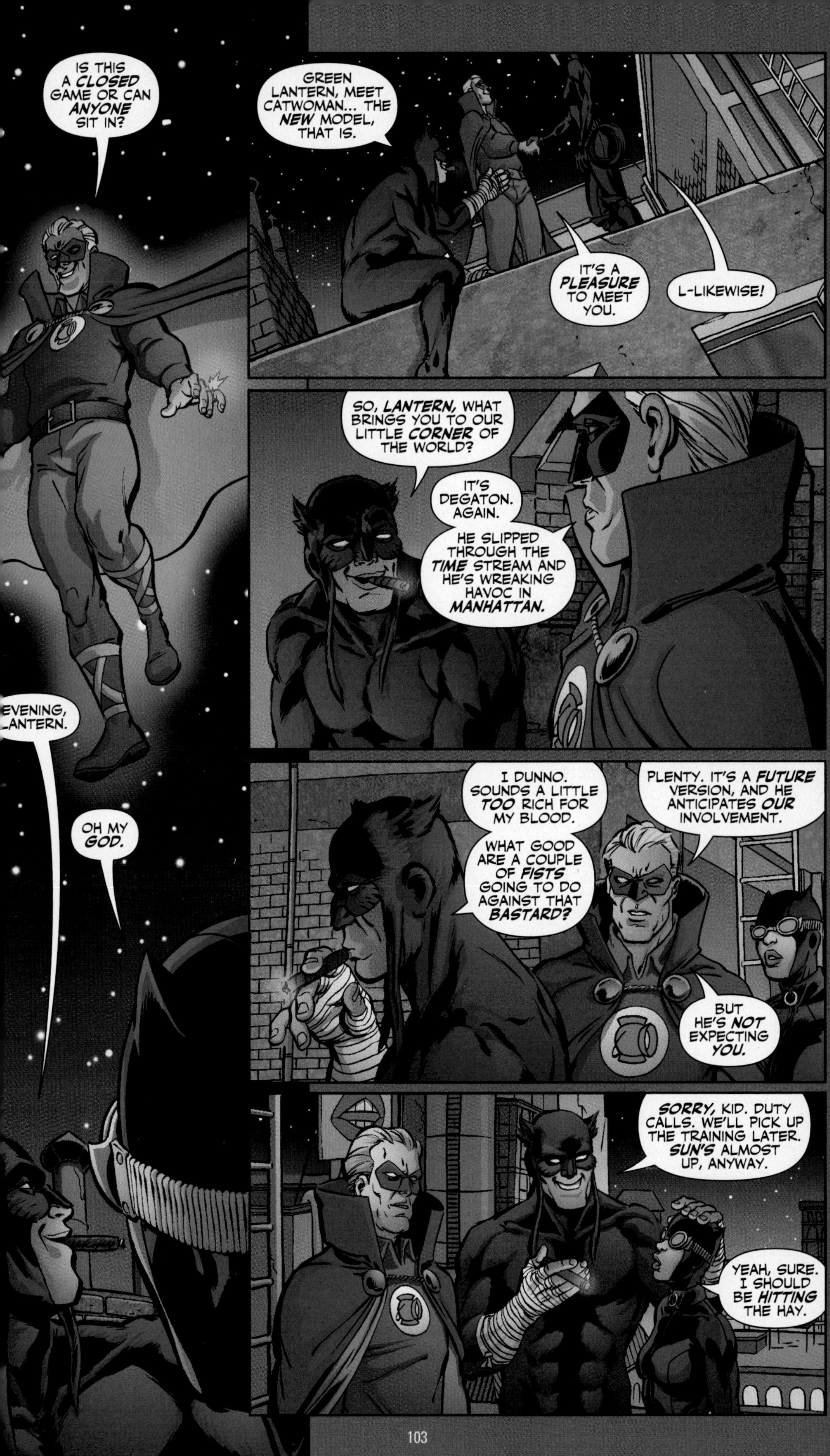
IS THIS A CLOSED GAME OR CAN ANYONE SIT IN?
EVENING, LANTERN.
OH MY GOD.
GREEN LANTERN, MEET CATWOMAN... THE NEW MODEL, THAT IS.
IT'S A PLEASURE TO MEET YOU.
L-LIKEWISE!
SO, LANTERN, WHAT BRINGS YOU TO OUR LITTLE CORNER OF THE WORLD?
IT'S DEGATON. AGAIN.
HE SLIPPED THROUGH THE TIME STREAM AND HE'S WREAKING HAVOC IN MANHATTAN.
I DUNNO. SOUNDS A LITTLE TOO RICH FOR MY BLOOD.
WHAT GOOD ARE A COUPLE OF FISTS GOING TO DO AGAINST THAT BASTARD?
PLENTY. IT'S A FUTURE VERSION, AND HE ANTICIPATES OUR INVOLVEMENT.
BUT HE'S NOT EXPECTING YOU.
SORRY, KID. DUTY CALLS. WE'LL PICK UP THE TRAINING LATER. SUN'S ALMOST UP, ANYWAY.
YEAH, SURE. I SHOULD BE HITTING THE HAY.

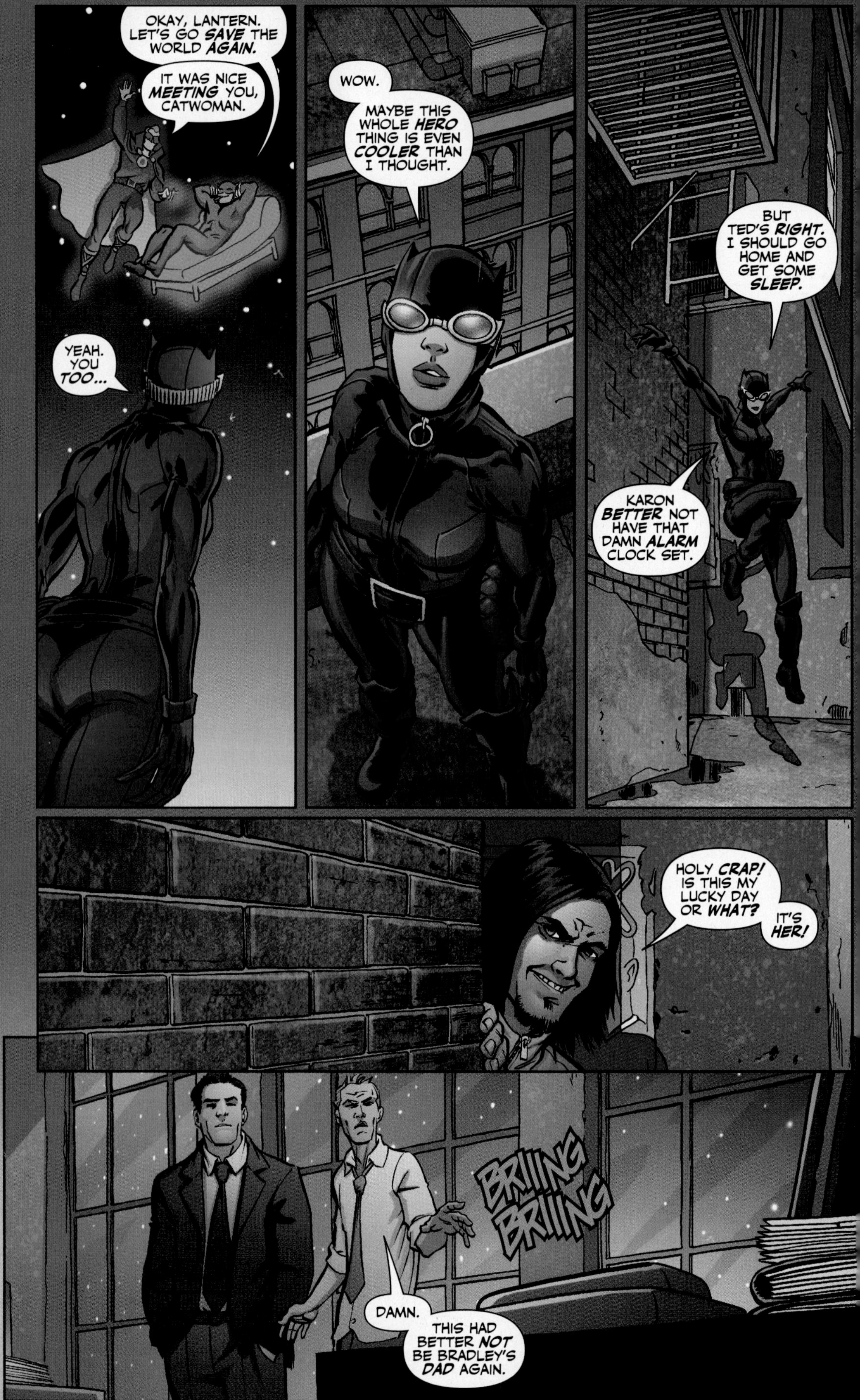

OKAY, LANTERN. LET'S GO SAVE THE WORLD AGAIN.
IT WAS NICE MEETING YOU, CATWOMAN.
YEAH. YOU TOO...
WOW.
MAYBE THIS WHOLE HERO THING IS EVEN COOLER THAN I THOUGHT.
BUT TED'S RIGHT. I SHOULD GO HOME AND GET SOME SLEEP.
KARON BETTER NOT HAVE THAT DAMN ALARM CLOCK SET.
HOLY CRAP! IS THIS MY LUCKY DAY OR WHAT?
IT'S HER!
BRIING BRIING
DAMN.
THIS HAD BETTER NOT BE BRADLEY'S DAD AGAIN.

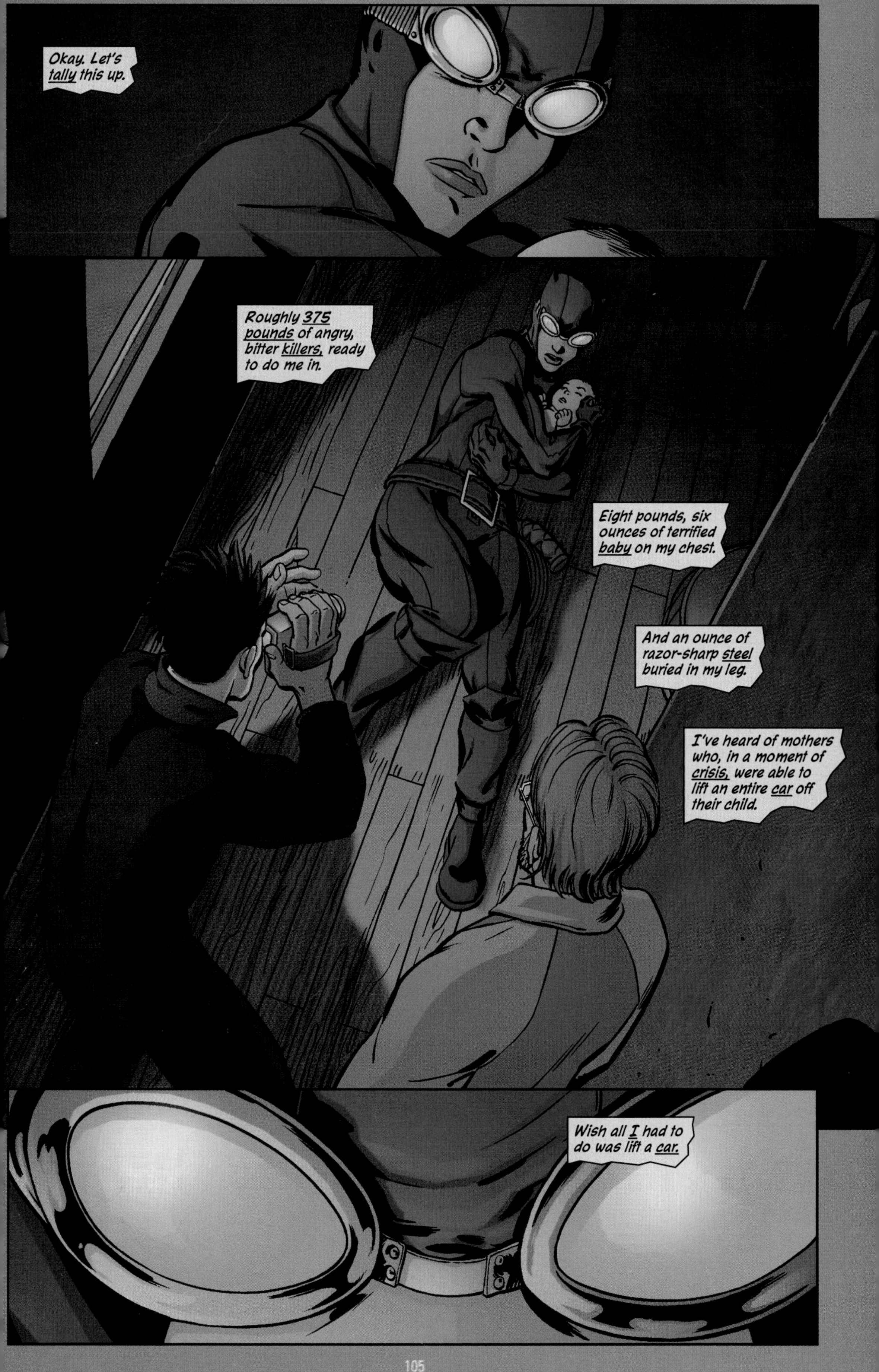
Okay. Let's tally this up.
Roughly 375 pounds of angry, bitter killers, ready to do me in.
Eight pounds, six ounces of terrified baby on my chest.
And an ounce of razor-sharp steel buried in my leg.
I've heard of mothers who, in a moment of crisis, were able to lift an entire car off their child.
Wish all I had to do was lift a car.

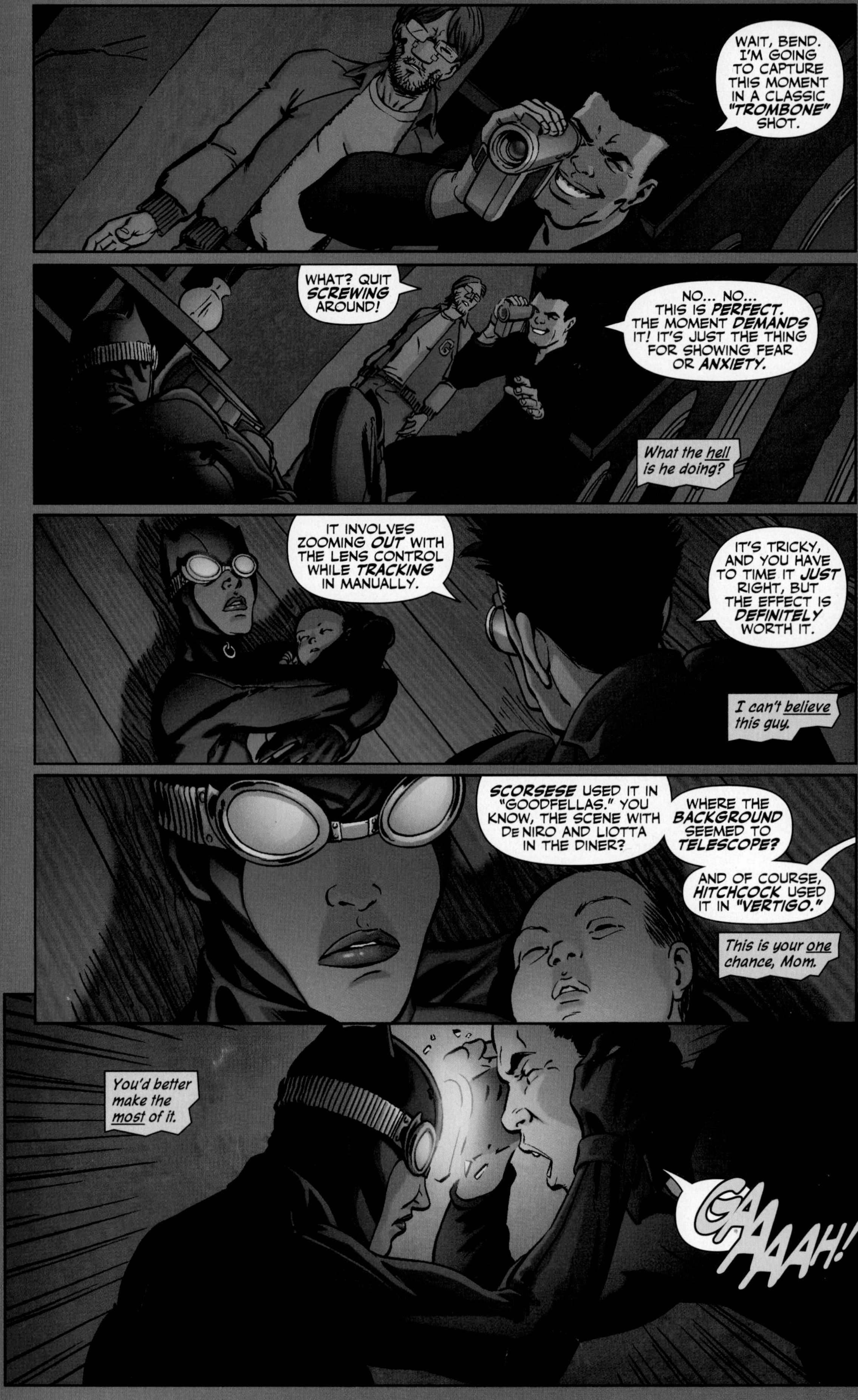
WAIT, BEND. I'M GOING TO CAPTURE THIS MOMENT IN A CLASSIC "TROMBONE" SHOT.
WHAT? QUIT SCREWING AROUND!
NO... NO... THIS IS PERFECT. THE MOMENT DEMANDS IT! IT'S JUST THE THING FOR SHOWING FEAR OR ANXIETY.
What the hell is he doing?
IT INVOLVES ZOOMING OUT WITH THE LENS CONTROL WHILE TRACKING IN MANUALLY.
IT'S TRICKY, AND YOU HAVE TO TIME IT JUST RIGHT, BUT THE EFFECT IS DEFINITELY WORTH IT.
I can't believe this guy.
SCORSESE USED IT IN "GOODFELLAS." YOU KNOW, THE SCENE WITH DE NIRO AND LIOTTA IN THE DINER?
WHERE THE BACKGROUND SEEMED TO TELESCOPE?
AND OF COURSE, HITCHCOCK USED IT IN "VERTIGO."
This is your one chance, Mom.
You'd better make the most of it.
GAAAAH!

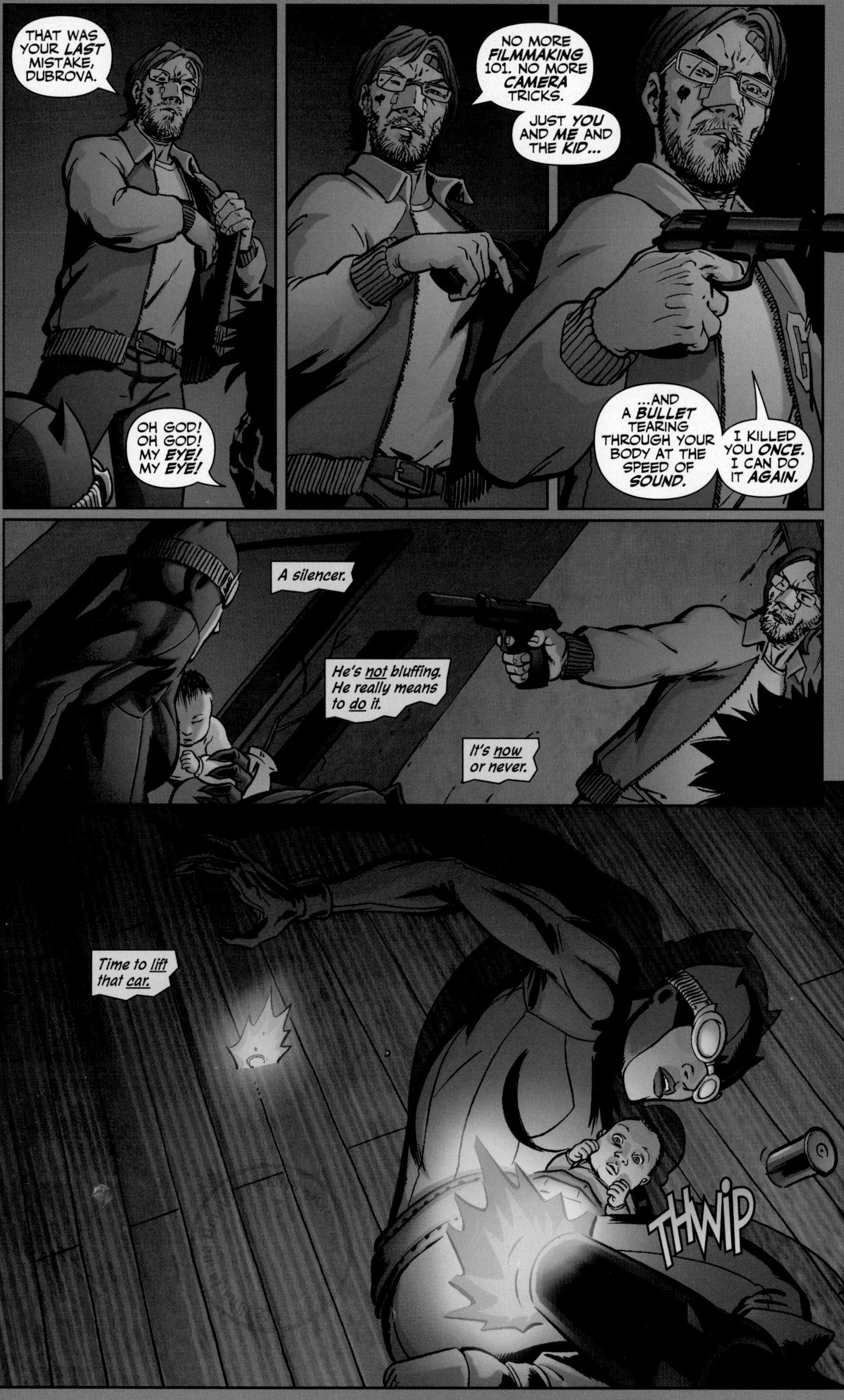
THAT WAS YOUR LAST MISTAKE, DUBROVA.
OH GOD! OH GOD! MY EYE! MY EYE!
NO MORE FILMMAKING 101. NO MORE CAMERA TRICKS.
JUST YOU AND ME AND THE KID...
...AND A BULLET TEARING THROUGH YOUR BODY AT THE SPEED OF SOUND.
I KILLED YOU ONCE. I CAN DO IT AGAIN.
A silencer.
He's not bluffing. He really means to do it.
It's now or never.
Time to lift that car.
THWIP

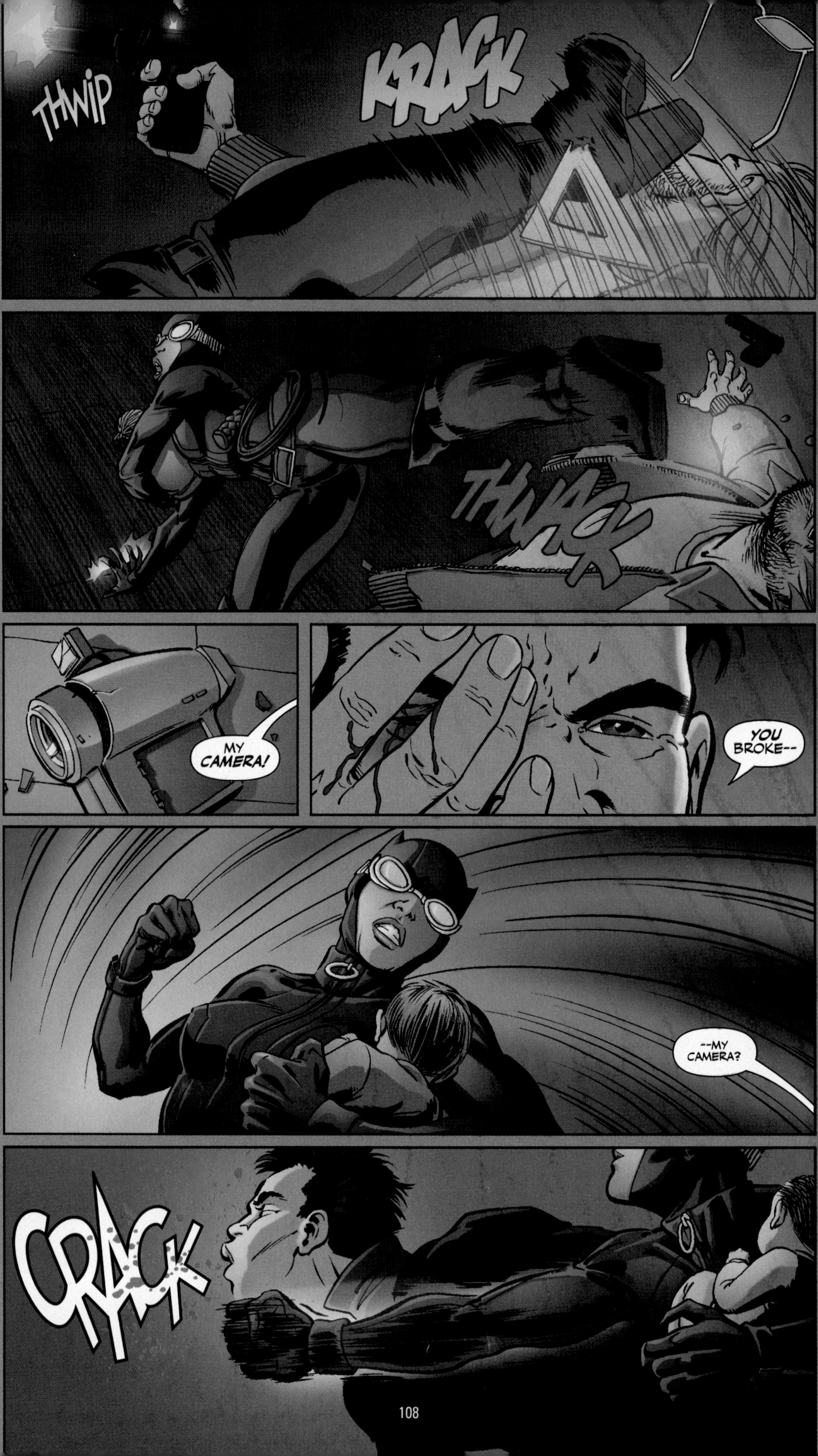
THWIP
KRACK
THWACK
MY CAMERA!
YOU BROKE--
--MY CAMERA?
CRACK

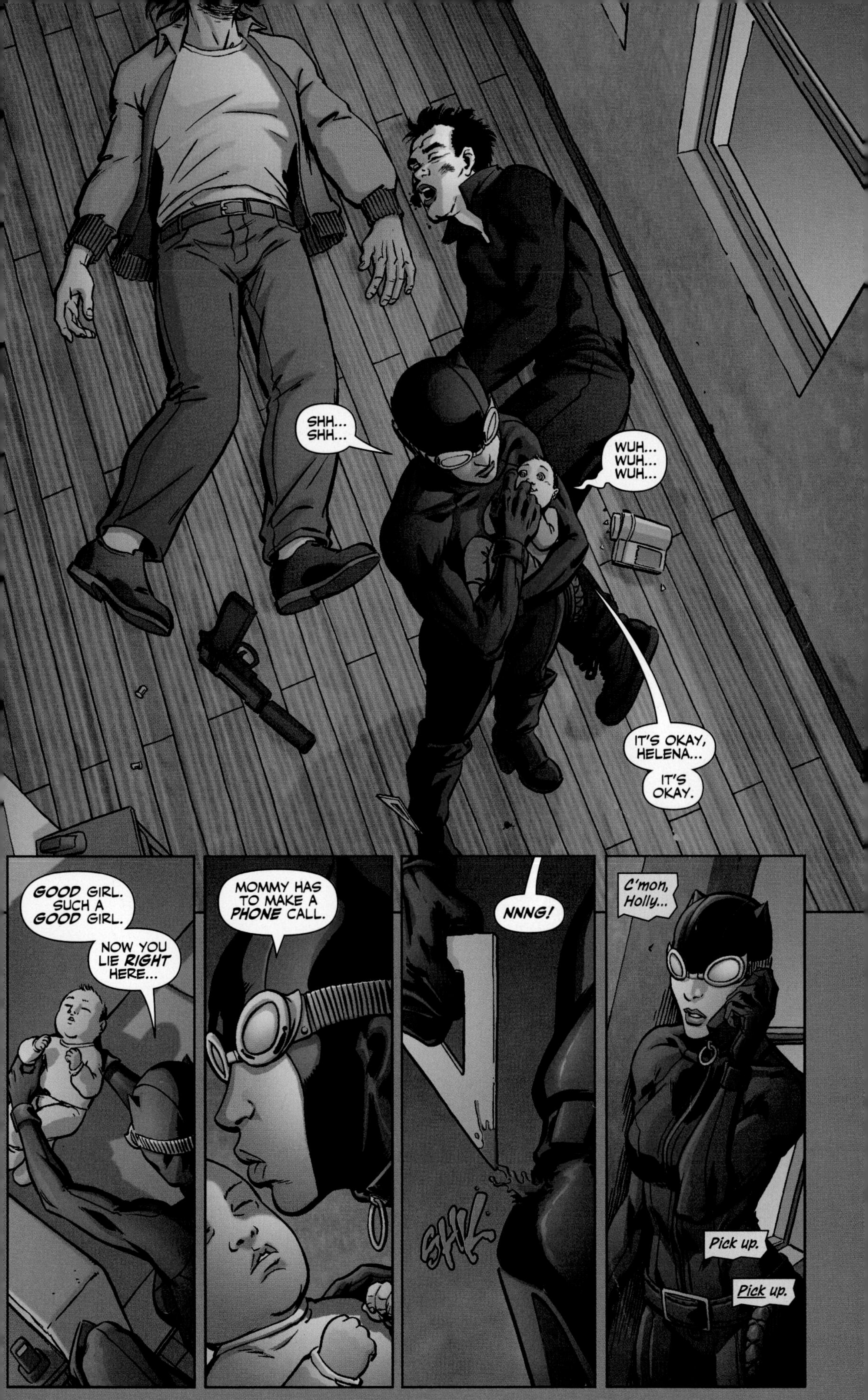
SHH... SHH...
WUH... WUH... WUH...
IT'S OKAY, HELENA...
IT'S OKAY.
GOOD GIRL. SUCH A GOOD GIRL.
NOW YOU LIE RIGHT HERE...
MOMMY HAS TO MAKE A PHONE CALL.
NNNG!
C'mon, Holly...
Pick up.
Pick up.

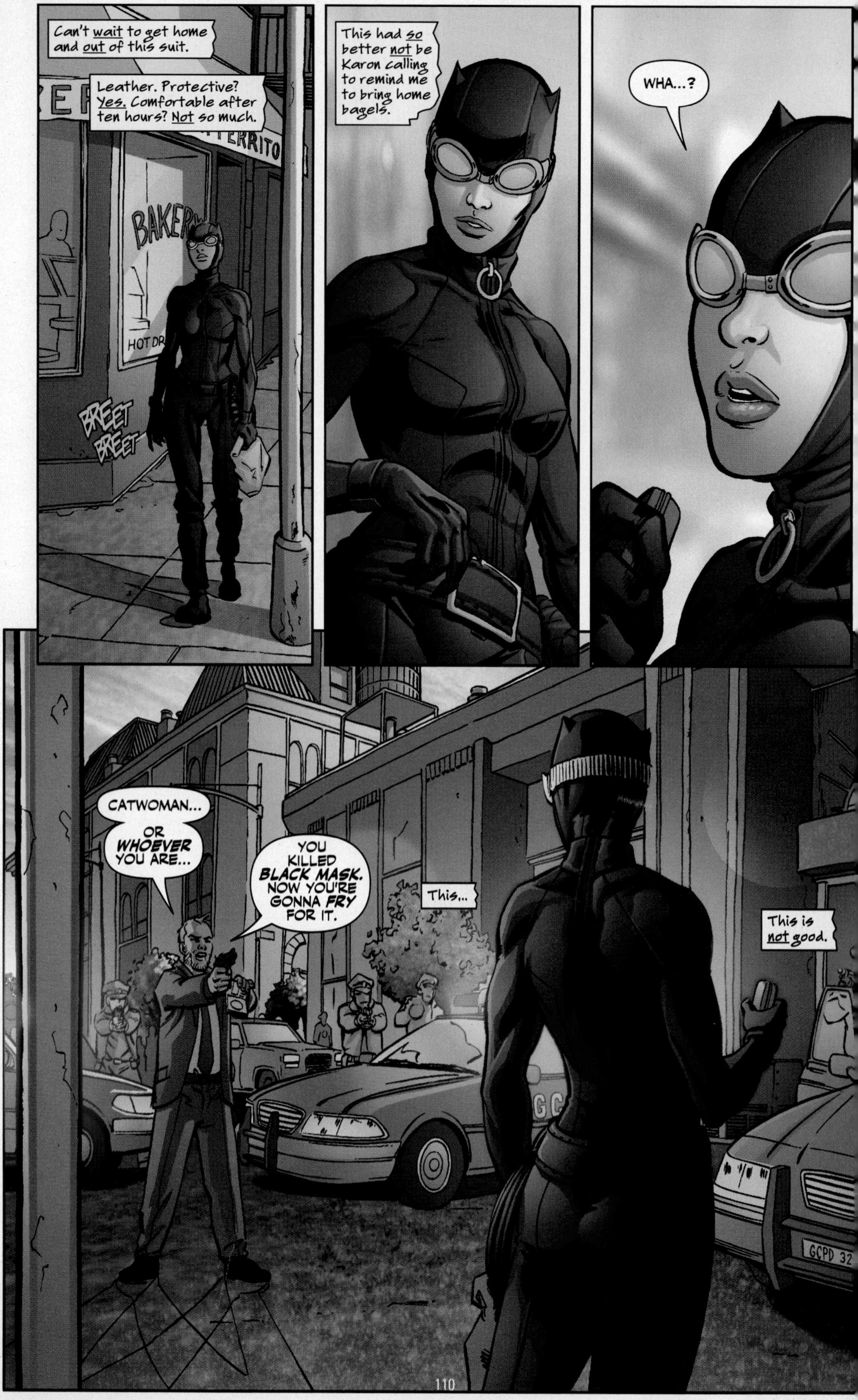

Can't wait to get home and out of this suit.
Leather. Protective? Yes. Comfortable after ten hours? Not so much.
BAKERY
TERRITO
HOT DR
BREEET BREEET
This had so better not be Karon calling to remind me to bring home bagels.
WHA...?
CATWOMAN...
OR WHOEVER YOU ARE...
YOU KILLED BLACK MASK. NOW YOU'RE GONNA FRY FOR IT.
This...
This is not good.
GCPD 32

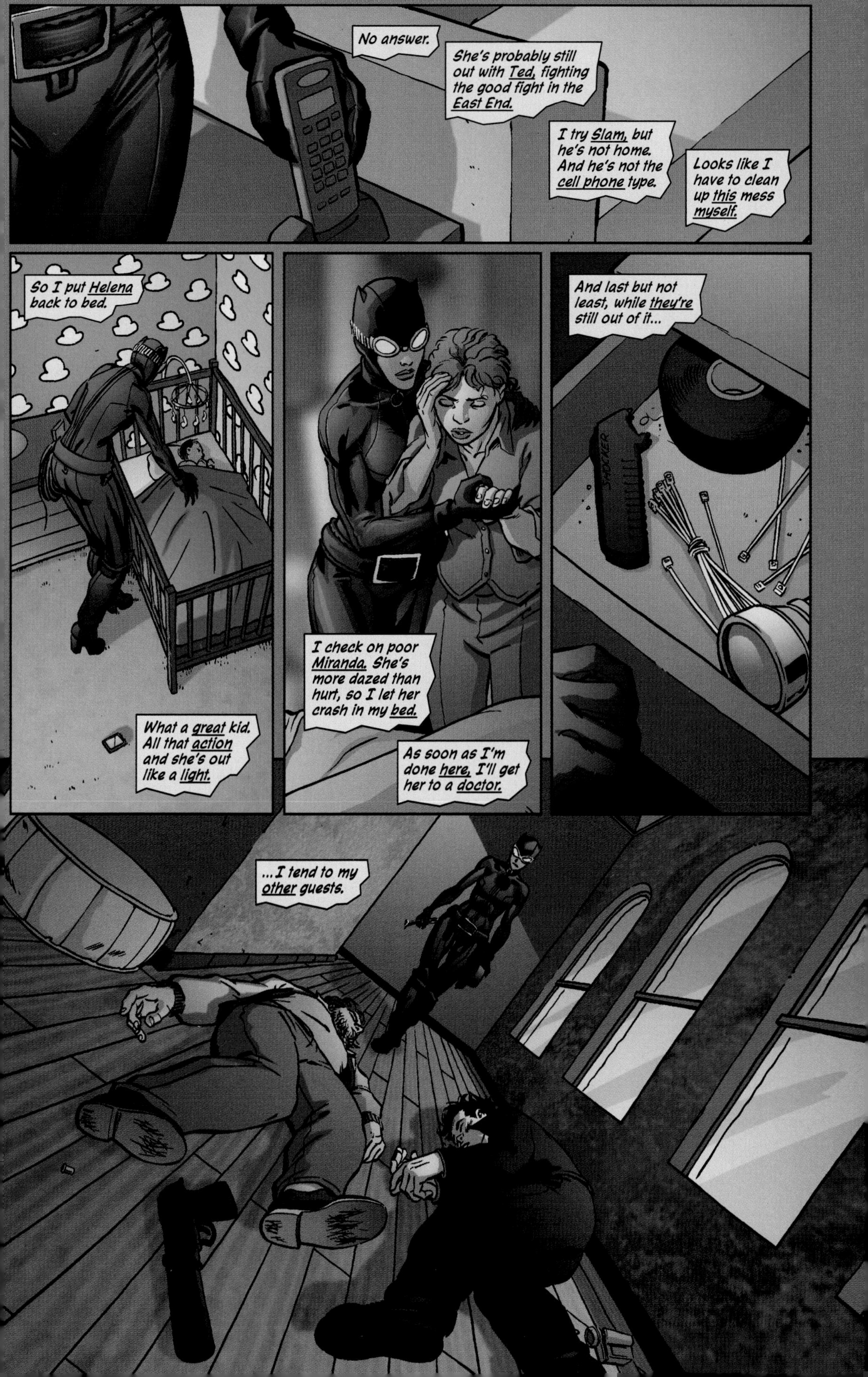
No answer.
She's probably still out with Ted, fighting the good fight in the East End.
I try Slam, but he's not home. And he's not the cell phone type.
Looks like I have to clean up this mess myself.
So I put Helena back to bed.
What a great kid. All that action and she's out like a light.
I check on poor Miranda. She's more dazed than hurt, so I let her crash in my bed.
As soon as I'm done here, I'll get her to a doctor.
And last but not least, while they're still out of it...
SHOCKER
...I tend to my other guests.

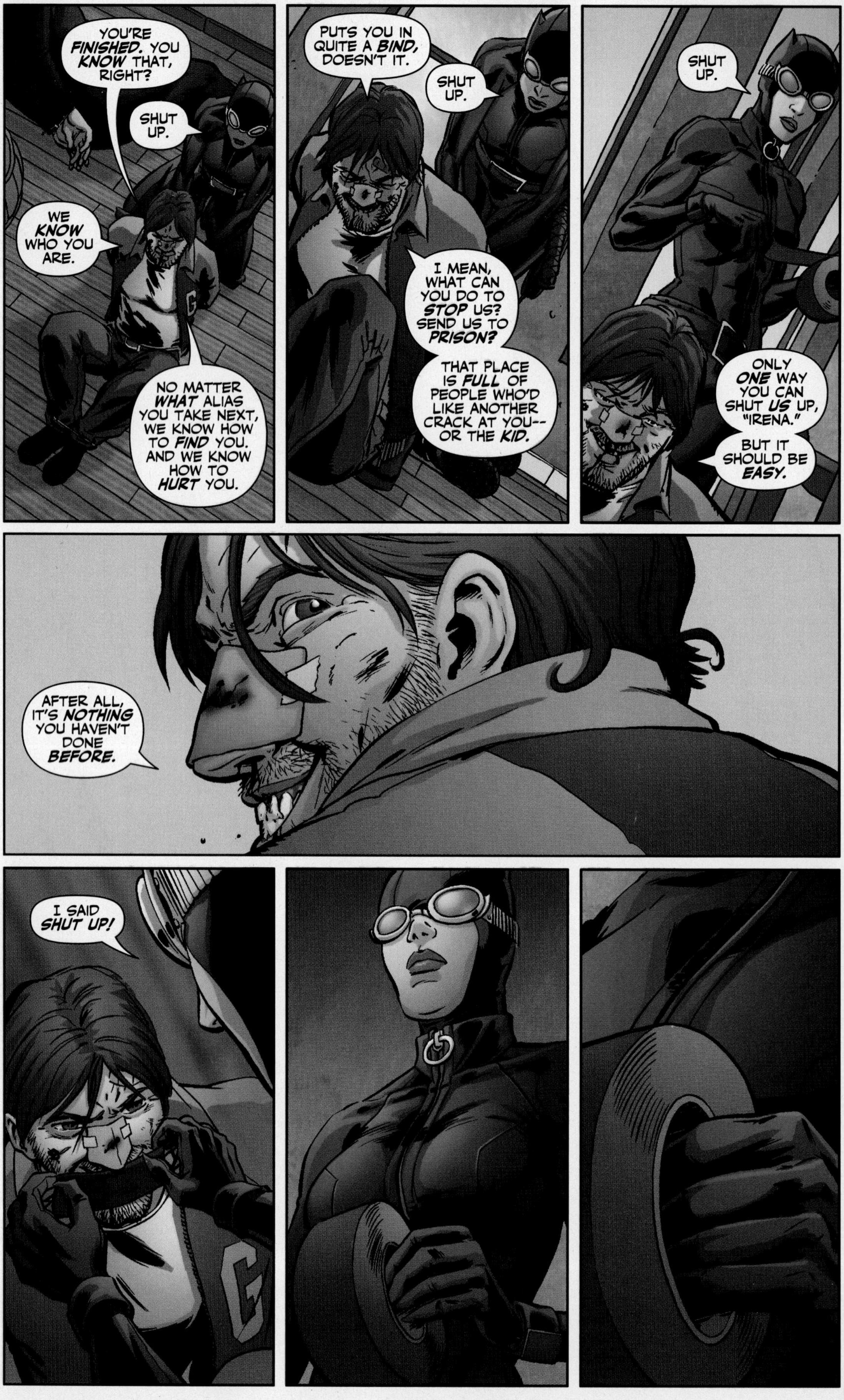
YOU'RE FINISHED. YOU KNOW THAT, RIGHT?
SHUT UP.
WE KNOW WHO YOU ARE.
NO MATTER WHAT ALIAS YOU TAKE NEXT, WE KNOW HOW TO FIND YOU. AND WE KNOW HOW TO HURT YOU.
PUTS YOU IN QUITE A BIND, DOESN'T IT.
SHUT UP.
I MEAN, WHAT CAN YOU DO TO STOP US? SEND US TO PRISON?
THAT PLACE IS FULL OF PEOPLE WHO'D LIKE ANOTHER CRACK AT YOU-- OR THE KID.
SHUT UP.
ONLY ONE WAY YOU CAN SHUT US UP, "IRENA."
BUT IT SHOULD BE EASY.
AFTER ALL, IT'S NOTHING YOU HAVEN'T DONE BEFORE.
I SAID SHUT UP!

NEVER MIND HOW I *GOT* THIS NUMBER.

I *NEED* IT DONE. AND I NEED IT DONE *QUICKLY*.

THE CLOCK IS *RUNNING* AND THE STAKES ARE HIGH. *VERY* HIGH.

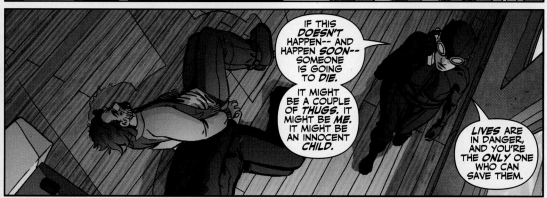

IF THIS *DOESN'T* HAPPEN-- AND HAPPEN *SOON*-- SOMEONE IS GOING TO *DIE*.

IT MIGHT BE A COUPLE OF *THUGS*. IT MIGHT BE *ME*. IT MIGHT BE AN INNOCENT *CHILD*.

LIVES ARE IN DANGER, AND YOU'RE THE *ONLY* ONE WHO CAN SAVE THEM.

BUT... BUT I *CAN'T*. YOU OF *ALL* PEOPLE SHOULD UNDERSTAND *WHY*.

I ONLY UNDERSTAND *TWO* THINGS.

ONE, MY BABY'S *LIFE* IS ON THE LINE.

AND TWO...

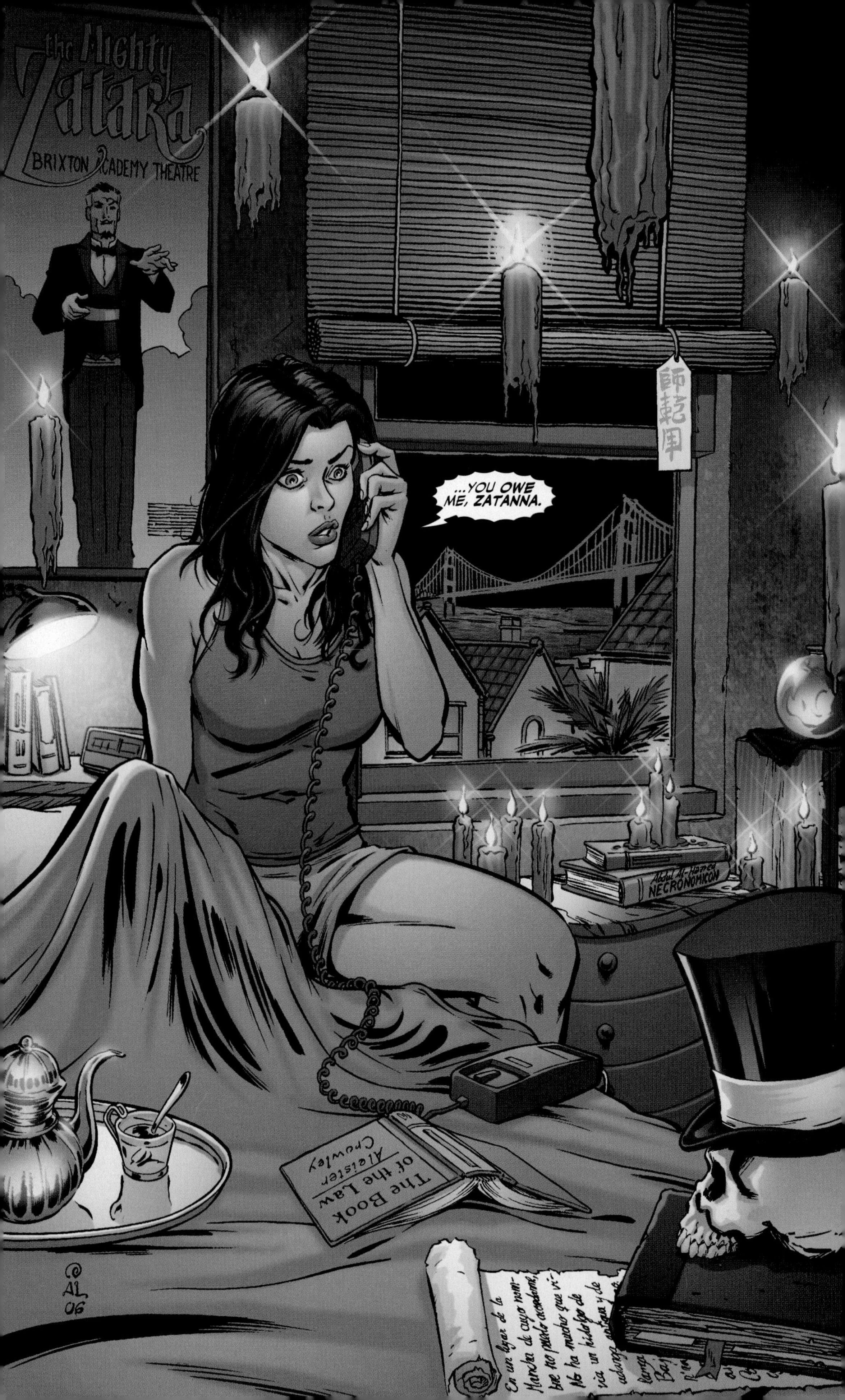
the Mighty Zatara
BRIXTON ACADEMY THEATRE
...YOU OWE ME, ZATANNA.
Abdul Al-Hazred
NECRONOMICON
The Book of the Law
Aleister Crowley

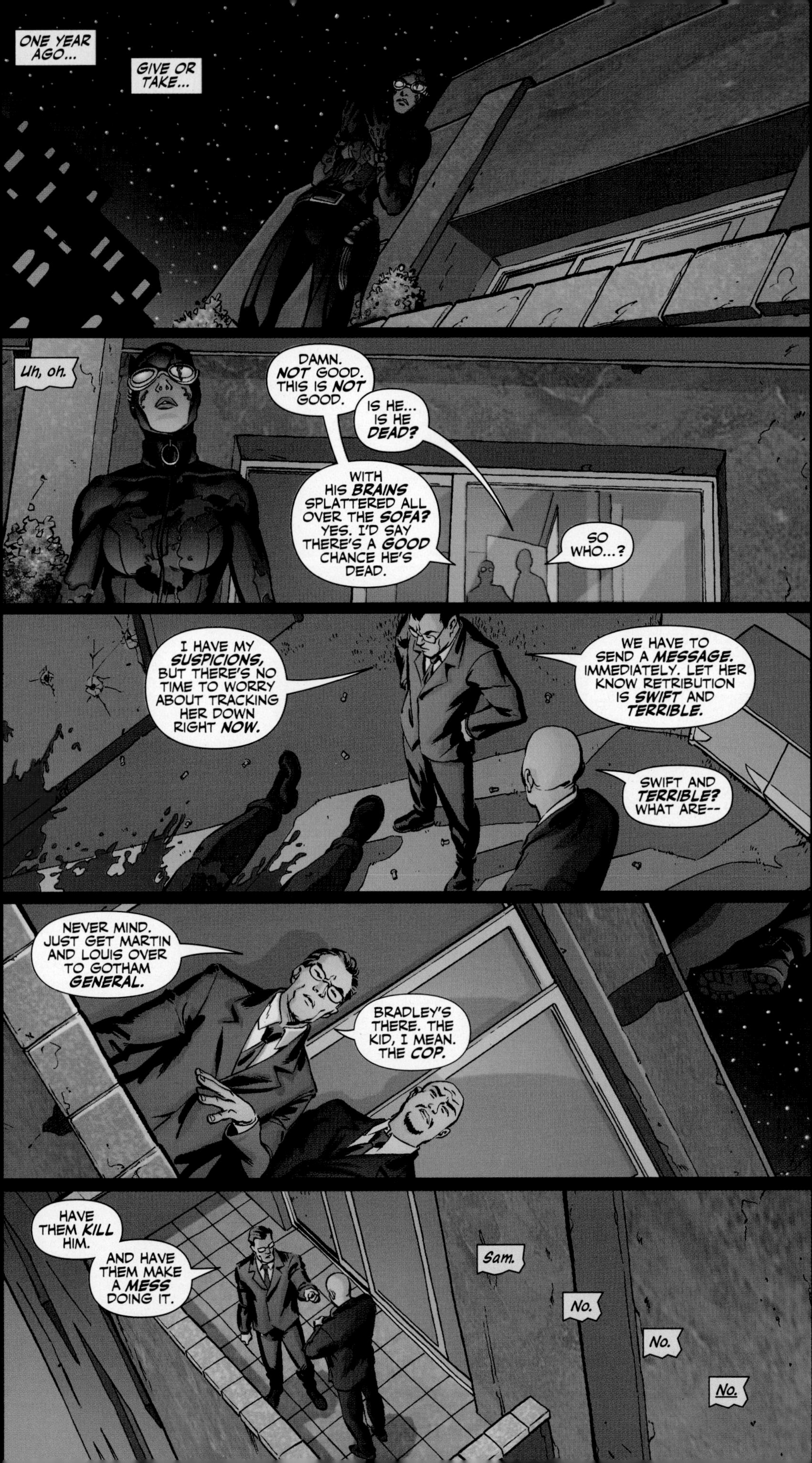
ONE YEAR AGO...
GIVE OR TAKE...
Uh, oh.
DAMN. NOT GOOD. THIS IS NOT GOOD.
IS HE... IS HE DEAD?
WITH HIS BRAINS SPLATTERED ALL OVER THE SOFA? YES. I'D SAY THERE'S A GOOD CHANCE HE'S DEAD.
SO WHO...?
I HAVE MY SUSPICIONS, BUT THERE'S NO TIME TO WORRY ABOUT TRACKING HER DOWN RIGHT NOW.
WE HAVE TO SEND A MESSAGE. IMMEDIATELY. LET HER KNOW RETRIBUTION IS SWIFT AND TERRIBLE.
SWIFT AND TERRIBLE? WHAT ARE--
NEVER MIND. JUST GET MARTIN AND LOUIS OVER TO GOTHAM GENERAL.
BRADLEY'S THERE. THE KID, I MEAN. THE COP.
HAVE THEM KILL HIM.
AND HAVE THEM MAKE A MESS DOING IT.
Sam.
No.
No.
No.

NOW.

RRRIP

OWW!

YOU MUST THINK THAT WAS PRETTY *FUNNY*, RIGHT? WELL KEEP LAUGHING. LAUGH IT *UP*.

BECAUSE PRETTY *SOON*, CATWOMAN OR IRENA DUBROVNA OR *WHATEVER* YOUR NAME IS...

IT'S GOING TO BE NOTHING BUT *TEARS* FOR YOU.

TEARS OVER THE WAY AN OBSCURE CRIMINAL NAMED *ANGLE MAN* RUINED YOUR LIFE.

TEARS OVER THE WAY HE *DROWNED* YOU IN MISERY.

TEARS OVER THE WAY HE LET EVERY MURDEROUS *LUNATIC* WITHIN A HUNDRED MILES KNOW *JUST* WHERE TO *FIND* YOU.

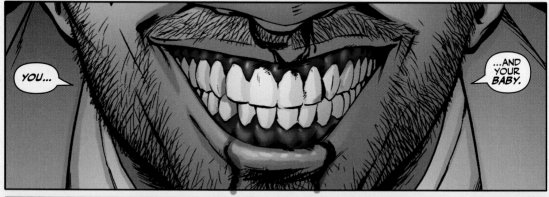

YOU...

...AND YOUR *BABY*.

RRRIP

OWW!

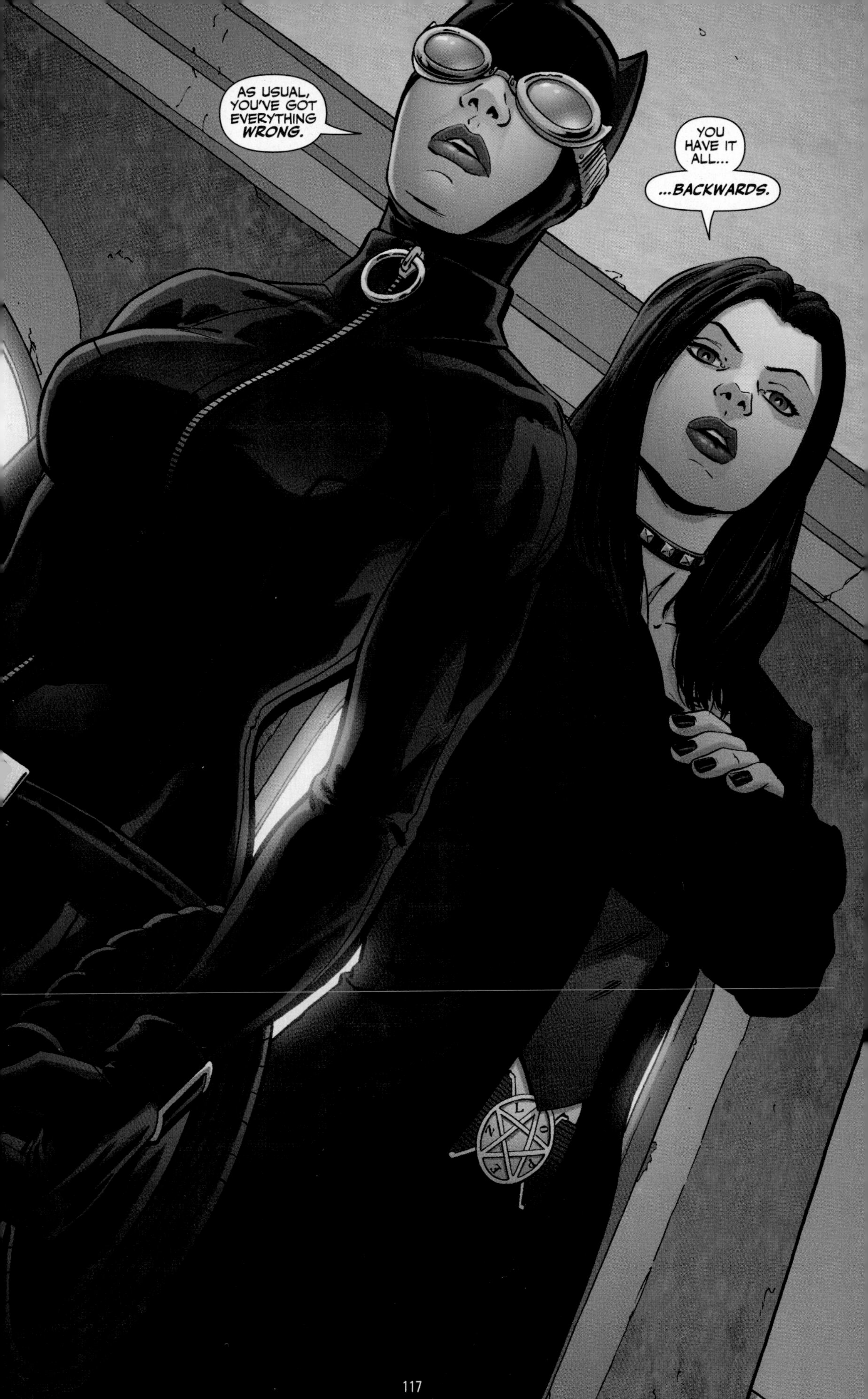

AS USUAL, YOU'VE GOT EVERYTHING *WRONG.*
YOU HAVE IT ALL...
...BACKWARDS.

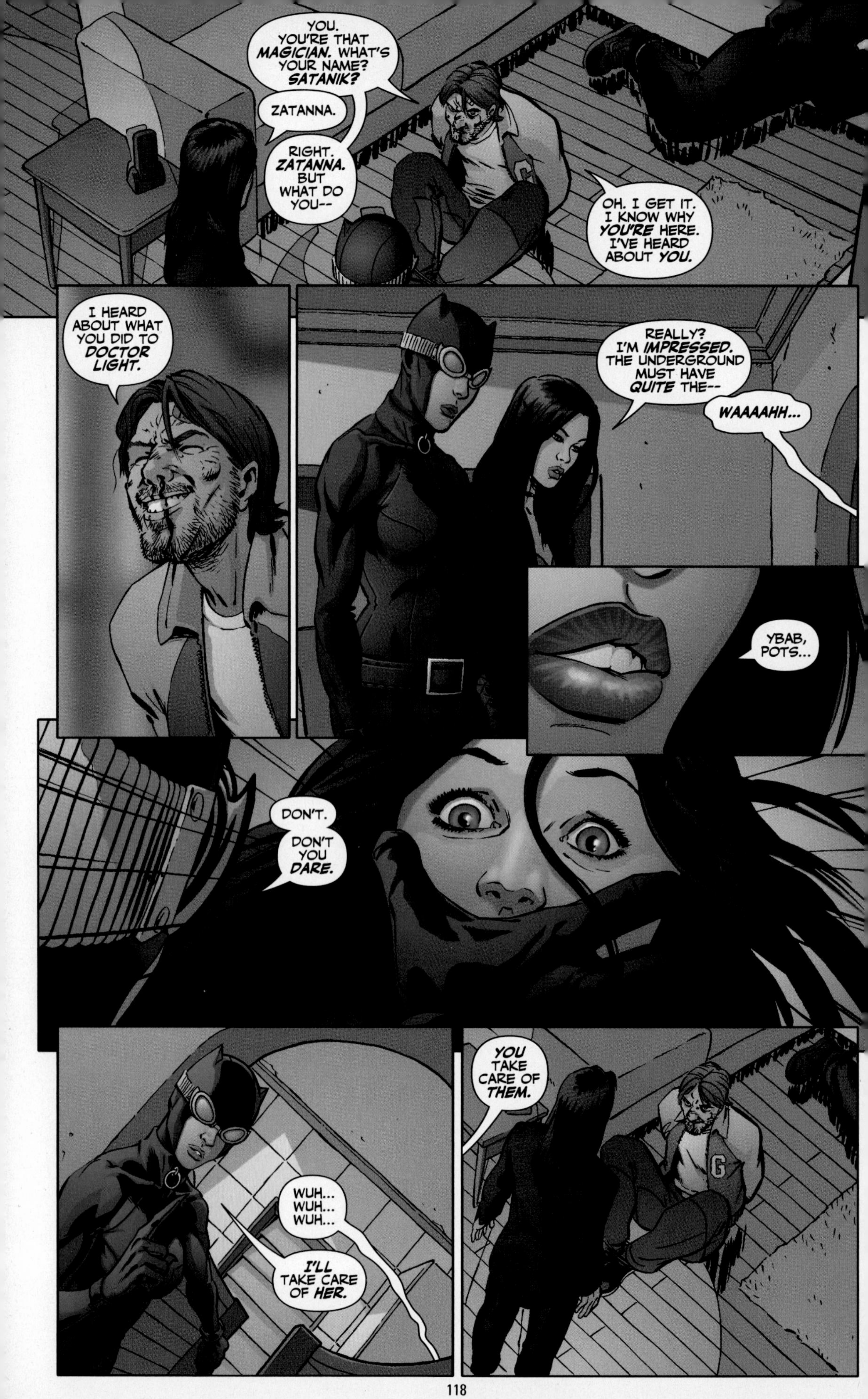
YOU. YOU'RE THAT MAGICIAN. WHAT'S YOUR NAME? SATANIK?
ZATANNA.
RIGHT. ZATANNA. BUT WHAT DO YOU--
OH. I GET IT. I KNOW WHY YOU'RE HERE. I'VE HEARD ABOUT YOU.
I HEARD ABOUT WHAT YOU DID TO DOCTOR LIGHT.
REALLY? I'M IMPRESSED. THE UNDERGROUND MUST HAVE QUITE THE--
WAAAAHH...
YBAB, POTS...
DON'T. DON'T YOU DARE.
WUH... WUH... WUH...
I'LL TAKE CARE OF HER.
YOU TAKE CARE OF THEM.

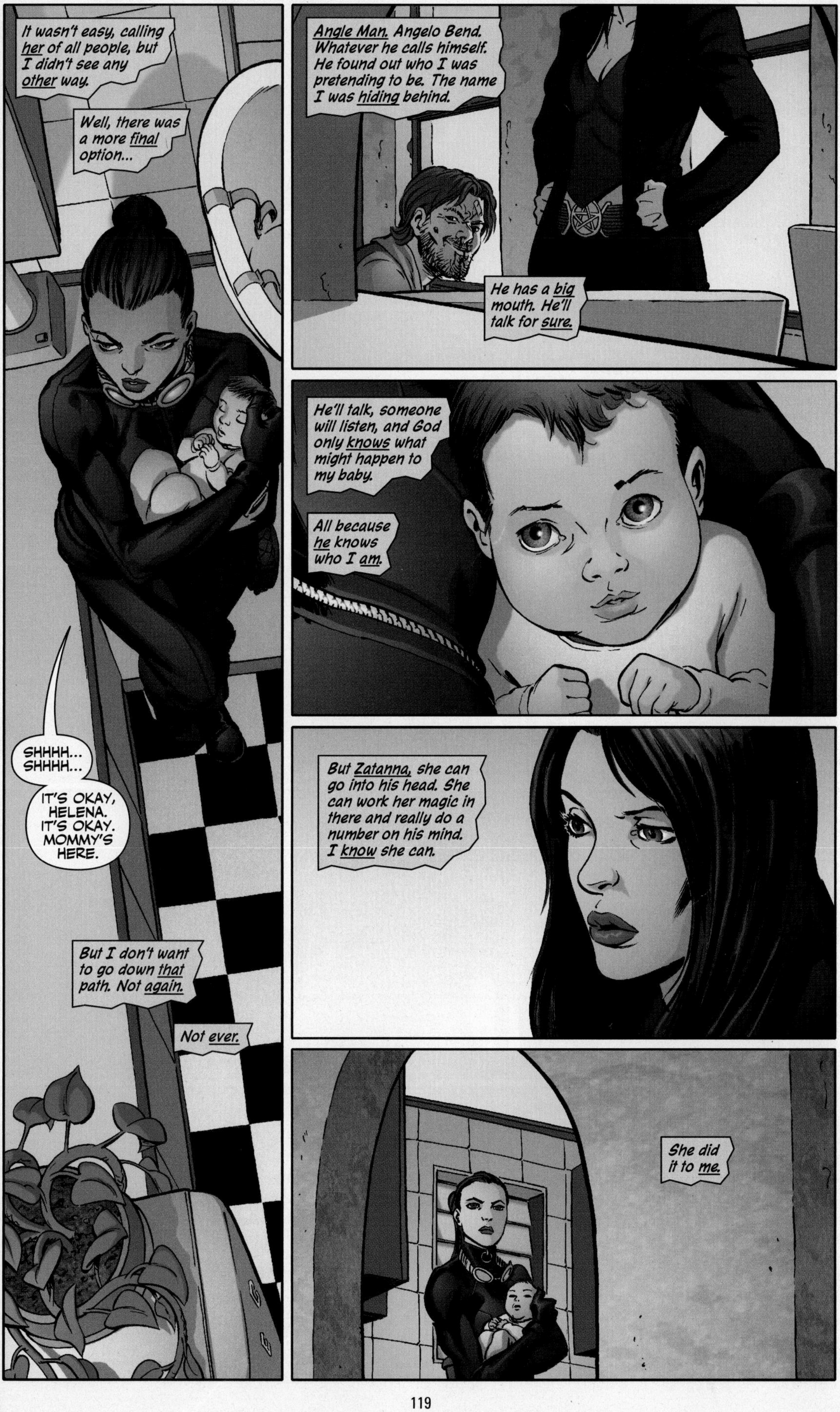
It wasn't easy, calling her of all people, but I didn't see any other way.
Well, there was a more final option...
SHHHH... SHHHH...
IT'S OKAY, HELENA. IT'S OKAY. MOMMY'S HERE.
But I don't want to go down that path. Not again.
Not ever.
Angle Man. Angelo Bend. Whatever he calls himself. He found out who I was pretending to be. The name I was hiding behind.
He has a big mouth. He'll talk for sure.
He'll talk, someone will listen, and God only knows what might happen to my baby.
All because he knows who I am.
But Zatanna, she can go into his head. She can work her magic in there and really do a number on his mind. I know she can.
She did it to me.

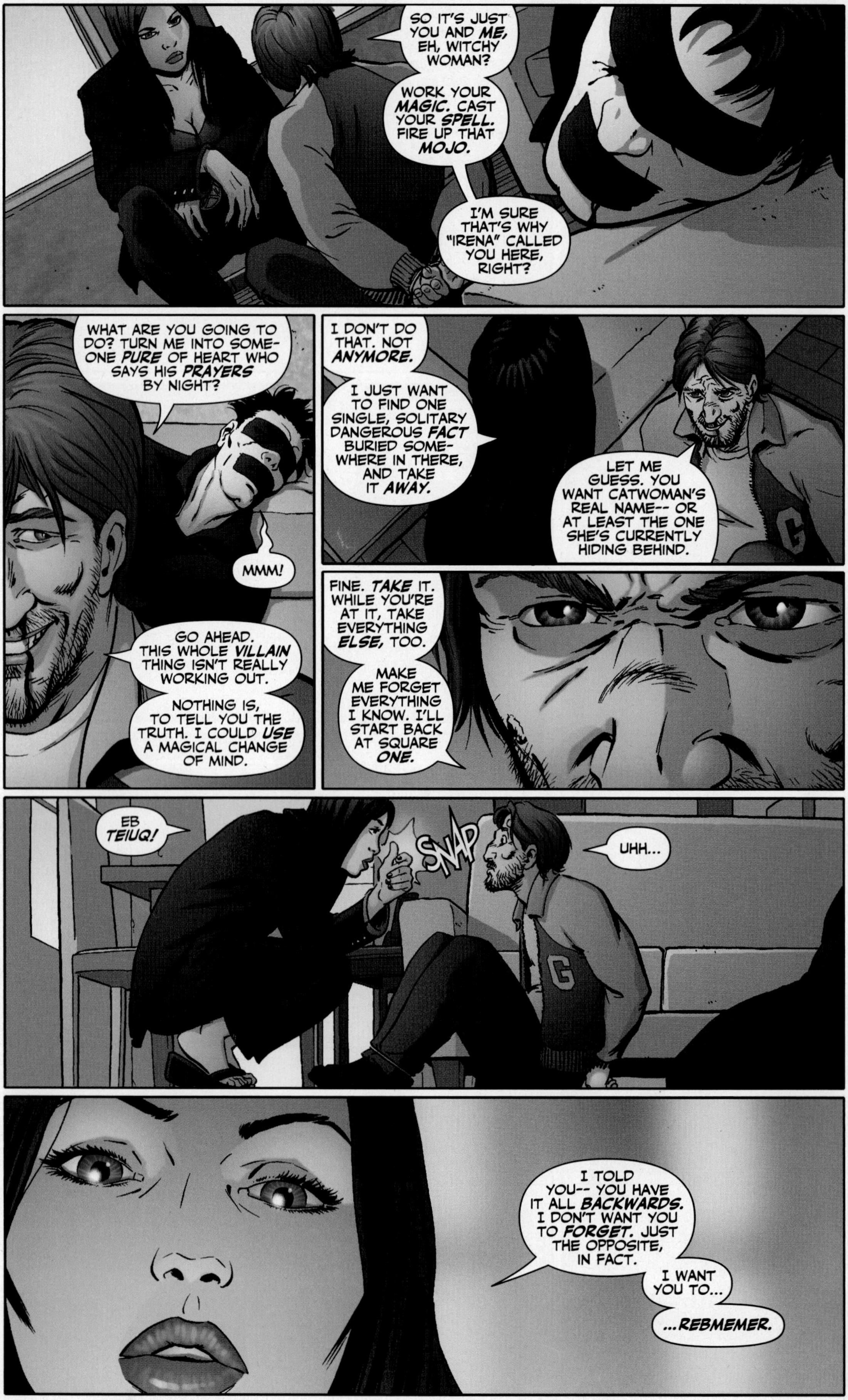
SO IT'S JUST YOU AND ME, EH, WITCHY WOMAN?
WORK YOUR MAGIC. CAST YOUR SPELL. FIRE UP THAT MOJO.
I'M SURE THAT'S WHY "IRENA" CALLED YOU HERE, RIGHT?
WHAT ARE YOU GOING TO DO? TURN ME INTO SOME-ONE PURE OF HEART WHO SAYS HIS PRAYERS BY NIGHT?
MMM!
GO AHEAD. THIS WHOLE VILLAIN THING ISN'T REALLY WORKING OUT.
NOTHING IS, TO TELL YOU THE TRUTH. I COULD USE A MAGICAL CHANGE OF MIND.
I DON'T DO THAT. NOT ANYMORE.
I JUST WANT TO FIND ONE SINGLE, SOLITARY DANGEROUS FACT BURIED SOME-WHERE IN THERE, AND TAKE IT AWAY.
LET ME GUESS. YOU WANT CATWOMAN'S REAL NAME-- OR AT LEAST THE ONE SHE'S CURRENTLY HIDING BEHIND.
FINE. TAKE IT. WHILE YOU'RE AT IT, TAKE EVERYTHING ELSE, TOO.
MAKE ME FORGET EVERYTHING I KNOW. I'LL START BACK AT SQUARE ONE.
EB TEIUQ!
SNAP
UHH...
I TOLD YOU-- YOU HAVE IT ALL BACKWARDS. I DON'T WANT YOU TO FORGET. JUST THE OPPOSITE, IN FACT.
I WANT YOU TO...
...REBMEMER.

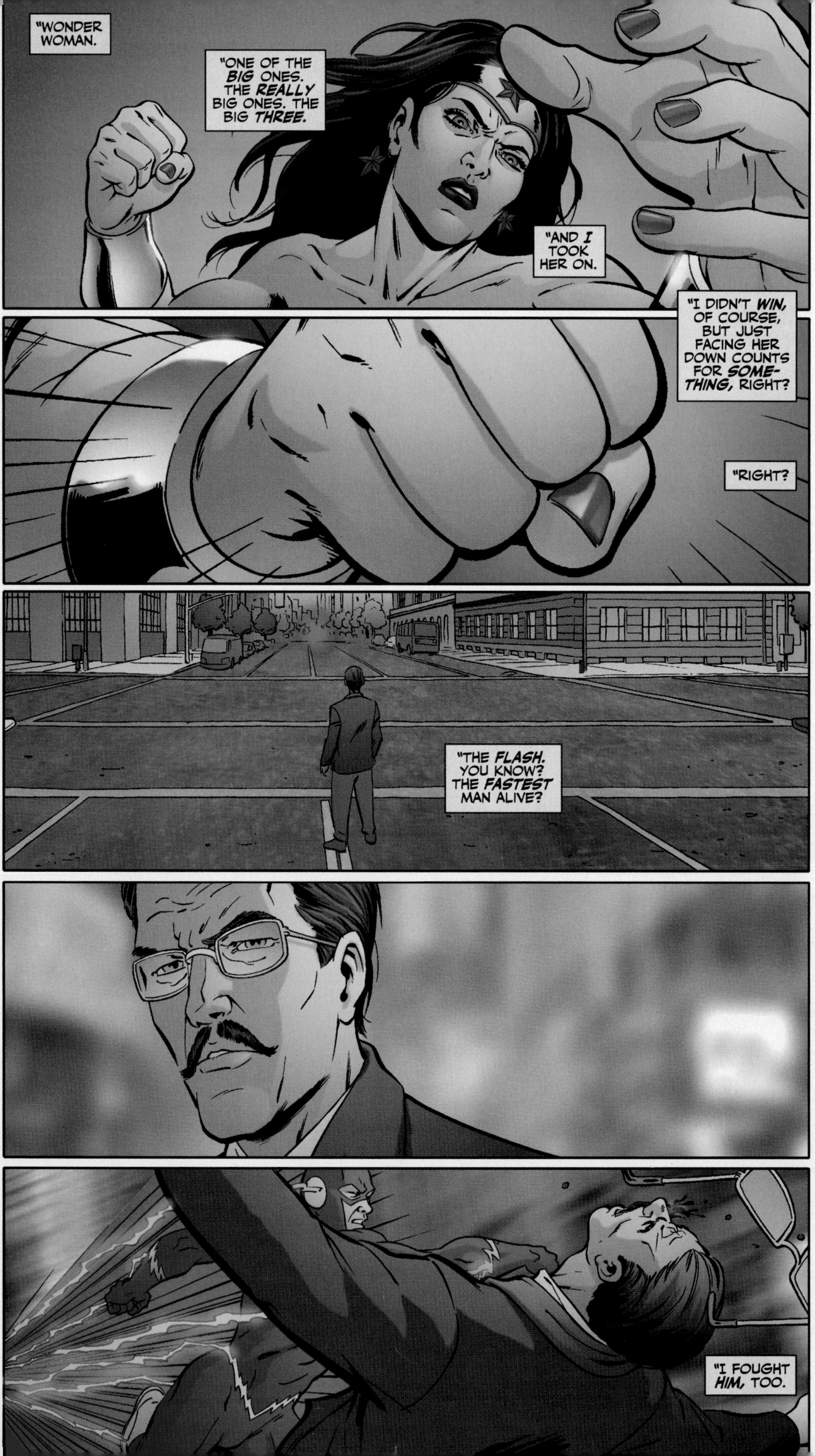
"WONDER WOMAN.
"ONE OF THE BIG ONES. THE REALLY BIG ONES. THE BIG THREE.
"AND I TOOK HER ON.
"I DIDN'T WIN, OF COURSE, BUT JUST FACING HER DOWN COUNTS FOR SOMETHING, RIGHT?
"RIGHT?
"THE FLASH. YOU KNOW? THE FASTEST MAN ALIVE?
"I FOUGHT HIM, TOO.

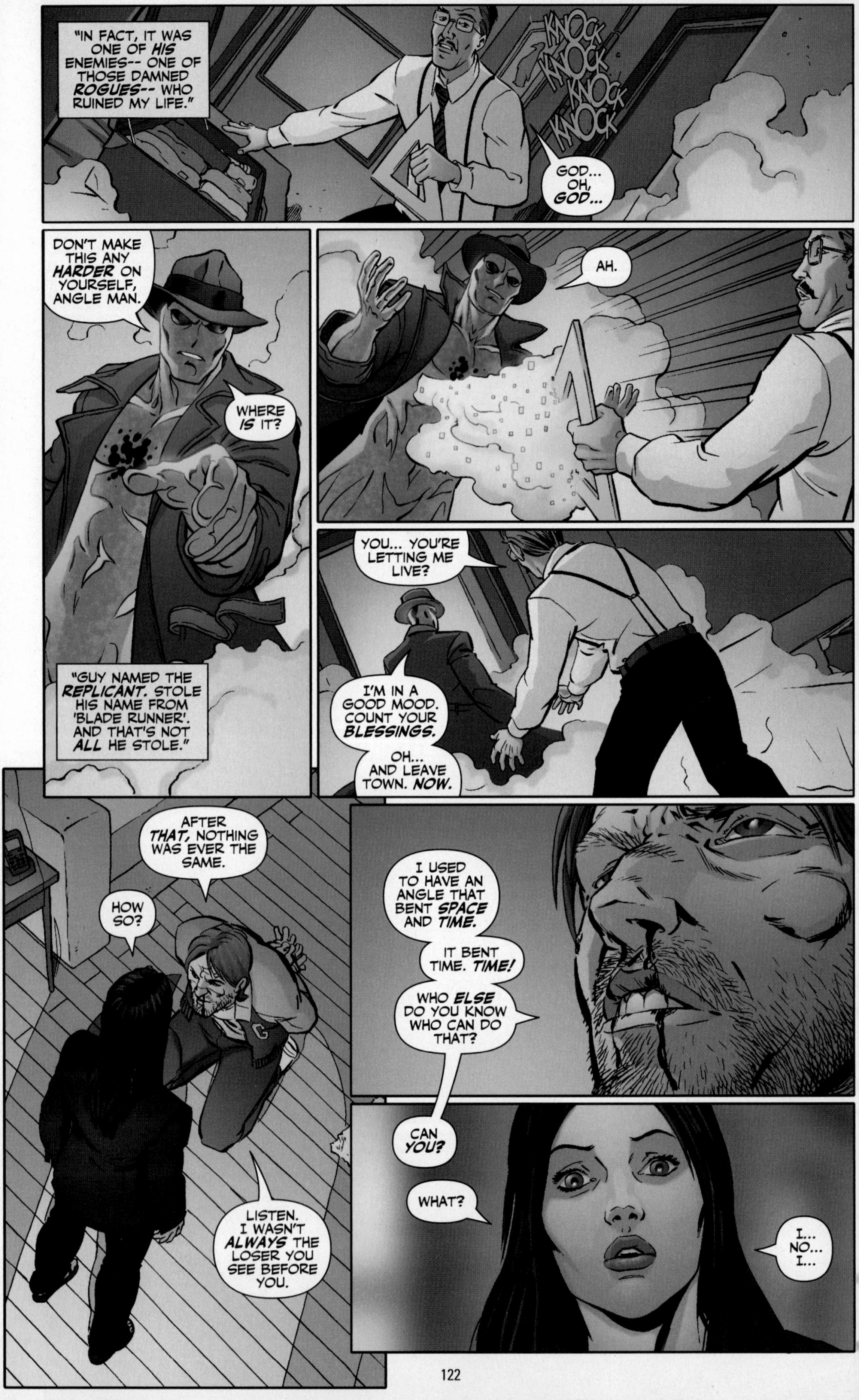
"IN FACT, IT WAS ONE OF HIS ENEMIES-- ONE OF THOSE DAMNED ROGUES-- WHO RUINED MY LIFE."
KNOCK KNOCK KNOCK KNOCK
GOD... OH, GOD...
DON'T MAKE THIS ANY HARDER ON YOURSELF, ANGLE MAN.
WHERE IS IT?
"GUY NAMED THE REPLICANT. STOLE HIS NAME FROM 'BLADE RUNNER'. AND THAT'S NOT ALL HE STOLE."
AH.
YOU... YOU'RE LETTING ME LIVE?
I'M IN A GOOD MOOD. COUNT YOUR BLESSINGS.
OH... AND LEAVE TOWN. NOW.
AFTER THAT, NOTHING WAS EVER THE SAME.
HOW SO?
LISTEN. I WASN'T ALWAYS THE LOSER YOU SEE BEFORE YOU.
I USED TO HAVE AN ANGLE THAT BENT SPACE AND TIME.
IT BENT TIME. TIME!
WHO ELSE DO YOU KNOW WHO CAN DO THAT?
CAN YOU?
WHAT?
I... NO... I...

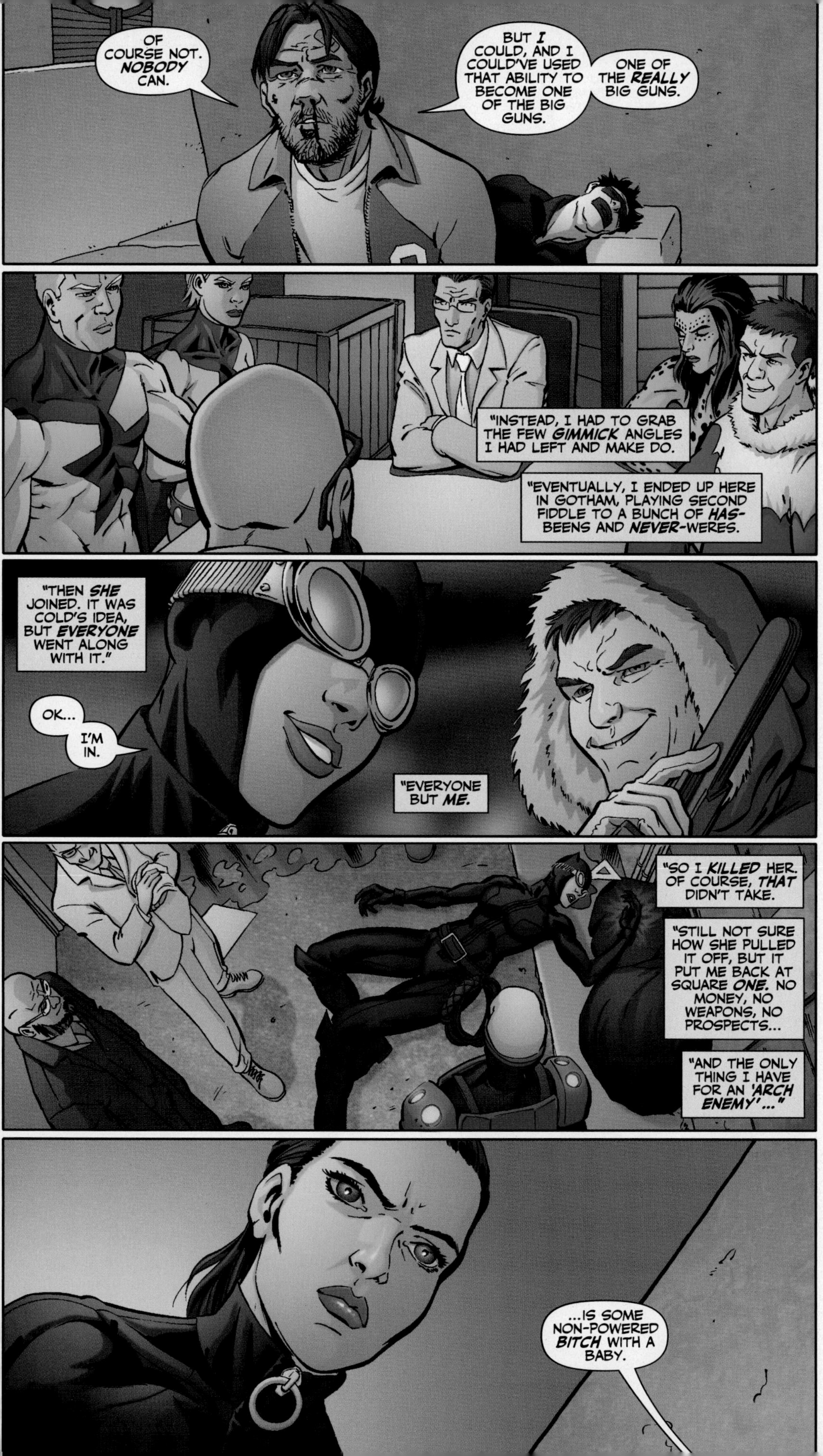
OF COURSE NOT. NOBODY CAN.
BUT I COULD, AND I COULD'VE USED THAT ABILITY TO BECOME ONE OF THE BIG GUNS.
ONE OF THE REALLY BIG GUNS.
"INSTEAD, I HAD TO GRAB THE FEW GIMMICK ANGLES I HAD LEFT AND MAKE DO.
"EVENTUALLY, I ENDED UP HERE IN GOTHAM, PLAYING SECOND FIDDLE TO A BUNCH OF HAS-BEENS AND NEVER-WERES.
"THEN SHE JOINED. IT WAS COLD'S IDEA, BUT EVERYONE WENT ALONG WITH IT."
OK...
I'M IN.
"EVERYONE BUT ME.
"SO I KILLED HER. OF COURSE, THAT DIDN'T TAKE.
"STILL NOT SURE HOW SHE PULLED IT OFF, BUT IT PUT ME BACK AT SQUARE ONE. NO MONEY, NO WEAPONS, NO PROSPECTS...
"AND THE ONLY THING I HAVE FOR AN 'ARCH ENEMY'...
...IS SOME NON-POWERED BITCH WITH A BABY.

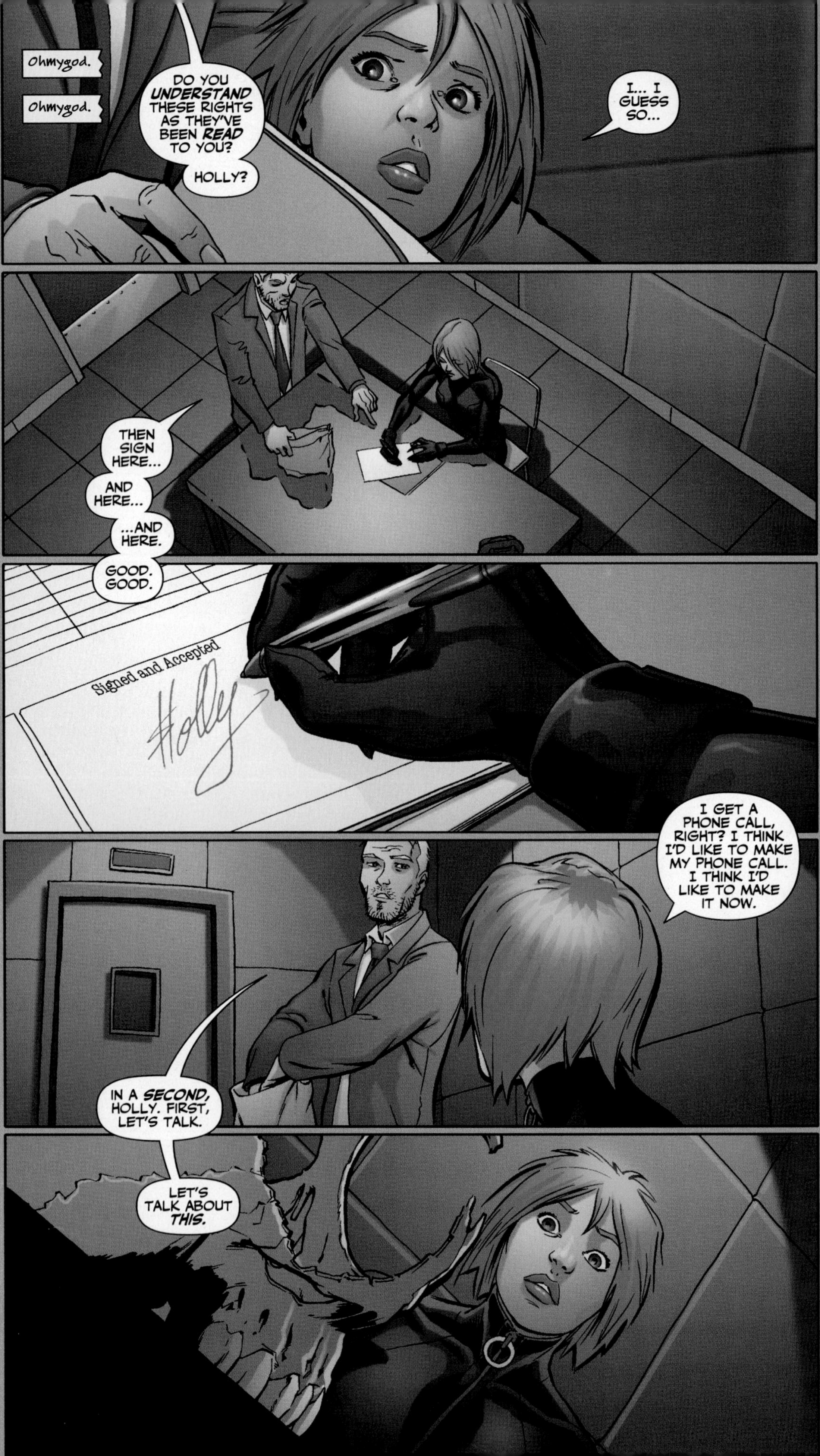
Ohmygod.
Ohmygod.
DO YOU UNDERSTAND THESE RIGHTS AS THEY'VE BEEN READ TO YOU?
HOLLY?
I... I GUESS SO...
THEN SIGN HERE...
AND HERE...
...AND HERE.
GOOD. GOOD.
Signed and Accepted
Holly
I GET A PHONE CALL, RIGHT? I THINK I'D LIKE TO MAKE MY PHONE CALL. I THINK I'D LIKE TO MAKE IT NOW.
IN A SECOND, HOLLY. FIRST, LET'S TALK.
LET'S TALK ABOUT THIS.

I THOUGHT ALL YOU HAD TO DO WAS MUMBLE A FEW WORDS *BACKWARDS* AND HIS MIND WOULD BE *WIPED.*

WHAT'S *TAKING* SO LONG?

IT *ALWAYS* TAKES LONG. EVEN WITH MAGIC, YOU HAVE TO FIND OUT WHERE THE INFORMATION IS BEFORE YOU CAN *REMOVE* IT.

YOU, FOR INSTANCE, TOOK AT *LEAST* EIGHT HOURS.

WHY DO YOU THINK WE WENT TO ALL THE *TROUBLE* OF TAKING YOU UP TO THE LEAGUE'S *SATELLITE?*

I'M *FLATTERED.*

BUT BEFORE I SET MY *BABY* DOWN AND CLAW YOUR EYES OUT IN *GRATITUDE,* LET'S *CHANGE* THE SUBJECT.

LET'S.

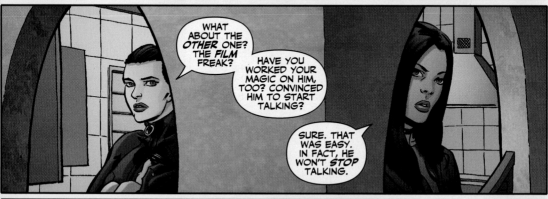

WHAT ABOUT THE *OTHER* ONE? THE *FILM* FREAK?

HAVE YOU WORKED YOUR MAGIC ON HIM, TOO? CONVINCED HIM TO START TALKING?

SURE. THAT WAS EASY. IN FACT, HE WON'T *STOP* TALKING.

WAIT A MINUTE... WAIT A MINUTE...

YOU AIN'T HEARD NOTHING YET...

WHAT HE'S TALKING *ABOUT,* THOUGH...

I HAVE *NO* IDEA.

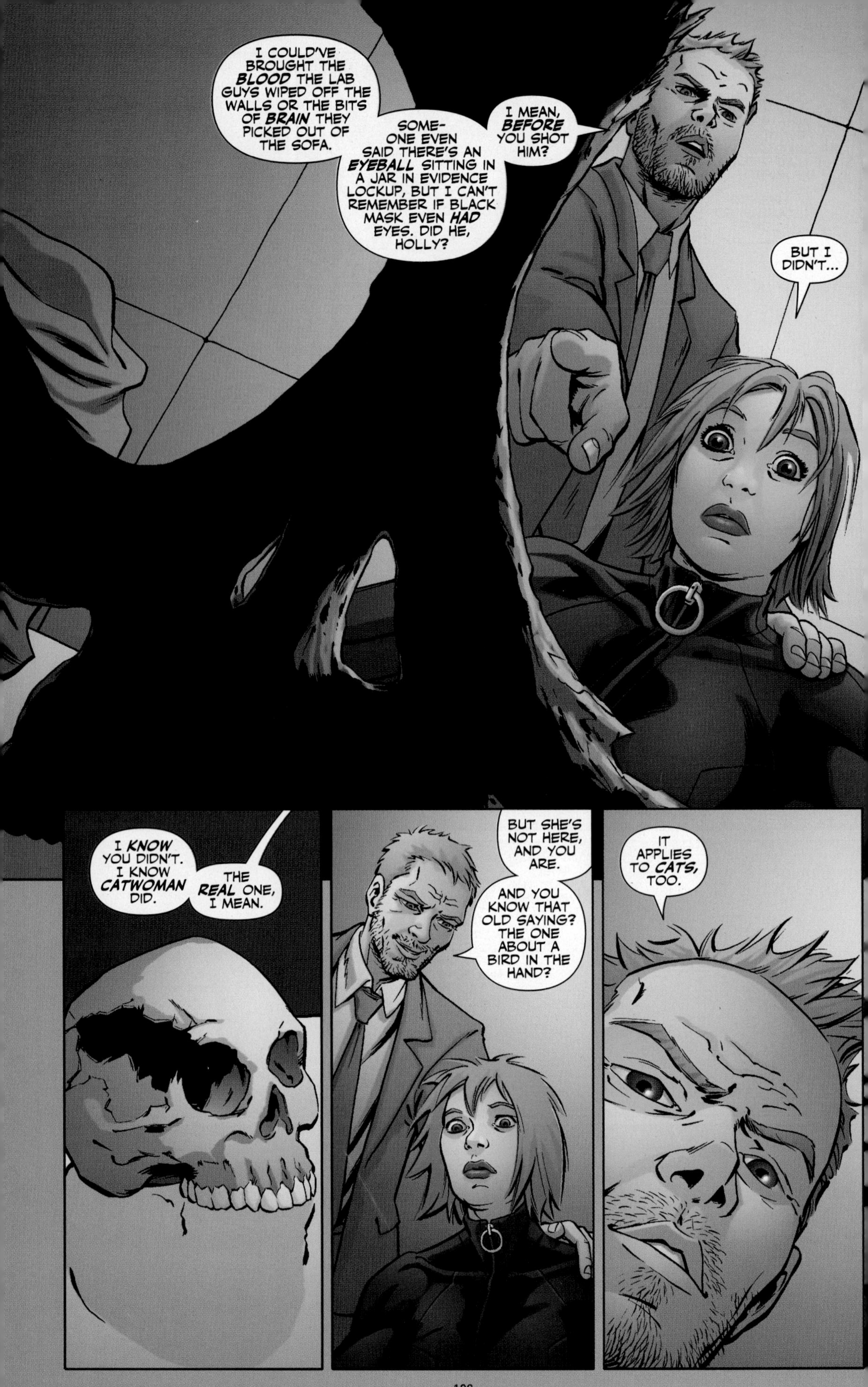
I COULD'VE BROUGHT THE BLOOD THE LAB GUYS WIPED OFF THE WALLS OR THE BITS OF BRAIN THEY PICKED OUT OF THE SOFA.
SOME-ONE EVEN SAID THERE'S AN EYEBALL SITTING IN A JAR IN EVIDENCE LOCKUP, BUT I CAN'T REMEMBER IF BLACK MASK EVEN HAD EYES. DID HE, HOLLY?
I MEAN, BEFORE YOU SHOT HIM?
BUT I DIDN'T...
I KNOW YOU DIDN'T. I KNOW CATWOMAN DID.
THE REAL ONE, I MEAN.
BUT SHE'S NOT HERE, AND YOU ARE.
AND YOU KNOW THAT OLD SAYING? THE ONE ABOUT A BIRD IN THE HAND?
IT APPLIES TO CATS, TOO.

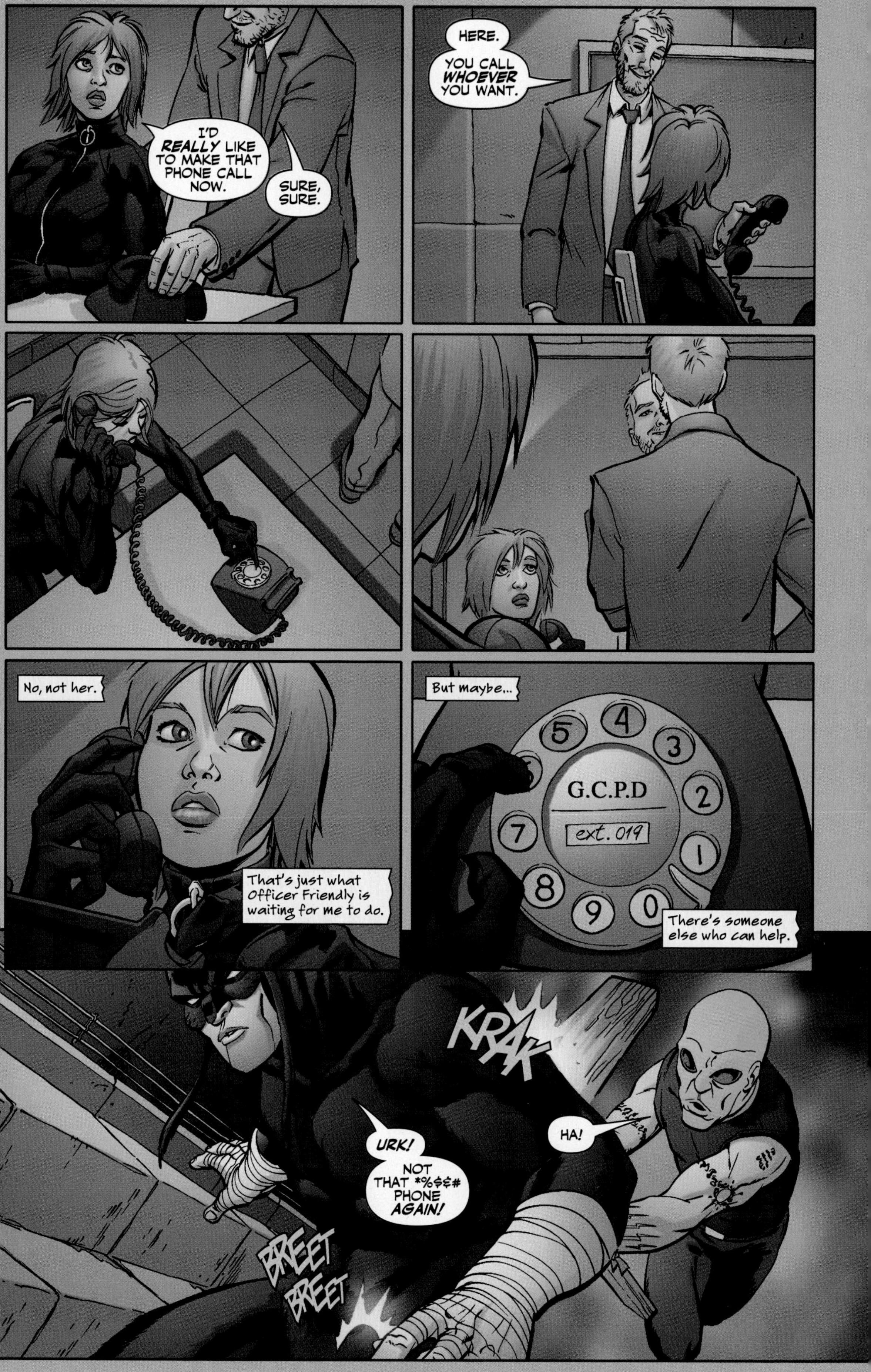
I'D REALLY LIKE TO MAKE THAT PHONE CALL NOW.
SURE, SURE.
HERE.
YOU CALL WHOEVER YOU WANT.
No, not her.
That's just what Officer Friendly is waiting for me to do.
But maybe...
G.C.P.D
ext. 019
There's someone else who can help.
KRAK
HA!
URK!
NOT THAT *%$&# PHONE AGAIN!
BREET BREET

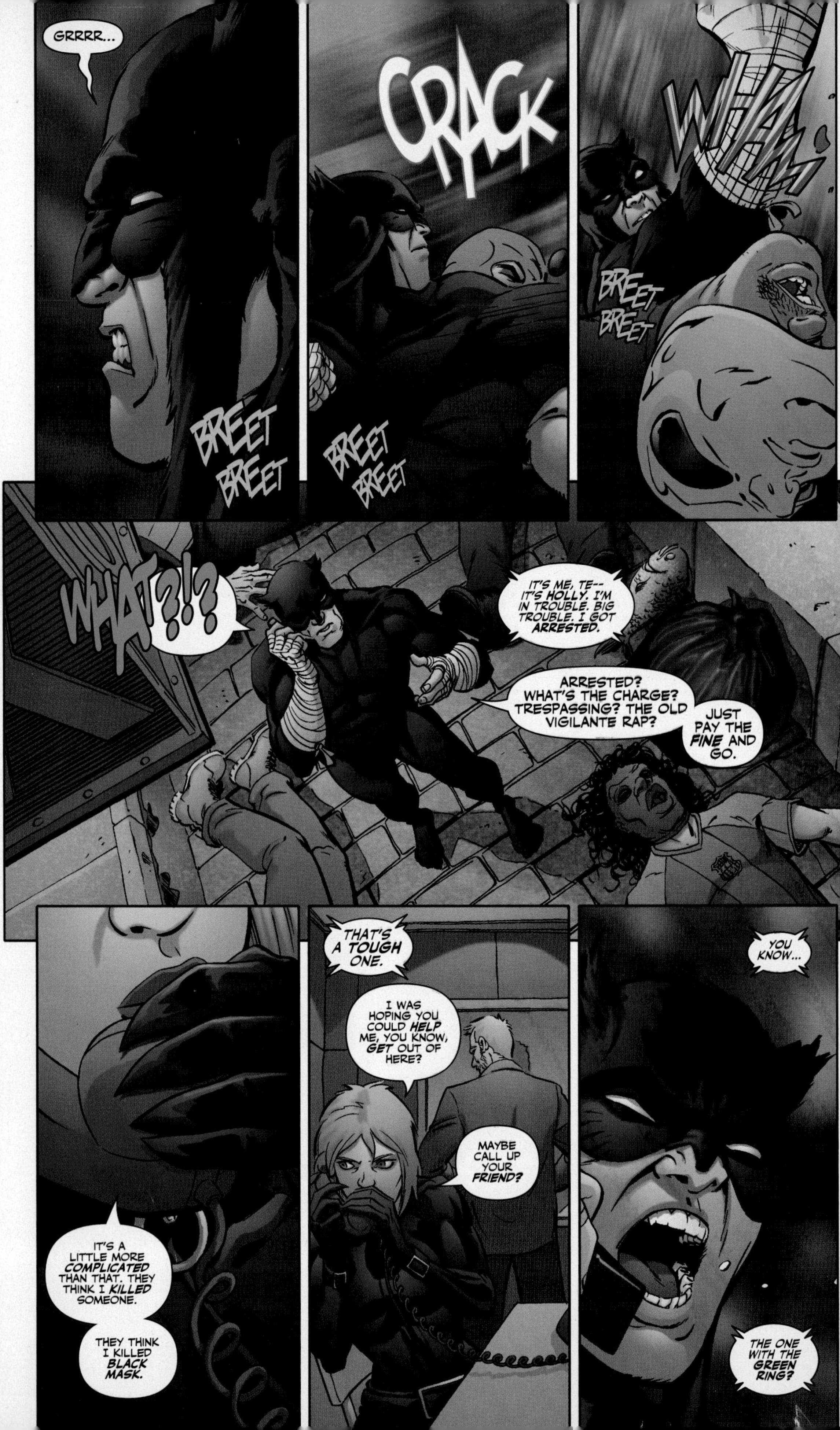
GRRRR...
BREET BREET
CRACK
BREET BREET
WHAM
BREET BREET
WHAT?!?
IT'S ME, TE-- IT'S HOLLY. I'M IN TROUBLE. BIG TROUBLE. I GOT ARRESTED.
ARRESTED? WHAT'S THE CHARGE? TRESPASSING? THE OLD VIGILANTE RAP?
JUST PAY THE FINE AND GO.
IT'S A LITTLE MORE COMPLICATED THAN THAT. THEY THINK I KILLED SOMEONE.
THEY THINK I KILLED BLACK MASK.
THAT'S A TOUGH ONE.
I WAS HOPING YOU COULD HELP ME, YOU KNOW, GET OUT OF HERE?
MAYBE CALL UP YOUR FRIEND?
YOU KNOW...
THE ONE WITH THE GREEN RING?

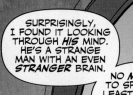

FINISHED? FINALLY?

SURPRISINGLY, I FOUND IT LOOKING THROUGH *HIS* MIND. HE'S A STRANGE MAN WITH AN EVEN *STRANGER* BRAIN.

NO *MEMORIES* TO SPEAK OF, AT LEAST NOT IN THE *NORMAL* SENSE. JUST FILM CLIP AFTER FILM CLIP AFTER FILM CLIP.

IT WAS LIKE A *MASTER* CINEMA HISTORY CLASS, EVERY GENRE AND ERA COVERED IN *DETAIL.* EVENTUALLY WE GOT TO 1942-- AND "CAT PEOPLE"...

AND "*IRENA* DUBROVNA," THE LEAD CHARACTER'S NAME.

YES. "*FINALLY.*"

I *TOLD* YOU IT WOULD TAKE A WHILE TO *FIND* THE INFORMATION THEY HAD ON YOU... "IRENA."

VAL LEWTON. NICE.

THOUGH *PERSONALLY,* I'VE ALWAYS PREFERRED HIS MORE OBSCURE FILM, "THE SEVENTH VICTIM."

SUICIDE AND *SATANISM* IN 1940s GREENWICH VILLAGE. *YOU* WOULD.

BUT YOU DID IT, RIGHT? YOU MADE THEM *FORGET* WHAT THEY KNEW ABOUT ME, RIGHT? ABOUT ME AND MY *BABY?*

OF COURSE.

AS FAR AS *THEY'RE* CONCERNED, YOUR NAME IS *CATWOMAN,* AND IRENA DUBROVNA IS JUST A *CHARACTER* IN AN OLD MOVIE.

BE GLAD THEY NEVER DISCOVERED WHO "*SELINA KYLE*" IS.

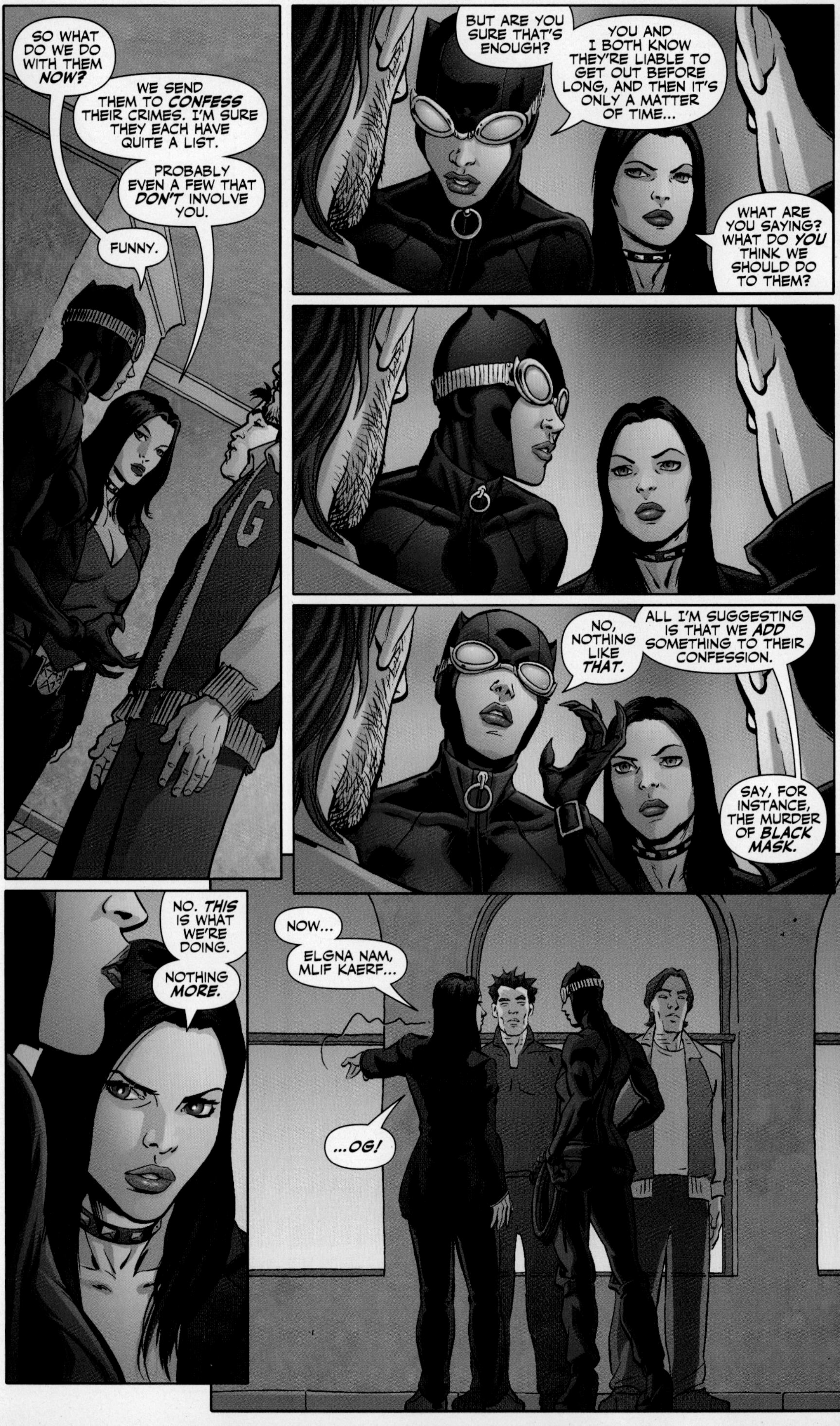
SO WHAT DO WE DO WITH THEM NOW?
WE SEND THEM TO CONFESS THEIR CRIMES. I'M SURE THEY EACH HAVE QUITE A LIST.
PROBABLY EVEN A FEW THAT DON'T INVOLVE YOU.
FUNNY.
BUT ARE YOU SURE THAT'S ENOUGH?
YOU AND I BOTH KNOW THEY'RE LIABLE TO GET OUT BEFORE LONG, AND THEN IT'S ONLY A MATTER OF TIME...
WHAT ARE YOU SAYING? WHAT DO YOU THINK WE SHOULD DO TO THEM?
NO, NOTHING LIKE THAT.
ALL I'M SUGGESTING IS THAT WE ADD SOMETHING TO THEIR CONFESSION.
SAY, FOR INSTANCE, THE MURDER OF BLACK MASK.
NO. THIS IS WHAT WE'RE DOING.
NOTHING MORE.
NOW...
ELGNA NAM, MLIF KAERF...
...OG!

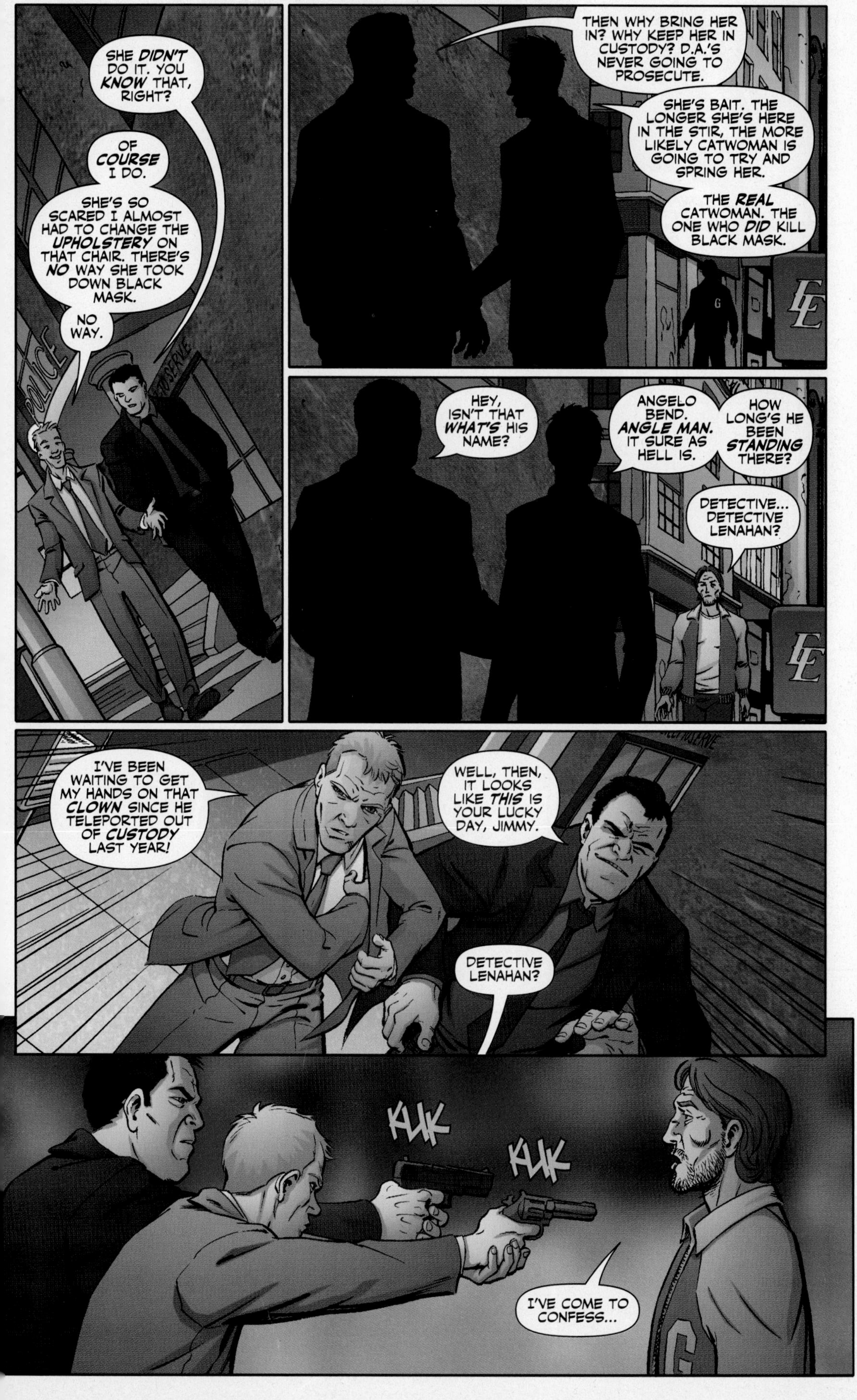
SHE DIDN'T DO IT. YOU KNOW THAT, RIGHT?
OF COURSE I DO.
SHE'S SO SCARED I ALMOST HAD TO CHANGE THE UPHOLSTERY ON THAT CHAIR. THERE'S NO WAY SHE TOOK DOWN BLACK MASK.
NO WAY.
THEN WHY BRING HER IN? WHY KEEP HER IN CUSTODY? D.A.'S NEVER GOING TO PROSECUTE.
SHE'S BAIT. THE LONGER SHE'S HERE IN THE STIR, THE MORE LIKELY CATWOMAN IS GOING TO TRY AND SPRING HER.
THE REAL CATWOMAN. THE ONE WHO DID KILL BLACK MASK.
HEY, ISN'T THAT WHAT'S HIS NAME?
ANGELO BEND. ANGLE MAN. IT SURE AS HELL IS.
HOW LONG'S HE BEEN STANDING THERE?
DETECTIVE... DETECTIVE LENAHAN?
I'VE BEEN WAITING TO GET MY HANDS ON THAT CLOWN SINCE HE TELEPORTED OUT OF CUSTODY LAST YEAR!
WELL, THEN, IT LOOKS LIKE THIS IS YOUR LUCKY DAY, JIMMY.
DETECTIVE LENAHAN?
KLIK
KLIK
I'VE COME TO CONFESS...

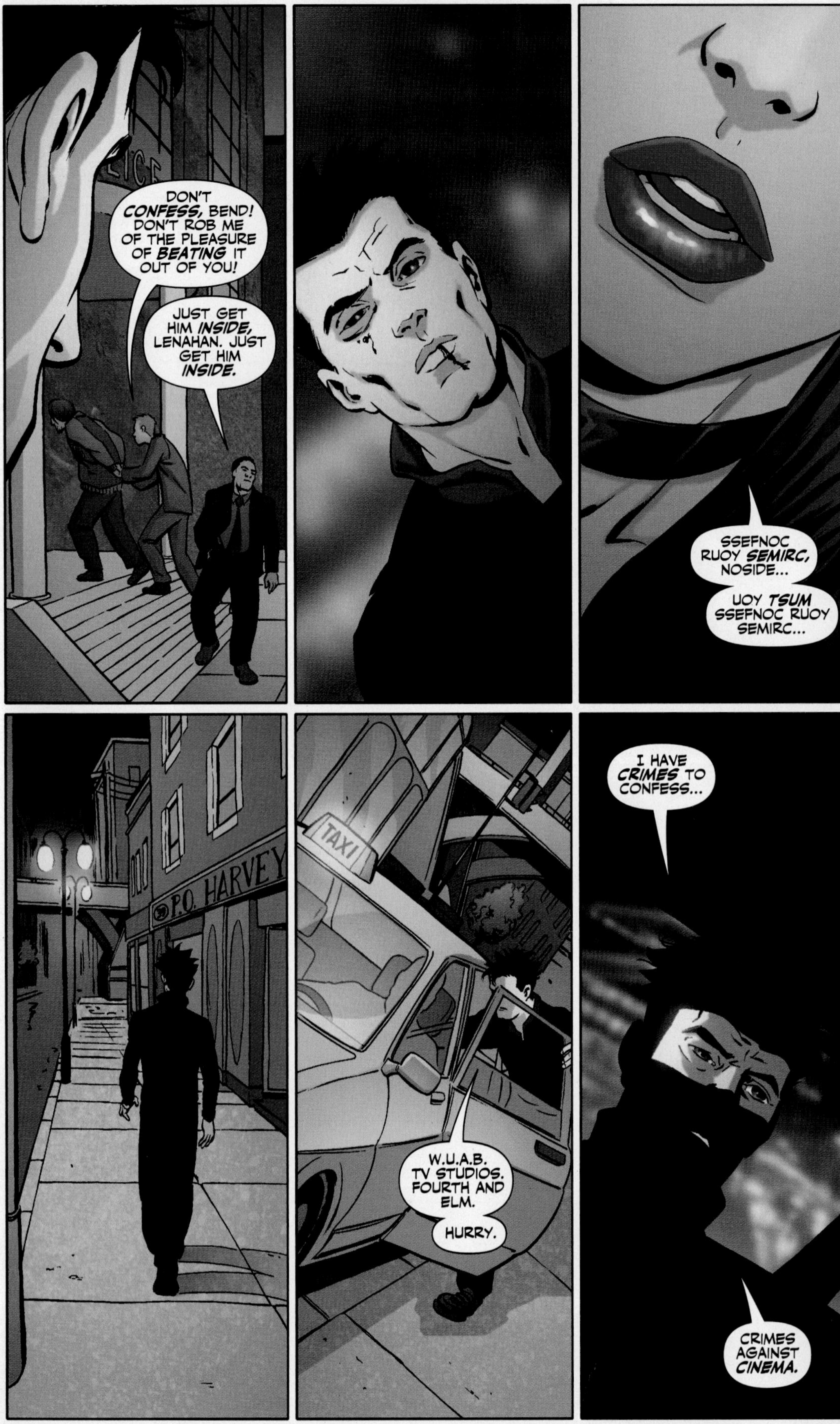
DON'T CONFESS, BEND! DON'T ROB ME OF THE PLEASURE OF BEATING IT OUT OF YOU!
JUST GET HIM INSIDE, LENAHAN. JUST GET HIM INSIDE.
SSEFNOC RUOY SEMIRC, NOSIDE...
UOY TSUM SSEFNOC RUOY SEMIRC...
P.O. HARVEY
TAXI
W.U.A.B. TV STUDIOS. FOURTH AND ELM.
HURRY.
I HAVE CRIMES TO CONFESS...
CRIMES AGAINST CINEMA.

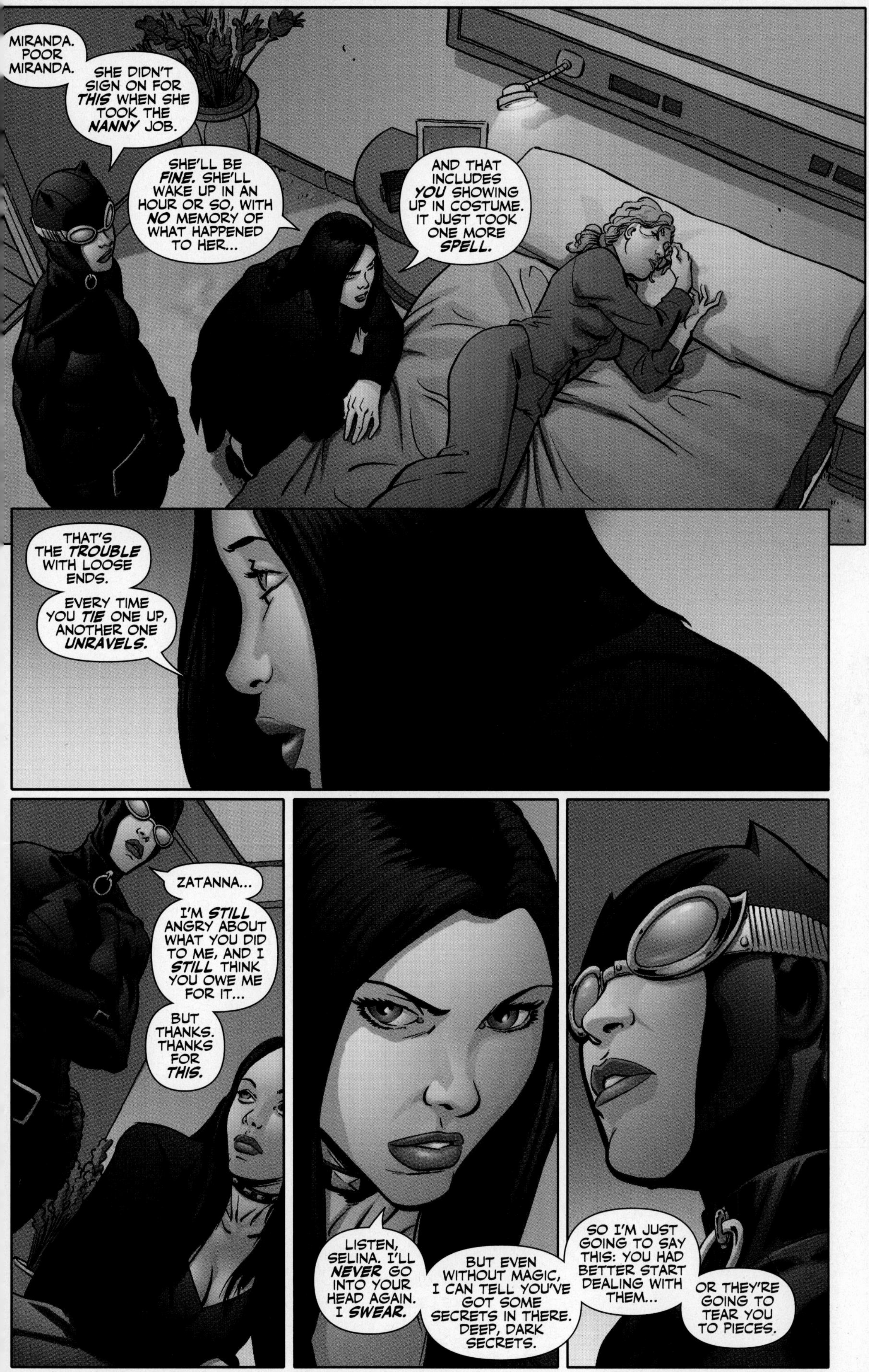
MIRANDA. POOR MIRANDA.
SHE DIDN'T SIGN ON FOR THIS WHEN SHE TOOK THE NANNY JOB.
SHE'LL BE FINE. SHE'LL WAKE UP IN AN HOUR OR SO, WITH NO MEMORY OF WHAT HAPPENED TO HER...
AND THAT INCLUDES YOU SHOWING UP IN COSTUME. IT JUST TOOK ONE MORE SPELL.
THAT'S THE TROUBLE WITH LOOSE ENDS.
EVERY TIME YOU TIE ONE UP, ANOTHER ONE UNRAVELS.
ZATANNA...
I'M STILL ANGRY ABOUT WHAT YOU DID TO ME, AND I STILL THINK YOU OWE ME FOR IT...
BUT THANKS. THANKS FOR THIS.
LISTEN, SELINA. I'LL NEVER GO INTO YOUR HEAD AGAIN. I SWEAR.
BUT EVEN WITHOUT MAGIC, I CAN TELL YOU'VE GOT SOME SECRETS IN THERE. DEEP, DARK SECRETS.
SO I'M JUST GOING TO SAY THIS: YOU HAD BETTER START DEALING WITH THEM...
OR THEY'RE GOING TO TEAR YOU TO PIECES.

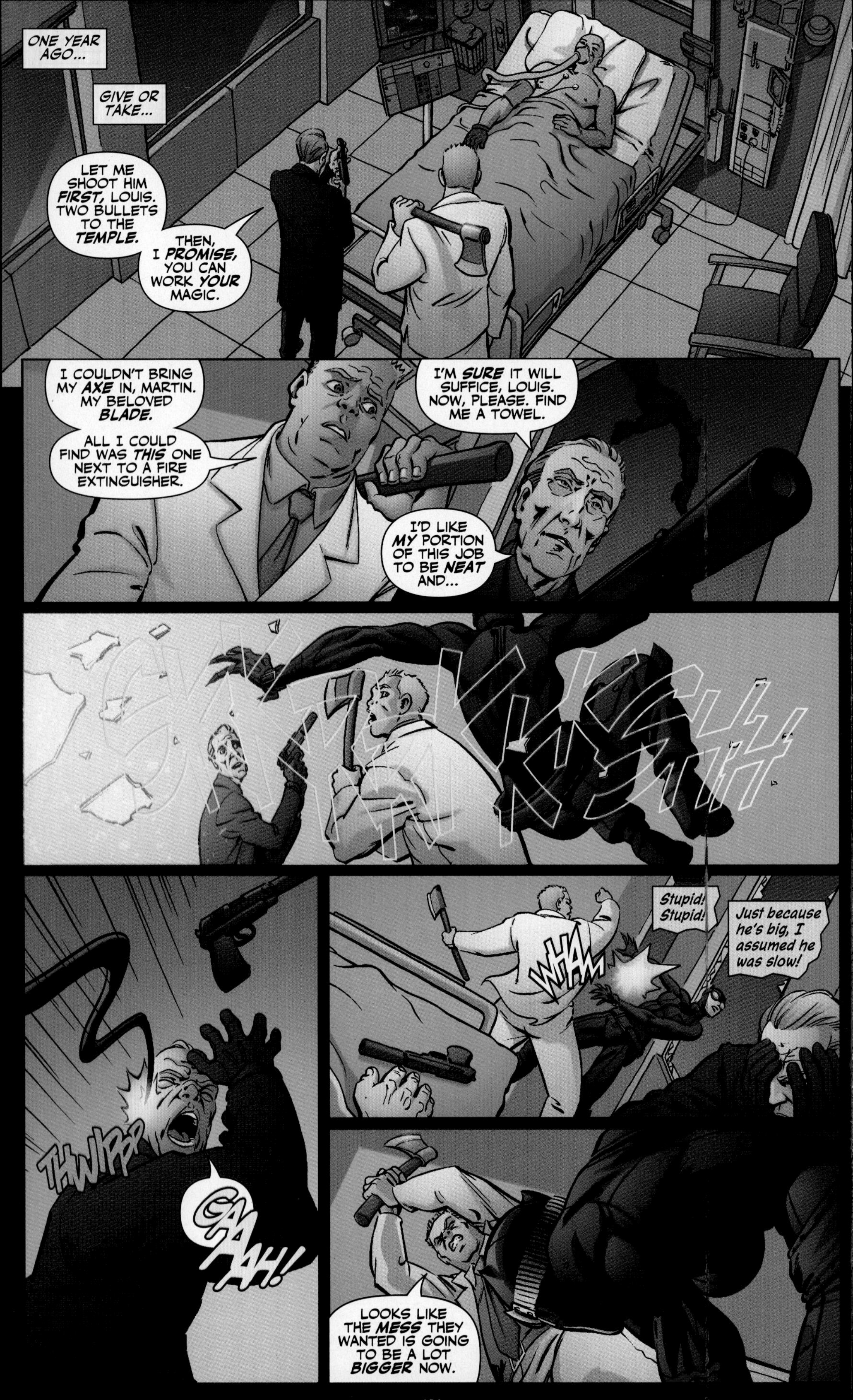
ONE YEAR AGO...
GIVE OR TAKE...
LET ME SHOOT HIM *FIRST*, LOUIS. TWO BULLETS TO THE *TEMPLE*.
THEN, I *PROMISE*, YOU CAN WORK *YOUR* MAGIC.
I COULDN'T BRING MY *AXE* IN, MARTIN. MY BELOVED *BLADE*.
ALL I COULD FIND WAS *THIS* ONE NEXT TO A FIRE EXTINGUISHER.
I'M *SURE* IT WILL SUFFICE, LOUIS. NOW, PLEASE. FIND ME A TOWEL.
I'D LIKE *MY* PORTION OF THIS JOB TO BE *NEAT* AND...
SKRAKKSSH
THWIPP
GAAAH!
WHAM
Stupid! Stupid!
Just because he's big, I assumed he was slow!
LOOKS LIKE THE *MESS* THEY WANTED IS GOING TO BE A LOT *BIGGER* NOW.

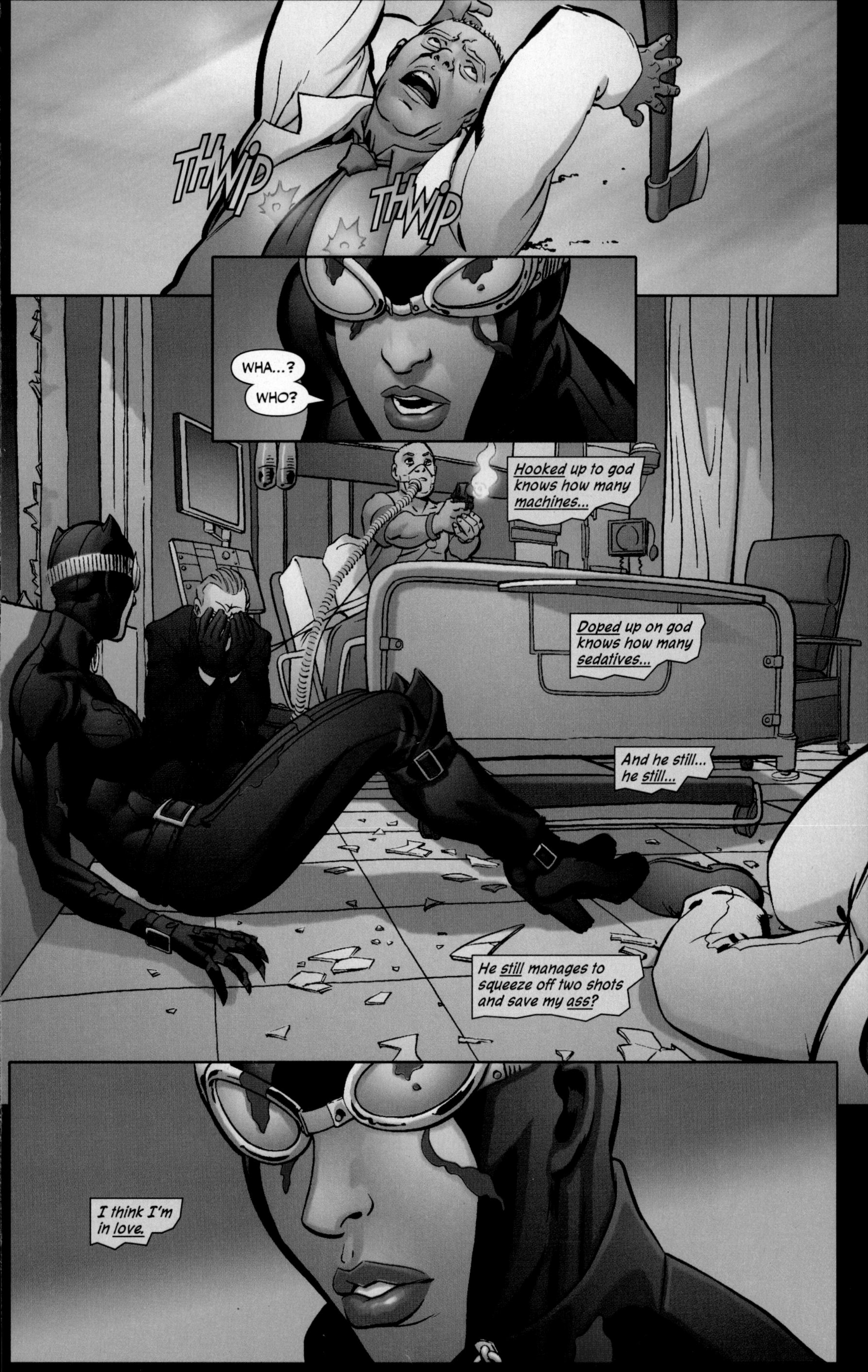
THWIP
THWIP
WHA...?
WHO?
Hooked up to god knows how many machines...
Doped up on god knows how many sedatives...
And he still... he still...
He still manages to squeeze off two shots and save my ass?
I think I'm in love.

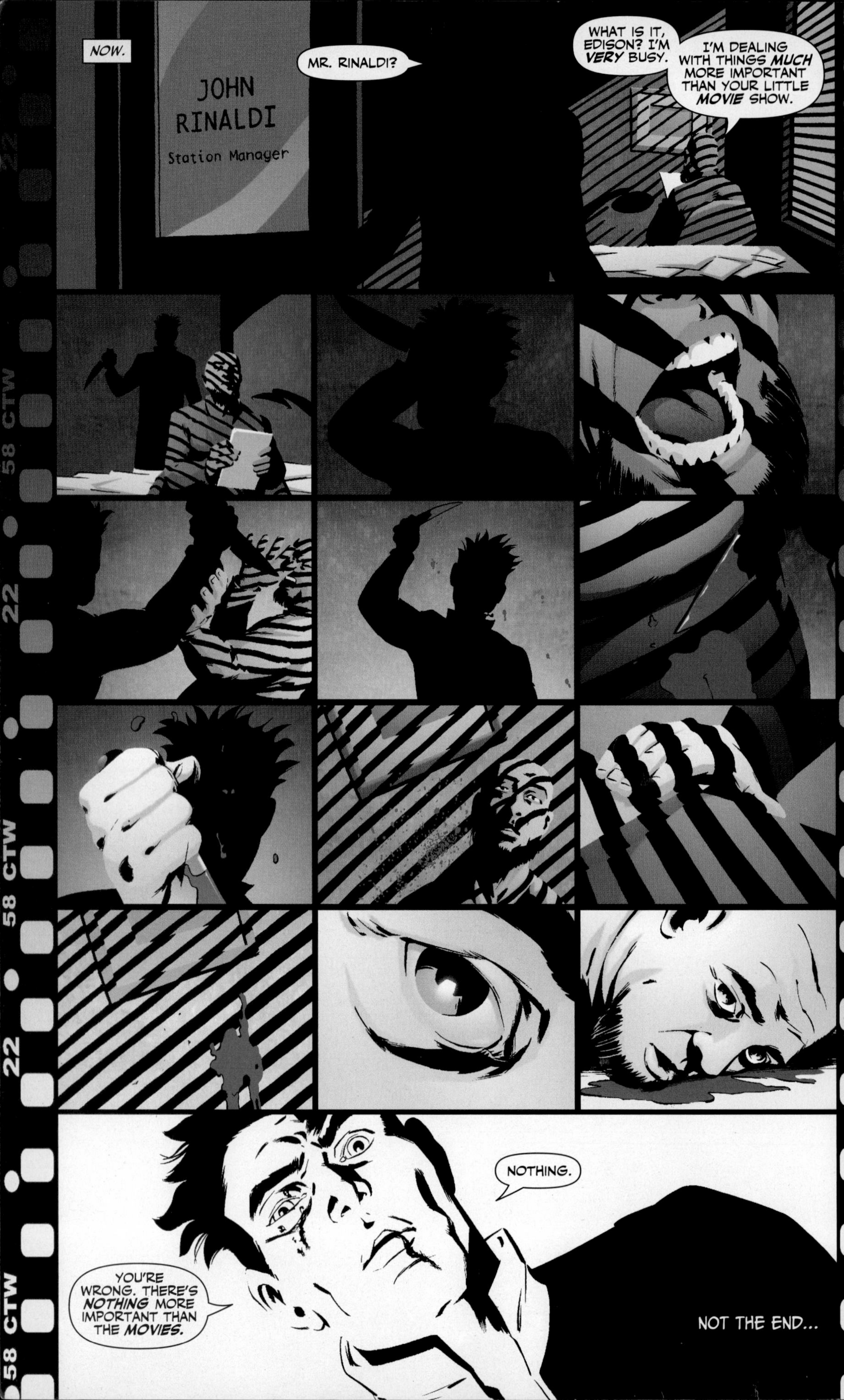
NOW.
JOHN RINALDI
Station Manager
MR. RINALDI?
WHAT IS IT, EDISON? I'M VERY BUSY.
I'M DEALING WITH THINGS MUCH MORE IMPORTANT THAN YOUR LITTLE MOVIE SHOW.
NOTHING.
YOU'RE WRONG. THERE'S NOTHING MORE IMPORTANT THAN THE MOVIES.
NOT THE END...

CAT WOMAN

THE REPLACEMENTS

COVER GALLERY

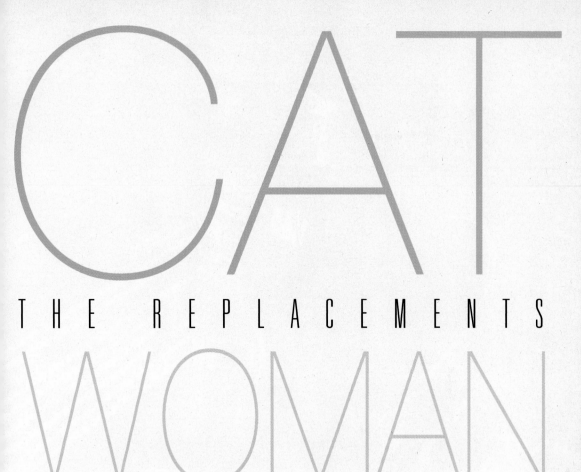

BY ADAM HUGHES

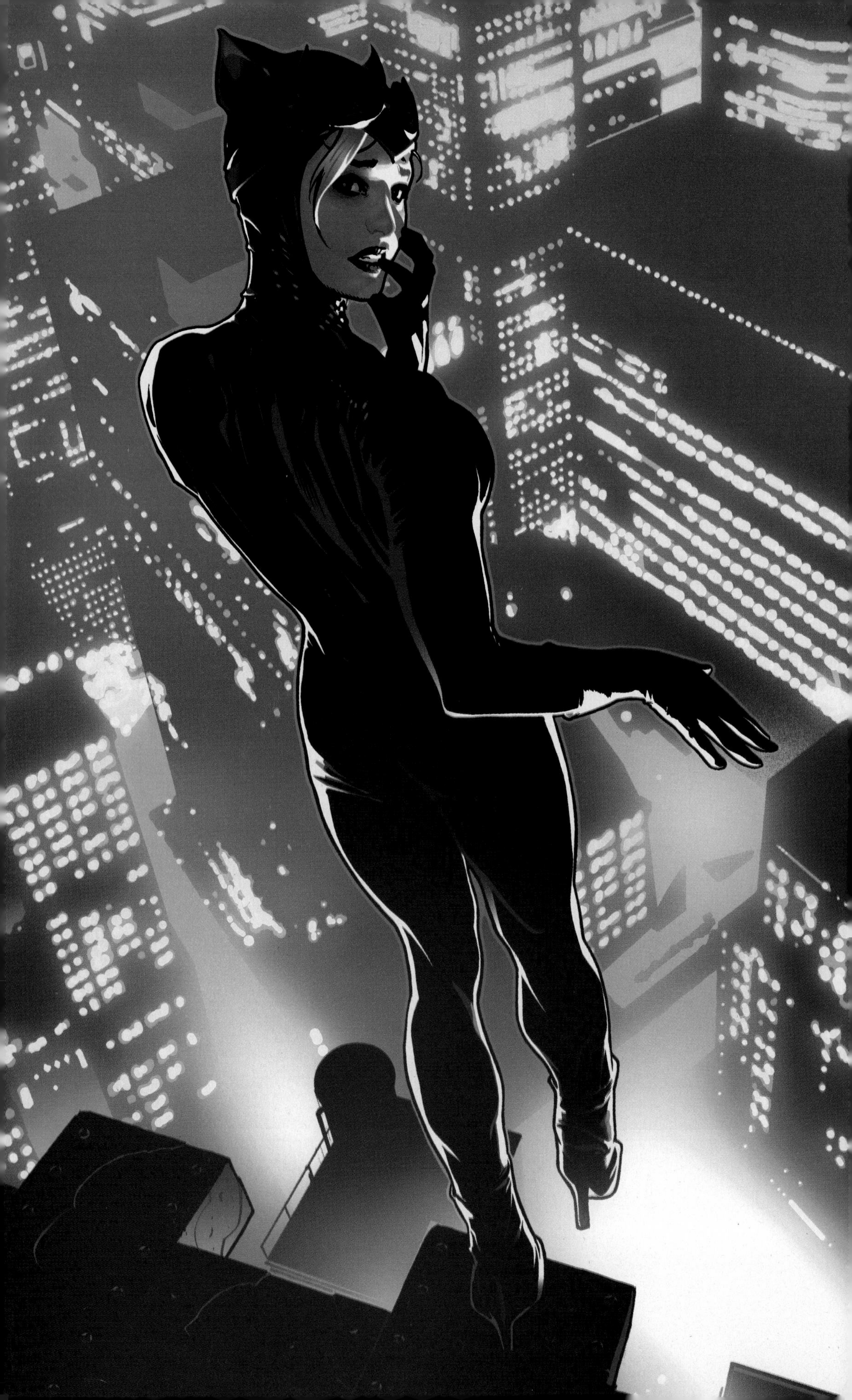

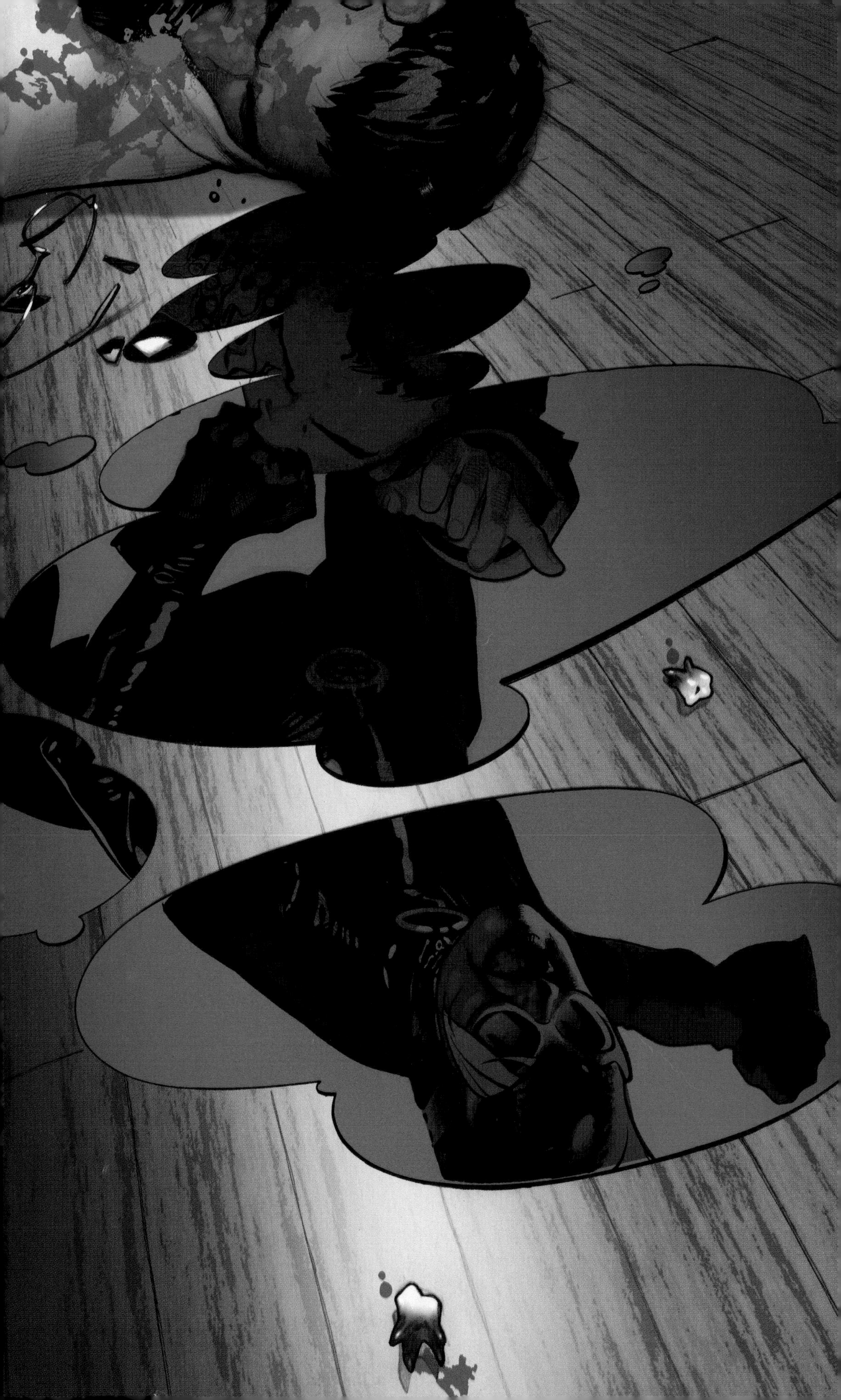

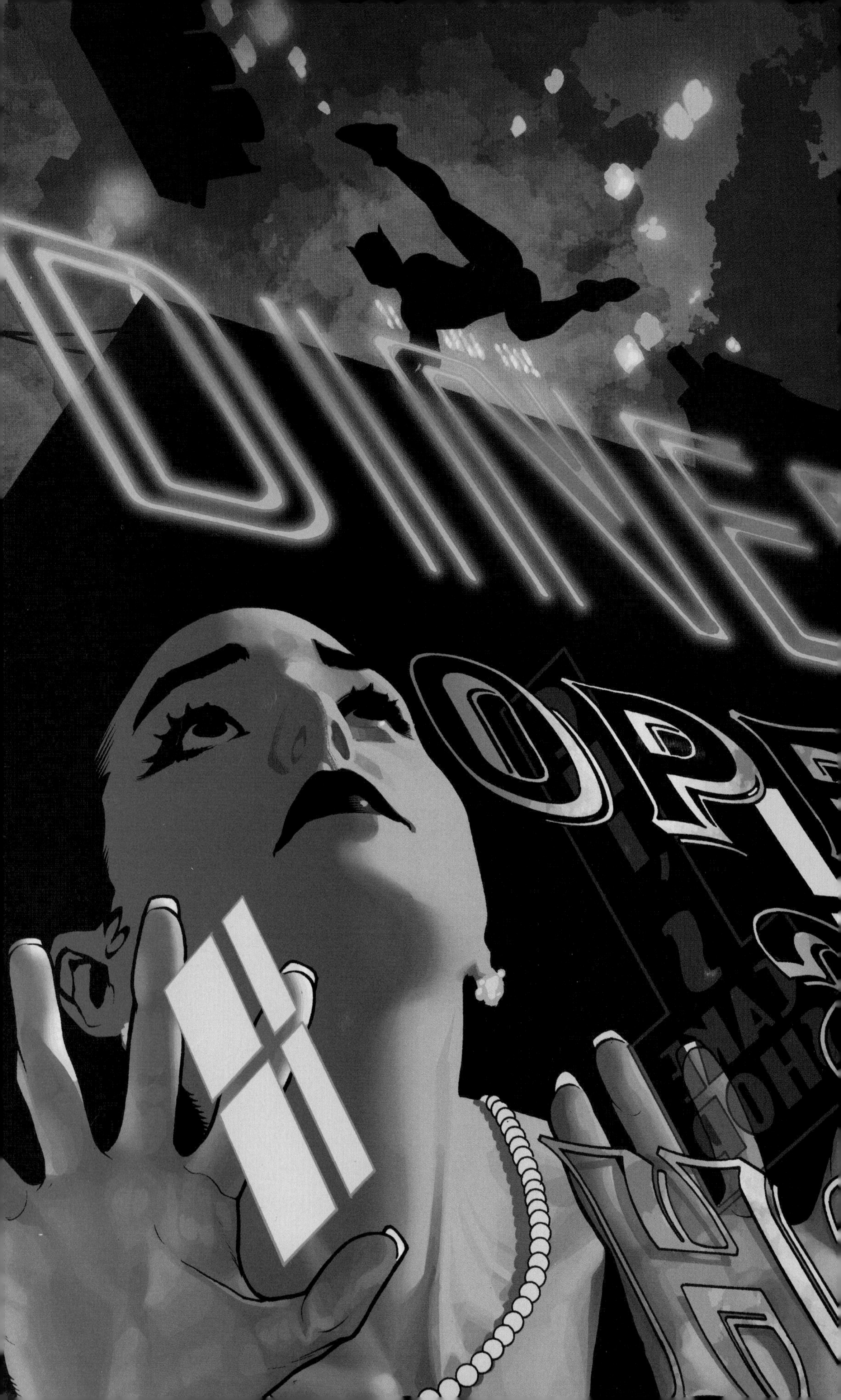

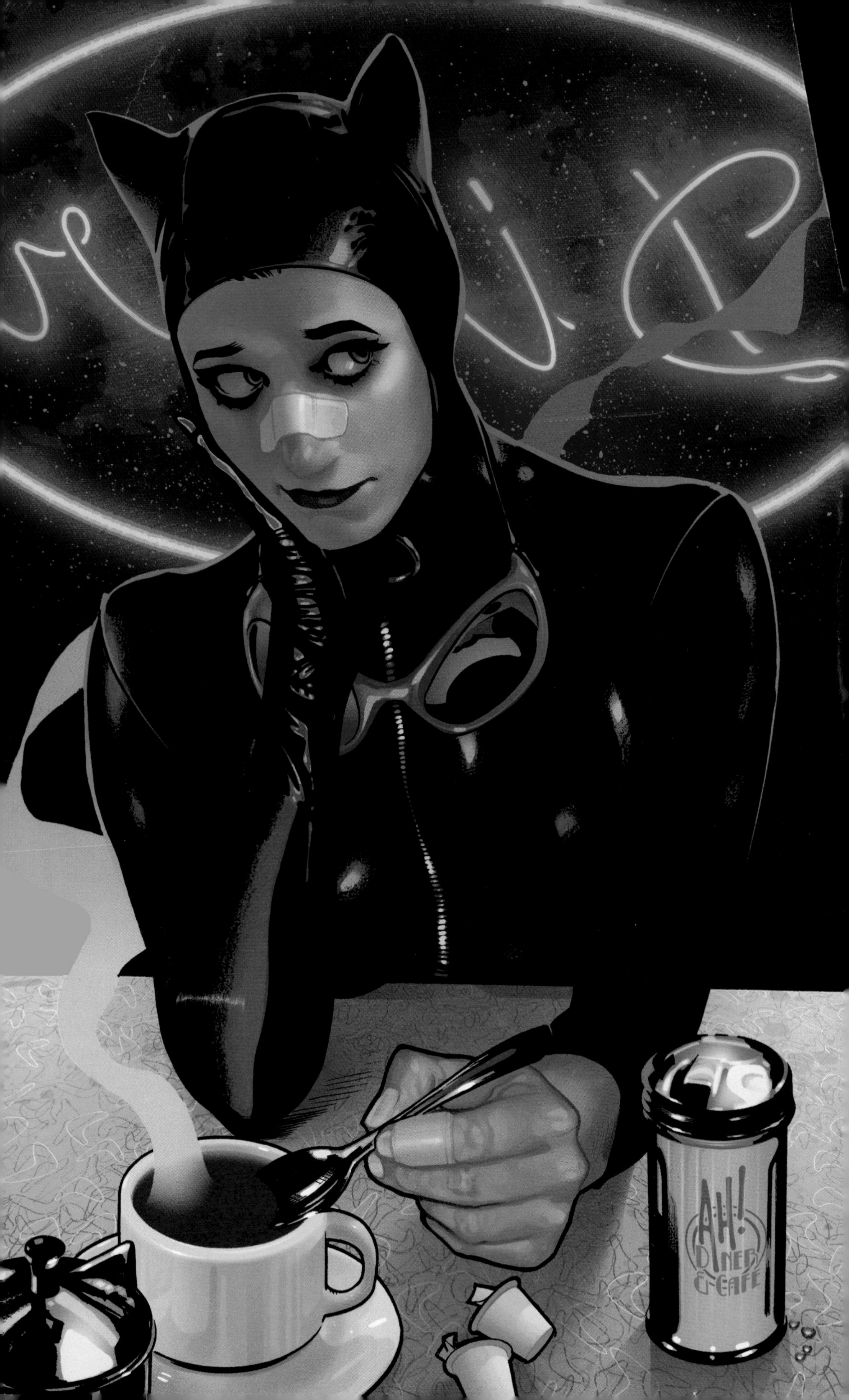
AH!
DINER
& CAFE

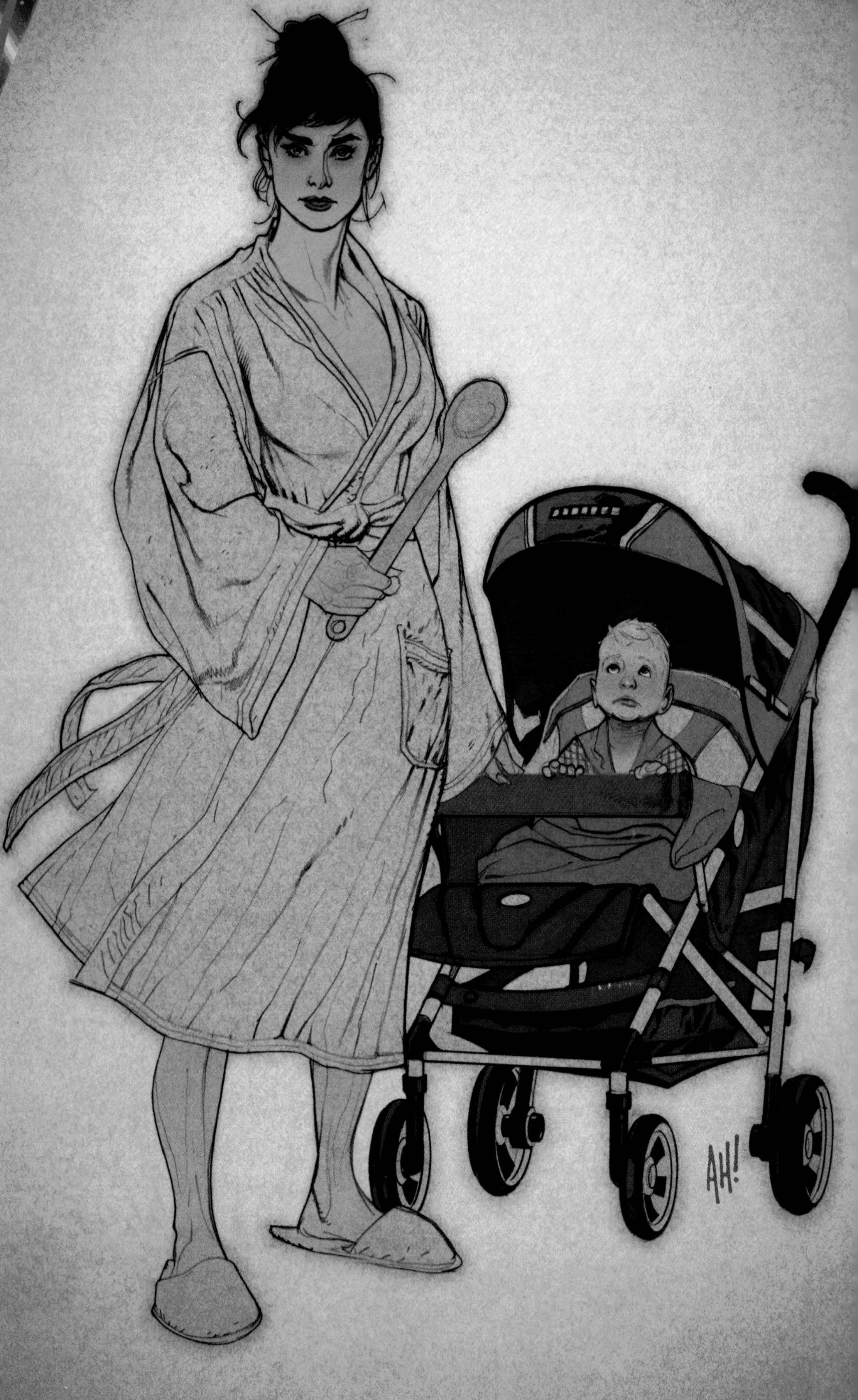
AH!

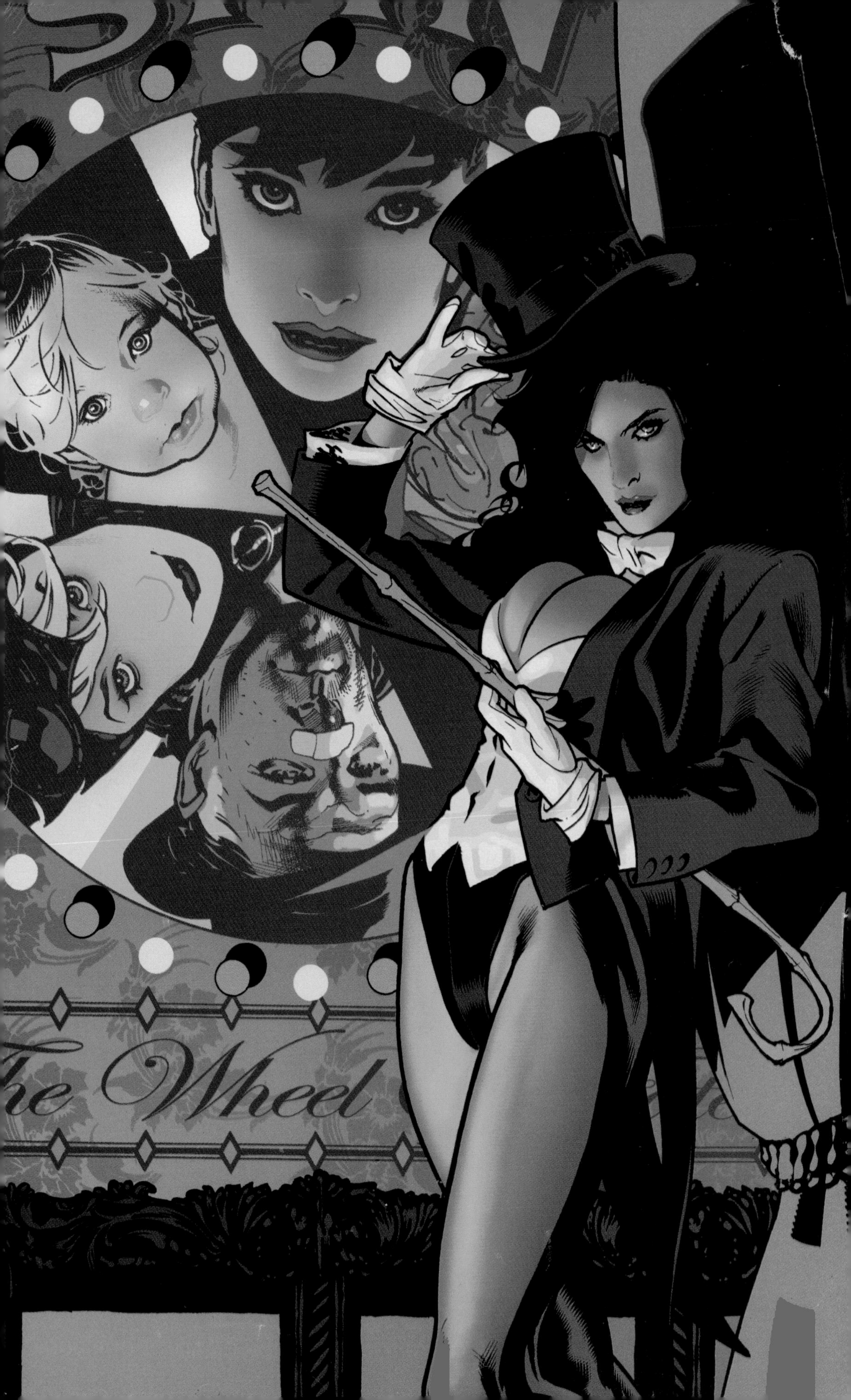
he Wheel

READ MORE OF THE DARK KNIGHT
DETECTIVE'S ADVENTURES
THESE COLLECTIONS
ROM DC COMICS:

BATMAN

BATMAN
HUSH
JEPH LOEB
JIM LEE
SCOTT WILLIAMS
VOLUME ONE

BATMAN: HUSH VOLUME 1

Jeph Loeb, Jim Lee and **Scott Williams** tell an epic tale of friendship, trust and betrayal, in the first volume of a tale that spans a lifetime of the Dark Knight.

"THE ACTION IS EXCITING AND THE DETAIL IS METICULOUS."
— CRITIQUES ON INFINITE EARTHS

BATMAN:
THE DARK KNIGHT RETURNS

BATMAN: THE DARK KNIGHT RETURNS
FRANK MILLER
with KLAUS JANSON and LYNN VARLEY

FRANK MILLER
KLAUS JANSON
LYNN VARLEY

BATMAN:
THE LONG HALLOWEEN

JEPH LOEB TIM SALE
BATMAN
THE LONG HALLOWEEN

JEPH LOEB
TIM SALE

BATMAN:
YEAR ONE

YEAR ONE
FRANK MILLER
DAVID MAZZUCCHELLI

FRANK MILLER
DAVID MAZZUCCHELLI

SEARCH THE GRAPHIC NOVELS SECTION OF
www.DCCOMICS.com
FOR ART AND INFORMATION ON ALL OF OUR BOOKS!

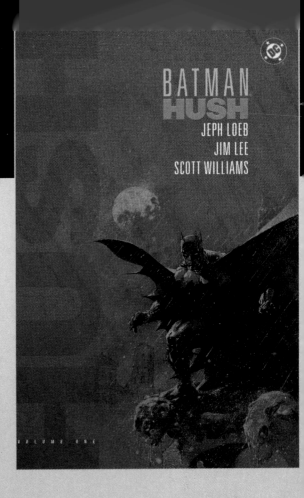